VILLAGE COMMUNITIES AND LAND TENURES IN WESTERN INDIA UNDER COLONIAL RULE

Village Communities and Land Tenures in Western India Under Colonial Rule

Edited by

BRAHMA NAND

MANOHAR
2009

First published 2009

ISBN 978-81-7304-820-3

Published by
Ajay Kumar Jain *for*
Manohar Publishers & Distributors
4753/23 Ansari Road, Daryaganj
New Delhi 110 002

Typset at
Chanakya Graphics
New Delhi-110 055

Printed at
Salasar Imaging Systems
Delhi 110 035

Contents

Acknowledgements	7
Introduction	9-58

PART I

Report on the Village Communities of the Deccan	59-128
Village Communities	62
Nature of Huks	87
Ready-Money Grants, Enams	96
General Observations	100

PART II

Land Tenures in the Bombay Presidency	129-238
Character of Land Tenures; Systems of Survey and Settlements	131
The Survey Tenure	147
Tenures in the Deccan	147
Tenures in Gujarat	149
Tenures in the Konkan	159
Inam Tenures	165
Land Tenures and Land Revenue Administration in the Town and Island of Bombay	167
Land Tenures in Sind	177
Suspensions and Remissions of Land Revenue	198
Glossary	239
Index	243

Acknowledgements

I am extremely grateful to Shriman Ruseed Wadiaji, an eminent Mumbaikar historian, for extending all possible help in making this compilation possible. Prof. Sabyasachi Bhattacharya, Chairman, Indian Council of Historical Research, New Delhi, has always been a source of inspiration and encouragement. My younger brother Prof. Shri Krishan, P.G. Centre Rewari, has extended help from time to time. My wife Sushila Rani and our children Anuj and Ajay have helped by sharing many responsibilities at home.

I would like to thank in particular Mr. O.P. Sharma of Chanakya Graphics for composing this work and Mr. Ramesh Jain and Ajay Jain of Manoher Publishers & Distributors for publishing it.

BRAHMA NAND

Introduction

This compilation of official documents from western India under British rule explores the twin aspects of social relationship in the rural society ; one is between the human beings themselves (i.e. the village community) and, the other between the human beings with reference to nature, especially the land (i.e. the land tenures). Taken together they provide a comprehensive overview of the rural society. Both these relationships were not stable or static as was assumed by many observers at that time and is still taken for granted by many contemporary writers. They were undergoing a continuous process of change. Some of these changes are clearly discernible in these documents while others can only be dimly perceived. The central concern of these essays, the historical constitution of the rural society, the distribution and redistribution of landed property and agrarian surplus, has not lost its relevance even today. Some of these issues emerged in my earlier study on the *Fields and Farmers in Western India, 1850-1950* (Bibliomatrix, New Delhi, 2003). However, on the completion of the volume, which had already become formidable in size for the contemporary readers, it was felt that some of the vital aspects had not received sufficient attention they deserved. One was the issue of famines in colonial India. Most of the existing studies were based on official sources and did not provide an authentic picture of the colonial social realities. The compilation of a companion volume based on unofficial historical narratives was published under the title *Famines in Colonial India : Some Unofficial Historical Narratives* (Kanishka, New Delhi, 2007). The second issue which did not receive its due attention was village communities and land tenures. The present volume is a result of the realisation of this inadequacy.

However, both these volumes on famines and village communities can be read separately and independently of the earlier work.

Village Community as an Ensemble of Social Relations

The village communities had their origins deep in the antiquity. They emerged as a complex ensemble of social relations. The authority of the village community as an autonomous institution seems to have been strengthened during the feudal era with the fragmentation of political authority. The local village officials appointed by the state tended to become hereditary which in times of political crises began to command considerable power and authority. The village became the only centre of stability, the only repository of civil rights in the apparently prevailing chaotic conditions. It was against this historical premises that R.N. Gooddine set out to make an enquiry into the village communities of the Deccan.[1]

Sir Henry Sumner Maine observed that the village communities in India had a striking resemblance to the Teutonic Townships or Marks of early Europe. Both had a group of families united by common kinship which exercised joint ownership over land. The domain which it occupied was distributed upon the same principles, if not in the same manner. While the Mark had been transformed into the manor which in the evolutionary process gave rise to the self-governing institutions in Europe, the Indian village community was a living and not a dead institution. In other words, European past was India's present. The village community was arrested in an early stage of development in India and the country itself was in a state of barbarism.[2]

Frederick Engels had pointed out that from India to Ireland common ownership in land was a survival of the tribal past though societies had much advanced beyond that stage. Sometimes the arable land was cultivated jointly for account of the community, and sometimes in detached parcels of land temporarily allocated to families by the community, while woodland and pasture land continued to be used in common.[3] In north India, the latter category of arable waste was referred as *gam shamlat* or village common.

B.H. Baden-Powell insisted that the village community had never enshrined communal ownership of land. The pattern of landholding were always heterogeneous, most often *ryotwari* or household based. In the North-Western Provinces and also in the Punjab, the village communities of the joint landlord type were in existence at the advent of British rule, but in Oudh and elsewhere the village communities were not really archaic, not ancient tribal idea of property. Here the universal joint character was a result of the British system and a large number of the village communities were of modern origin. The principle of joint inheritance and the custom of sharing, of pre-emption, and other means of excluding strangers, were all derived from the aboriginal tribal idea, that the family, not the individual, was the owner of property. It was equally true of the bhaichara villages where ancestral shares never were recognized, but where a special principle of allotting equal shares and holdings for individuals or families obtained : some tribal bond and traditional principle of association, must have furnished the scheme by which the body worked and held together. From the point of view of the state the village community was merely a tax-gathering agency. The village community had joint responsibility for the payment of land revenue which the government usually collected through a middleman, either a *zamindar,* or a *talukdar,* or a *lambardar.* The middleman was not the sole-proprietor or a lord of manor or an overlord interest in the property which found expression in a cash allowance included in the village revenue but paid through the treasury or the settlement was made with him as overlord and a sub-settlement with the village body.

Some of the real old bhaichara villages were of the ryotwari type where the family or individual plot was the holder's *dad ilahi* or gift of providence, or it was said that everyman's cultivation extended to what he could manage – *kasht hasb maqdur.* When the dense population began to press on land, the right to pre-emption became operative. This feature of joint communities gave every existing co-sharer a right to purchase in preference to an outsider and thus secure a livelihood for his family. It afforded a strong inducement to a village to hold together. Apart from bhaichara villages, later extension of cultivation occurred by voluntary association. In latter case, the body of different castes and families agreed together and clung together from the necessity of mutual aid and defence with no common bond of family descent and no idea of allotting land on ancestral shares. The settlers built a village residence and each took his land according to his power, i.e. according to the number of hands his family contained (or labourers he had induced to follow him), the number of ploughs and bullocks that he brought, and so forth. The leading men also dug the tank or sunk the wells and planted the village grove and had a sort of pre-eminence in virtue of this. Then the state, finding headman necessary, gave them further powers by granting them privileges and revenue-free holdings and gave them opportunity of becoming farmers of village revenue in later days. Beyond the bhaichara were *zamindari* and *pattidari* estates.

The landlord got a footing in the village in several ways, e.g., as a grant from the ruling prince, or by retaining a fragment of estate upon division or disruption in the ruling family or when a revenue farmer at an auction sale for arrears of revenue got the village as landlord or small clan and bodies of adventurers conquering or settling in a district as landlords. When the landlord died his family gradually multiplied into in a jointly entitled body, which formed, in time, a community of proprietors. The conquering clans and high caste families acknowledged no *raja* and divided the village land not by any ancestral shares but on principles of equal division by adopting curious methods of land measurement and making up *bighas* consisting of plots of each kind of soil with a view to equality. This particular form of holding 'by custom of the brotherhood' was really the true and original meaning of bhaichara though this term was applied by British administrators to all other types of joint villages. Also, during the early British rule a considerable number of estates passed into hands of auction-purchasers or revenue farmers and others who undertook the responsibility where original owners had fallen into poverty or decay or disappeared. A large number of estates were deserted, ownerless (*khana khali*) and abandoned. The revenue farmers or quasi-landlords crept into the place of owners to manage and restore the abandoned and deserted estates with their capital, means and energy. They were called *mustjirs* or *sadr-malguzars* (principal revenue payers). In process of time, the single landlord was represented by his sons and grandsons who jointly claimed the same right as their ancestor. Similarly, a zamindar, talukdar or grantee's right got divided after some generations in main shares (*pattis*) by names of heads of families. Thus pattidari villages blossomed out and enthusiastic historians spoke of them as *'primeval bodies, surviving unmoved the fall of empires !'* The happy picture of self-governing communities, careless of the world outside was more visionary than real though they had an advantage of union in times of war and trouble.[4]

Whereas Henry Maine believed that the village communities in the East and West had some common point of origin in history, B.H. Baden-Powell situated village communities in India in purely indigenous roots. The village communities were in existence in southern and western India though they sank into oblivion after the introduction of ryotwari settlement there. Initially, Thomas Munro in the Madras Presidency and Elphinstone in the Bombay Presidency had strongly recommended a settlement through the village communities and were in favour of preserving and strengthening these institutions. That of course did not happen and a direct settlement with individual cultivators was preferred by the government, setting in process the decline and decay of the village communities.

However the early British administrators like Thomas Munro, Elphinstone and Charles Metcalfe were fascinated by the functioning of the village communities. They appeared to be a simple form of self-government which protected the cultivators of every village from the oppression of the zamindars and government. These unique and excellent ancient institutions with their self-governing constitution resembling a corporation or township had survived wreck of dynasties and downfall of empires. Their organisation of offices, servants and internal economy had remained unchanged. Elphinstone in his Report on Bombay in 1819 observed that the village communities had miniature of all materials of a state and provided remedy for a bad government. They had *patel* (village headman) and *kulkarni* (accountant) as the main office-bearers assisted by a team of twelve artisans and village servants (the so-called *baru balotis*) such as carpenter, blacksmith, barber, priest, etc., who extended essential services to the village. The Patel who was originally an agent of the government became in historical course a representative of the ryots, protected and asserted their rights and made known wrongs of people. Under the British rule the right of the peasants to hold land at fixed rates was crushed under the increasing burden of land revenue demands and village communities disappeared.[5] In 1830, Charles Metcalfe described the village communities as little republics, isolated and independent of the onside world. They seemed to last where nothing else lasted. They had remained unchanged and survived the fall of dynasties and sweeping revolutions. Each village community formed a separate little state in itself.[6]

The stereotyped notions of the early colonial administrators prevailed throughout the nineteenth century. Marx emphasized in his writings that the Asian societies had three distinct features : oriental despotism based on irrigation, absence of private property in land, and cohesive village communities.[7] The peculiar characteristic of the Asian society was that it was basically stagnant, stationary and changeless in contradistinction to European societies. In *Capital,* vol. I, Marx observed :

> Those small and extremely ancient Indian communities, some of which have continued down to this day, are based on possession in common of the land, on the blending of agriculture and handicrafts, and on an unalterable division of labour, which serves, whenever a new community is started, as a plan and scheme ready cut and dried. Occupying areas of from 100 up to several thousand acres each forms a compact whole producing all it requires. The chief part of the products is destined for direct use by the community itself, and does not take the form of a commodity. Hence, production here is independent of that division of labour brought about, in Indian society as a whole, by means of the exchange of commodities. It is the surplus alone that becomes a commodity, and a portion of even that, not until it has reached the hands of the state into whose hands from time immemorial a certain quantity of these products has found its way in the shape of rent in kind. The constitution of these communities varies in different parts of India. In those of the simplest form, the land in tilled in common, and the produce divided among the members. At the same time, spinning and weaving are carried on in each family as subsidiary industries. Side by side with the masses thus occupied with one and the same work, we find the "chief inhabitant", who is judge, police and tax-gatherer in one ; the book-keeper, who keeps the accounts of the village and registers everything relating thereto ; another official, who prosecutes criminals, protects strangers travelling through and escorts them to the next village ; the boundaryman, who guards the boundaries against neighbouring communities ; the water

> overseer who distributes the water from the common tanks for irrigation ; the Brahmin, who conducts the religious services ; the school master, who on the sand teaches the children reading and writing ; the calender Brahmin, or astrologer, who makes known the lucky or unlucky days for seed-time and harvest, and for every other kind of agricultural work ; a smith and a carpenter, who make and repair all the agricultural implements ; the potter, who makes all the pottery of the village ; the barber, the washerman, who washes clothes, the silversmith, here and there the poet, who in some communities replaces the silversmith, in others the school-master. This dozen of individuals is maintained at the expense of the whole community. If the population increases, a new community in founded, on the pattern of the old one, on unoccupied land. The whole mechanism discloses a systematic division of labour ; but a division like that in manufactures is impossible, since the smith and the carpenter, etc., find an unchanging market, and at the most there occur, according to the sizes of the villages, two or three of each, instead of one. The law that regulates the division of labour in the community acts with the irresistible authority of a law of Nature, at the same time that each individual artificer, the smith, the carpenter and so on, conducts on his workshop all the operations of his handicraft in the traditional way, but independently, and without recognizing any authority over him. The simplicity of the organization for production in these self-sufficing communities that constantly reproduce themselves in the same form, and when accidentally destroyed spring up again on the spot and with the same name—this simplicity supplies the key to the secret of the unchangeableness of Asiatic societies, an unchangeableness in such striking contrast with the constant dissolution and refounding of Asiatic states and the never-ceasing changes of dynasty. The structure of the economic elements of society remains untouched by the storm clouds of the political sky.[8]

The notions of unchanging village communities, oriental despotism and absence of private property in land were rejected by many historians including D.D. Kosambi, Romila Thapar, Irfan Habib, Bipan Chandra and other.[9] The nature of class structure and class struggles, technological change and social dynamism was no way unique in India or in no way dissimilar to the West, they argued. The village community was more an idea than a fact, S.N. Mukherjee had observed.[10] This kind of statement is, of course, historically not valid. The problem was that from Munro to Maine and right up to Baden-Powell the village community was seen basically in relation to state, as a tax paying unit, not as an autonomous social unit or as a living reality. The village community was essentially an ensemble of social relations which evolved out of an inherent necessity of social interdependence and not as a tax gathering tool for the state. Louis Dumont observed that caste was ignored or underplayed in the prevalent ideology of the period as community was an egalitarian group. Dominance and hierarchy though not absolutely ignored, remained in the background.[11] Clive Dewey argued that the images of the village community were coloured with ideology of the observer. The conservatives approved it as a source of social cohesion while radicals or utilitarians condemned it as an obstacle to economic growth.[12]

To clear Clive Dewey's dilemma it should be noted that an image need not be a true reflection of the reality, it could be a distorted image depending on the mirror used for reflection. Also, Louis Dumont's assertion that caste and dominance are ignored or underplayed, is not true. The caste and *jajmani* system were intricately interwoven within the institution of village community and were an intrinsic part of it. Unlike Russia, where land was held on communal basis by *obschina* or village community and distributed periodically every 8 to 12 years among the peasant households by rotating strips of different quality or fertility of soil among them to ensure egalitarianism, in Deccan village communities were not egalitarian institutions. The egalitarianism of Russian obschina assured by periodic repartition of land and joint responsibility towards payment of redemption dues and state taxes was celebrated by Narodniks or populists and condemned as irrational and features of backwardness by Liberals and Marxists.[13] Peasant households had to retain abundant labour as a precondition for obtaining scarce land. With the exception of certain joint landlord type villages in north India, there was no communal ownership of land in India. There was considerable differentiation among different castes and groups reflected in wide disparities in resources and wealth. Against these disparities, village communities provided bonds of cohesion.

The distribution of agrarian surplus was in the form of differential remuneration to different categories of artisans who were often engaged in caste-based hereditary occupations or village officials or servants under the *barabaluta* system. Historically, it appears they arose to cope with the problem of increasing social division of labour and increasing class polarisation. Contrary to being antithetical to differentiation within rural society, they tried to institutionalise the existing pattern of social disparities. They began to collapse under the impetus of market economy and increasing intervention of the colonial state when the process of class polarisation went beyond this institutionalised limit. The independent middle peasantry began to lose control over land and other means of production and dwindle into dwarf-holding cultivators, tenants or wage labourers. The customary form of labour use was gradually displaced by contractual wage labour determined by market forces. The oldest form of labour co-operation, called *irjik* in Deccan and *sondhal* in Gujarat involved a simple free exchange of labour, found in many peasant communities all over the world, whereby families of small cultivators secured labour by lending personal services to one another especially when demand for labour was intense like transplantation and weeding of rice, sowing of sugar cane, when family labour proved inadequate. This system of labour exchange was based on reciprocity and did not involve any payment except that the participants received a meal from the owner of the field.[14]

Another form of labour cooperation which had semblence of communal responsibility was called *baluta.* The village artisans and servants provided their services to the entire village community and in exchange received fixed customary amount of grain and straw from each household. When the villages had initially settled as corporate units, they required services from certain categories of artisans or other servants which appeared very essential for the community as a whole such as carpenter, blacksmith, tanner, potter, barber, etc. As an inducement to settlement they had to be provided with subsistence for their families. The form in which this subsistence was to be granted could, of course, vary.[15] In the villages of Gujarat, Alexander Mackay during his visit around mid-nineteenth century observed that artisans and village servants were granted service land or *waola pasaita* as they were called. The interest in such land was usufructuary and lasted as long as the artisans rendered services to the village community. Such land held by artisans on the condition of services could not be sold. In the eventuality of the artisans ceasing to render the usual services, the land had to be returned back to the village community which transferred it to other artisan on similar condition.[16] The *bara balutedari* system prevailing in the villages of Deccan was an advance upon Gujarat. Rather than alienating land to artisans and binding them with land, the village communities in Deccan alienated a specific amount of produce of land based on household usage of their services, usually calculated on an annual basis. The claims of the artisans were limited in magnitude, well defined by custom and usage of the country and could not be extended arbitrarily. The artisans were usually paid in accordance with their importance for the agrarian economy. The remunerations or *huks* of he village servants were fixed and payable in kind. They were calculated according to the area of land cultivated or per family or according to the number of bullocks possessed by the peasant household. The carpenter received from 24 seers to 72 seers of grain per family, blacksmith often one-third of this and others one-fourth.[17]

The main concern of the enquiry by R.N. Gooddine was to define the customary rights and remuneration of the village officials inherited by the British from the previous social evolution which appeared vague and uncertain. The colonial rule had granted fixed salaries to the village officials but they continued to enjoy earlier rights and perquisites which was clearly unacceptable to the colonial rule as it attempted to appropriate maximum agrarian surplus for itself. As the colonial state consolidated its authority and tightened its tentacles around rural society it increasingly confronted the established loci of power. The settlement of a village was often accompanied by artisans and village servants whose number reached twelve, generally referred as bara baluta. These included patel, kulkarni, carpenter, blacksmith, tanner and shoemaker, potter, barber, washerman, astrologer, priest, goldsmith and mahars. The number varied in different villages with some additions or omissions. The latecomers could gain right to entry by contributing labour or money to the village community. Those with permanent rights of residence were called *gaokaris,* temporary residents were called *upris.*

Depending upon the nature and degree of control over land, the agrarian relations assumed different dimensions. The Kunbis or agriculturist class comprised of *thulwahiks* (in possession of land with permanent improvements like wells or enclosures) ; *mundwahiks* (in possession of simple lots) ; *upris* (cultivators without residential rights in the village) ; *owandkaris* (in possession of cultivating land but residing in another village). Land was also classified according to usage or purpose of utilisation. The entire land within village boundary was called *sewar*. It consisted of cultivable land, grass and pasture land (village common), land of extinct owner (*gatkulee*) hereditary owner (*miras*), land held as state grant or gift (*inam*). As privileged landowners *mirasdars* were vested with the rights of inheritance and proprietorship. They had acquired honours and immunity from patel's share of *huks* (perquisites) in kind on their land. Even if the mirasdar did not personally cultivate the land he could claim the established impost form the person who did, which was equivalent to the share of the village staff in production exclusive of the government dues. Besides these dues in kind, the patel received several other perks from the residents of the village such as a turban, shawl and cocoanut levied on the marriage of each member of a resident's family. In fact, R.N. Gooddine mentions three types of miras, according to its total, partial or non-exemption from impost. The mirasdars were also entitled to certain honours and privileges to display their social distinction such as priority of place in an assembly, at a festival or in a procession. The power and authority of patel also varied greatly. In some areas they had no claim to perks and depended entirely upon the government remuneration. In some cases they had sold their patelship partially, a half, a third or a fourth. There was inverse power relation within the village community ; the more powerful the patel, weaker the mirasdars and more powerful the mirasdars, weaker the authority of the patel. Where the responsibility for the government dues was entirely with the body of mirasdars, patelship was only nominal. The state under such circumstances circumvented the authority of the village community by imposing the higher rate of land revenue or an extra cess for compensating the patel. The central assumption of the colonial officials was that the land was state property and the position of the actual cultivator was merely that of a tenant. Accordingly, R.N. Gooddine regarded miras as a perpetual lease. In the event of miras being cultivated by others, patel often tried to enforce his right to perks, and privileges often resulting in conflicts and throwing off land out of cultivation. Under such circumstances, district officials acted as referees and often not without their own vested interests.

As the cultivators were broadly divided into two categories of mirasdars and upris, similarly village servants and artisans were divided into *balutee* (the effective) and *alootee* (the non-effective). The village servants were arranged hierarchically according to their importance and remuneration. The first class comprising carpenter, blacksmith, tanner and mahar received 30 sheaves per paeen ; the second class, potter, barber, washerman and mahar received 25 sheaves per paeen ; and the third class, astrologer, priest, maulana, mahar received 20 sheaves. The authority of patel in the village affairs was greatly undermined when individual ryots were made responsible for land revenue demand. Likewise, the privileges of mirasdars were clipped. In most villages the kulkarni enjoyed the same authority and perks or even more as patels. Even miras lands were not exempt from his levies. At district level deshmukh had the same duties as patel at the village level and deshpande as kulkarni. There was corresponding decline in their power and authority similar to patels and kulkarnis. R.N. Gooddine's enquiry revealed that there was no uniformity in the perks extracted by the village functionaries. It depended upon the power and authority of the individual determined by historical circumstances. Since it was not determined by the state but by balance of power between the powerful landholding interests on the one hand and the village functionaries on the other, such differences were not unexpected. The huks and perks of the patels and kulkarnis were more numerous than others. The dues collected by artisans and village servants were also put to close scrutiny by R.N. Gooddine. It was found that perhaps with the exception of the mahars who were the lowest in the social scale and derived the lowest huks or remuneration which converted into daily wages appeared to be below subsistence level on an average, the rest of the artisans and village servants were well provided for their services. Most of them received subsistence wages or even more. A well established hierarchy is revealed from the data gathered by R.N. Gooddine. It was kulkarni who received the highest perks in kind, followed by the three most important artisans, the carpenter, blacksmith and tanner, all linked intimately to the agricultural production by way of making and repairing tools and appliances, leather pots and ropes for irrigation. The changed position of the village functionaries is evident from the fact that while under the native states they were allowed to collect about 25 per cent in excess of government demand, the colonial government fixed their share at 6 per cent in the initial stage of their rule. Also, certain categories of land were granted exemption from government revenue demand in view of the services rendered to the state. They were referred as *inam* or *khairat* and denoted the privileged status of holders called *inamdars*.

The village community was an ensemble of social relations. It will not be appropriate to consider it merely as a tax-gathering tool for the state or an institution regulating the distribution or redistribution of agrarian surplus. It was a living social reality and functioned as an autonomous social unit. This point needs to be reiterated and emphasized as it has been overlooked in the existing writings. It is of vital importance if we are to understand the real nature of this institution. The village community, for instance, played a crucial role in social and political life of the rural people, especially in historical conditions where alternative institutions for this purpose were absent or were in nascent stage of evolution. For western India it can be illustrated with reference to the Deccan Peasant Uprising of 1875 and other similar revolts. In 1875, the Deccan peasantry made concerted attacks on the Marwari and Gujarati usurers, attacking and burning their houses and other property, depriving them of account books and bonds which were perceived as weapons or instruments of exploitation. The uprising was believed to be spontaneous in character but a close scrutiny of the records reveal that the village community was an instrumental force in organising the peasantry against the usury. Though participants belonged to different castes, they were united through the bonds of the village community, the majority of them being from the same ethnic group, i.e. the Maratha Kunbi. With the advent of British rule and market economy, the village community had lost its traditional strength but despite caste division and class disparities, the village community had retained a remarkable degree of influence and force in the Deccan, and socially the members of the village community met on a much more equitable basis and acted collectively in the face of a political crisis. During the Deccan Peasant Uprising of 1875, the village community imposed an organisational discipline upon all the members. Through *Sama Patras* (Common Agreement) village communities forbade all sections of rural society to assist moneylenders in any form. The boycott was near universal and complete. The barbers will not shave them, the washerman will not wash clothes for them, the mahars will not carry load for them. The village community declared that if any village servant broke the common agreement he would be denied his annual claims. If the 'Mokkadam' patel, priests or kulkarnis were to join and help the moneylenders, their hereditary rights were to be discontinued, and village community could engage new patel, priest or kulkarni. Those rayots who violated the rules established by the village community were neither to be allowed to inter-caste dinners nor inter-marry amongst their own caste groups. These Sama Patras were circulated among the neighbouring village communities with an appeal to assist them and to declare a similar strategy of common struggle against the common enemy.[18] In 1879, Vasudev Balwant Phadke in his rebellion against the British rule sought help from the caste heads and village communities to recruit soldiers for his fighting columns, which comprised men of different castes and occupations, including barbers, shoemakers, sweepers, basketmakers, mostly people of humble origin.[19] In the Native State of Baroda at Pilwai village in June 1898 about 300 Rajput landowners fought with sword, matchlock and canon against the State. The roads were barricaded by wooden logs, trees and shrubs. The assembly had reached about 3000 at the time of confrontation when troops opened fire. According to the unofficial reports about 300 or 400 among landowners were killed about 1062 houses were burnt, property worth about Rs. 3 lakh was destroyed.[20] That showed the mighty capacity of the village community to fight against the extreme odds. The community feeling has not completely vanished though it has been greatly diminished. In the recent spate of farmers' distress suicides in Maharashtra, the village community had tried unsuccessfully to mobilize financial help for the distressed farmers in numerous cases.[21] Actually, the odds of the contemporary civilisation are too complex and difficult for these primitive institutions to cope with or to overcome with their diminished capabilities and resources. But the community feeling has not died out completely.

Land and Power in the Countryside

Land was a symbol of power and authority in the countryside. It was the most significant among the means of production in the agrarian economy. A person without land was a person of no consequence in the rural society. The system of ownership rights and distribution of land had been determined by a long period of social evolution. When western India came under colonial control there were numerous land tenures in existence and though they were greatly modified in accordance with the requirements of the new rulers it was not possible to do away with them altogether. In this process of transformation English had created caricatures of various systems of landed property in India, Marx had lamented. He observed :

> If any nation's history, then the history of the English in India is a string of futile and really absurd (in practice infamous) economic experiments. In Bengal they created a caricature of large-scale English landed estates ; in south-eastern India a caricature of small parcelled property ; in the north-west they did all they could to transform the Indian economic community with common ownership of the soil into a caricature of itself.[22]

The British policy with regard to land tenure and revenue system was governed basically by the pragmatic considerations more than anything else. This has been ignored by those writers who trace the genealogical roots of legislation to various streams of ideologies. Like all social forms, the legal system has an historical dimension. The relationship among various groups and classes of rural society had been established by a long historical process and law mediated and reinforced these relationships. Since social relationships were undergoing a perpetual process of change, law also underwent a process of gradual restructuring accordingly. As the Governor-General-in-the-Council remarked,

> .... it has often been necessary to subordinate what would prima-facie appear to be economic expediency to considerations based on the actual social conditions and mutual relations of the classes concerned which have been determined by a long course of agrarian and in some cases also of political history.[23]

During the pre-British period the mirasdari system prevailed in the Deccan. The mirasdars were privileged cultivators with heritable and transferable right in lands which were held at a fixed assessment. The status of mirasdar carried a degree of distinction and there was no forfeiture of his land for default of payment. The mirasi right was long respected. The mirasdar had the privilege of re-entry within a period of 30 years after relinquishment of land. The family members were held jointly responsible for the payment of revenue. By the early nineteenth century no such joint ownership had survived as would warrant the village system of revenue management. The holders of mirasi lands were not exclusively descendants of old Marathi families. The energetic cultivators, both kunbis and others may have acquired mirasi land by purchase or by taking the burden of the revenue upon themselves.[24] There was another group of cultivators called upri which meant 'stranger' or 'coming from another place', and implied that the cultivator was of an inferior status with no hereditary claim to the land, though he may have been long resident and in possession. The upri was virtually tenant-at-will. He cultivated the common lands of the village or those of absentee mirasdars ; but had no proprietary interest of any kind in either. When the original holder had disappeared, the holding was known as *gatkul,* i.e. the family (*kula*) was lost or had disappeared (*gata*). When the rayatwari system was introduced in western India under the British rule both mirasi and upri tenures were merged into survey tenure with no privilege attached to mirasi tenure and dispriviIege attached to upri tenure. The ordinary survey tenure was defined as the right of occupancy of government land continuable in perpetuity on the payment of government demand and transferable by inheritance, sale, gift or mortgage.[25]

The colonial state had allowed at least one-third of the total cultivated land to be retained in the ownerships of the privileged class of landowners including inamdars, talukdars and *khots,* etc., while making settlement of land revenue demand. These were known as alienated lands on which government had parted with revenue rights, absolutely or partially, levying only a quit-rent called *judi* or *salami*. In Deccan, inamdars held alienated or revenue-free lands called *inams* or *muaphee.* These inams were divided into four groups according to the basis of exemption in assessment and consisted of : (1) political inams granted for civil or military services or pensions, (2) service inams granted on the basis of services rendered or renderable for each village or district, (3) religious endowments, i.e. holdings alienated to religious or charitable institutions and tenable in perpetuity or so long as the institution may be in existence, and (4) personal inams alienated during pre-British period under various denominations and which were for most part continuable in perpetuity and were transferable without any restriction whatsoever.[26] Apart from inams, there were other alienated lands also, referred by various names like *udhad jamabandi, palnook,* etc. These lands were cultivated by Brahmins and other influential classes. When rayatwari system was established it was deemed desirable to make some temporary concession with the view of conciliating these classes and promoting the immediate popularity of the British rule, and hence, these tenures, and privileges connected with them were continued under the British rule.[27]

The talukdari estates prevailed in the districts of Ahmedabad, Kheda, Broach and Panch Mahals in Gujarat. The leading characteristic of talukdari tenure was that a talukdari estate was held neither in gift from the crown (i.e. alienated) nor in occupancy (i.e. unalienated) but with full proprietary rights antedating the advent of British rule, and including ownership of mines, minerals and trees.

All talukdari estates were held subject to the payment of *jama* (land revenue) to the government which was either udhad (fixed in perpetuity) or fluctuating. The talukdars of Gujarat were historically identical with the ruling families of Kathiawad and other agencies. The talukdars comprised men of varying position, ranging from jurisdictional chiefs holding talukdari villages in British districts and the holders of recognised chieftainships such as *sanand, gamph,* etc., to the holders of a few acres in a coparcenary estate, who were fast being converted into yeoman cultivators. The bulk of the smaller estates were held by co-sharers whose increasing number threatened the estates with rapid disruption. Except where rapid sub-division of shares had forced the talukdar to the plough, he lived upon the rent of the land and regarded manual labour as degrading.[28]

Under *narvadari* and *bhagdari* tenures the land consisted of certain main divisions (*muksh bhag*). The head of each estate or the main division was called a *muksh bhagdar,* and was responsible for the payment of government assessment on the whole share. All sub-sharers, who had equal rights, were called pattidars, and were descendants of the old proprietary cultivators. Both the tenures involved joint responsibility for the payment of the government revenue. The narvadari tenure prevailed chiefly in Kheda district, a few villages being in Ahmedabad and Surat, while the bhagdari tenure was confined to Broach. All persons cultivating *narva* or bhagdari lands were tenants of the bhagdars. They included tenants-at-will, holding at the pleasure of the narvadars, who could eject them or increase their rents at discretion ; and customary tenants, who could not be ejected so long as they paid the customary rental, which was either a fixed share of the produce or more commonly the customary *bighoti* rates. The bhagdari tenure differed from the narvadari in one respect only, viz., that in the former there was always fixed bighoti assessment on each field while in the latter the revenue was fixed in the lump sum.[29]

In parts of Kheda and Ahmedabad districts, certain villages known as Mehwasi were held by descendants of Mehwasi Koli or Rajput Chiefs, once great freebooters and terror of the country. The tenure was similar to talukdari in Ahmedabad. The villages in Kheda were held on the udhad jama, the revenue was fixed and not liable to revision. The principal shareholders were generally Thakors, and were called muksh bhagdars (in Mehwasi villages the sub-sharers were known as *bhayats*). Under udhad jamabandi tenure, lands were liable to a fixed cess (jama) only, such jama remaining intact even at a general revision of assessment. Apart from them wholly or partially alienated lands were extensive, and of various denominations, the principal being *chakariat* (for service), *pasaita* (in charity), *haria* (for defence), *wazifa* (religious). These were again *nakra* (rent-free) or *salamia* (liable to quit rent).[30]

In the Ratnagiri and Kolaba districts of the Konkan region, Khoti land tenure prevailed. Most of the land in Ratnagiri district was under the control of landlords called khots. The khots usually had a large share of the best land as their private holding called *khot khasgi* which was cultivated through forced labour. The rest of the land was called *khot nisbat* and it was leased out to the cultivators for a share of produce as rent. The khot could lease out all waste land called *gaveek* and thus add to his income. He could also till or sub-let all land temporarily or permanently abandoned by *dharekaris* or occupancy tenants. Until a right of re-entry was asserted and established, khot could assume the management of such lands. In dharekari villages, he received a varying allowance or a fixed percentage for the collection of land revenue in addition to many privileges incidental to their position as heads of villages where there were no hereditary officers to take precedence of them, the khots enjoyed the right of exacting from all their tenants, except the peasant proprietors, one day's forced labour in eight, *athvethi,* of forcing them to plough khot khasgi, *nagar vethi*, of compelling them to carry their palanquins and attending their household work. For this, the tenants received nothing beyond a subsistence allowance of grain.

The khoti tenure in Konkan districts closely resembled feudalism. In Europe, feudalism arose from or was influenced by, the benefices, or grants of Roman provincial land by the chieftains of the tribes which overran the Roman Empire. The Ratnagiri district was originally *kulargi,* that is to say, the agrarian system was practically that of village communities. But during the medieval period, the region was subject to wars, marauders, etc., so, to collect the government revenue more easily, and to bring land under cultivation, benefices were bestowed, in other words, grants were made of khoti *watans*. The khot became the headman, the lord of the manor. The parallel may be pressed still closer without violating the facts. The land in a manor was divided into : (1) the demesne lands, i.e. the portion kept by the lord for himself or his family ; (2) bookland or charter land, held by deed under certain rents and free services, very similar to the free socage lands ; (3) folkland, not held by deed, but distributed among the common people at the lord's pleasure who might resume the occupation thereof at his discretion ; (4) the lord's waste, common both to the lord and his tenants. The first division can be compared to what they called khot khasgi, i.e. the land kept by the khot and his family, number (4) was disappearing owing to the increasing population and competition for land. The second and third divisions were called khot nisbat, i.e. khoti land cultivated by tenants. As to number (2), any land held on a quasi-freehold tenure, whether granted by the khot himself, or of more ancient date than the tenure of the khot, could not be held at the pleasure of the superior holder, the tenant had a right of permanent occupancy.[31]

The position of the free peasant proprietor or dharekari was similar to the mirasdar of Deccan. He paid nothing beyond the assessment and so long as he paid it, the khot could not oust him. He had the right to inherit, sell, mortgage or dispose of his estate in any way he pleased. He had the right of re-entry after a lapse of many years like mirasdars. The dharekaris often leased out their fields to other cultivators who occupied the same position as tenants of khoti land. The villages of peasant proprietors, called kulargi, were mostly situated along the coast and were extremely populous. They contained most of the *bagayat* land which was greatly improved by digging well, embanking from the sea, and even by laborious process of covering the bare rock with earth brought from a distance. They enjoyed water communication with markets for the sale of produce, and subsidiary employment in fishing. The capital sunk in agricultural improvement in these villages was vastly greater than in khoti. The average rate of land revenue assessment in these villages was Rs. 3-8-9 per acre compared to Rs. 1-3-4 in the khoti villages.[32]

The quasi-dharekaris or reduced peasant holders paid from one and a half times to double the quantity of grain at which their fields were rated. Like freeholders or dharekaris, these reduced holders could not be ousted so long they paid the assessment, and the khots could not raise their rents. They had also the privilege which other khoti tenants did not possess, of disposing off their lands by sale and mortgage. The main categories of the reduced holders were the one-and-a-half payers, *didhivalas* who gave the khot one-and-a-half maund of grain for every maund of assessment ; the one and three-quarter payers, *pavnedonpatkaris,* who gave one and three-quarter maunds for each maund of assessment ; the double payer, *dupatkaris,* giving two maunds for each maund of assessment. Another category of reduced holders called *daspatkaris* was superior to other reduced holders. Like dharekaris, they paid the government assessment, *dast,* but in addition gave the Khot a fixed cash bonus of 8 annas on every maund of assessment. They were called daspatkaris literally ten times payers, because they paid Rs. 10 for each *khandi* of assessment.[33]

There were a certain number of occupants generally known as *watandar kuls* or occupancy tenants, who could not be disposed by the khots and whose rights were heritable but not transferable. They were descendants of those cultivators who held land in the village before the khots obtained their grants. They were mostly Kunbis or Marathas. The tenants-at-will whose status was equivalent to upris in Deccan, cultivated *gayal* (or deserted fields) and *gaveek* (or waste) lands of the village.[34] The tenants called waste tillers or *badhekaris* may or may not have been the residents of the same village in which they cultivated as annual tenants. An outside tenant was called *dulandi.* The tenants-at-will were liable to ejectment at the will of the superior holder, and in the absence of any special agreement, were also liable to have their rents raised from time to time. Generally, there was little difference in the rents exacted from the khot's tenants whether permanent or temporary. As the tenants-at-will occupied the worst part of *varkas* land, they were allowed by the khots slightly lower grain rents to encourage them to cultivate. The khot had no claim on them for the exaction of atveth or forced labour.[35] The Khoti Act (Act I of 1880) laid down that all tenants who had continuously held land since the beginning of 1845 had an occupancy right. About 90 per cent of the khot's tenants could have acquired occupancy right but khots subverted the process by entering the khot nisbat land cultivated by tenants in their own names.[36] The occupancy rights were transferable by inheritance only, and not by sale or mortgage ; and were liable to forfeiture in case the tenant left the village without making arrangements for the cultivation of the land and the payment of the rent, even for a small period.[37]

The rent paid by a khot's tenant consisted either of a definite proportion of the actual harvest determined by the appraisement of the standing crop ; or a grain or cash payment fixed on the basis of the average yield of the land without reference to the actual produce of the year. The first and most common mode of payment was called *thal* or settlement and the crop inspection was called *abhavani* or appraisement. The khoti abhavanis were generally an overstatement of the value of standing crop. The tenants paid one-half, one-third or one-fourth of the produce as rent, and were called accordingly *ardhelis, tirdhelis,* or *chauthelis.* In rice lands the khot collected at one-half or even a little more, in medium varkas one-third ; and in inferior varkas lands at one-fourth. The Brahmins and in some cases Marathas paid one-fourth share of produce as rent.[38] The tenant had to contribute a share towards *gaon khurch* or *ghurputtee.* The annual dues to the village mahar and temple guru were paid by the tenant. They also paid for the annual field sacrifices. This increased the real payment for medium varkas to about half the produce. The second mode for rent payment was by contract without reference to the harvest called *makta* in the north and *khand* in the south. The tenants who opted for it were called *khand karis.* The rents were liable to periodic, if not yearly, enhancement. A considerable proportion of rice lands were held on payment of grain contracts. On small plots and gardens within village boundaries, the rent was usually paid in lump sum cash covering all demands and called *ukta tharav.* Neither thal nor makta rents were payable during the periodic fallows. In addition to rent, the khots levied from the tenants an extra cess. The collection of these extra demands depended almost entirely on the personal power and influence of the khot. The khots also used to make irregular demands on tenants for grass and firewood called *karsai.*[39]

The *izafat* tenure was a variety of service tenure, of hereditary district officers, chefly deshmukhs and deshpandes. The *shilotri* tenure prevailed on lands that had been embanked and reclaimed from the sea and the permanence of which was dependent on the embankments being kept up. The reclamations were commonly known as *khars.* Under shilotri proper, the khar belonged to the person by whom it was reclaimed and who had a proprietary right, but let out these lands at will and levied an additional maund of rice per bigha for the repair of the outer embankments. On lands which lapsed to the government an equivalent of shilotri maund was levied. The shilotri lands in which reclamations were made by associations of ryots were called *kularg.* In kularg khars the tenants carried out repairs jointly.[40]

The zamindari tenure prevailed over greater part of the Sind province. Most of the lands were held by large landowners, who leased them out to *haris* or tenants. This tenure evolved under the period of the successive waves of Mohammedan invasions in which the weak had no security of life and property save in the protection of some powerful individual. It was equally necessary for the State, which had no agency at its command adequate to the task of collecting revenue from a vast number of petty cultivators and was therefore, compelled to make its settlement with as few and wealthy individuals as possible. In course of time the zamindari rights in the land were purchased by the tenant or lapsed on demise without heir or otherwise fell into disuse, and thus a class of peasant proprietors sprang up. There were few tenant rights in existence in Sind. The smaller zamindars cultivated for themselves and the larger through the yearly tenants who paid superior landowners a proportion of the crop. In Upper Sind, a species of the hereditary tenancy existed which was locally termed *maurusi haripan.* The hereditary tenant paid a quit rent under the name *lapo,* zamindari, *malkano, tobro* or *deh khurch* to the proprietor. The quit rent differed in different villages, and even on different crops grown, but seldom exceeded 6 to 8 annas per acre and could not be enhanced. Besides the *maurusi haris,* there existed a class of occupancy tenants who paid lapo to the zamindar and also a proportion of the crop as rent, in accordance with the custom of the country, and as long as they did so, they could not be ousted from their tenancies. In these cases the zamindar paid the assessment to the government.[41]

Eclipse of the Power and Privileges Under Colonial Rule

The power and privileges of the traditional landed aristocracy, village communities and their hereditary revenue officials, as well as mercantile classes began to get eroded with the onset of the colonial rule.[42] The position of the mirasdars and inamdars in Deccan, talukdars in Gujarat, zamindars in Sind and khots in the Konkan region began to decline. The colonial rule had unleashed the forces of market economy which were hostile to the conditions upon which their existence was premised. In Germany, the *junkers* or landlords had adapted themselves to the changing conditions and by using agricultural machinery and wage labour began to produce for the market economy and ultimately transformed themselves to evolve into the capitalist farmers. In India, the landed aristocracy was incapable of doing so or was incapacitated by the prevailing colonial conditions which prevented and made such a transformation impossible. The powerful traditional mercantile class was displaced first from the international trade and then from the regional trade and part of their capital was subsumed by the East India Company to its own advantage, in the role of interest-bearing capital and the rest of it retreated into the country hinterland flourishing there in the form of usury.

The mirasdars, according to Ravinder Kumar, emerged as rich peasants in the nineteenth-century Maharashtra by transferring the burden of land revenue to the upris.[43] It is an absurd proposition. The historical evidence shows that numerous mirasdars were becoming pauper cultivators. The mirasi lands of such cultivators were sold in Pandharpur taluka of Sholapur district in 1842. In 1856, there were 332 cases in Ahmednagar district in which mirasdars were disposed by Decrees of Civil Courts, in Satara 46 such cases occurred, and in Sholapur 14 cases were recorded. The total number of sales and transfers were reported to be much higher. In all, 4386 cases of sales and transfer took place in Ahmednagar. In Satara district, there were 19 sales and 382 transfers of miras land. In Sholapur district, 210 cases of transfer occurred, of which 33 were by sale, 48 by deed of mortgage, and 129 at the owner's request. In 1862, out of 151 numbers put to auction in Satara district, only 13 realised sums more than 8 years assessment and were given to the highest bidders as miras, 77 fetched less than six years assessment and were sold as gatkul.[44] By mid-nineteenth century, numerous changes were taking place within the mirasdari tenure. The mirasdars did not constitute a homogeneous category any more and considerable leasing-in and leasing-out of land was going on among mirasdars themselves as well as from mirasdars to upris. In various talukas of Ahmednagar district, within mirasdars about 12 to 22 per cent of survey numbers were leased out from one section to another ; and of the mirasdari lands, 10 to 30 per cent were leased out to the upris.[45] The social and economic boundary between the mirasdars and upris was getting blurred with the introduction of the rayatwari system. Both were merged into survey tenure which was heritable and transferable and held by individual cultivators subject to the payment of land revenue to the government. The privilege and distinction attached with the mirasdari tenure became null and void with a single stroke of colonial legislation, viz., 'The Bombay Survey Settlement Act, 1865' (Act I of 1865).

The inamdars, who were holding wholly or partially alienated lands, free from the obligation to pay land revenue and constituted a privileged class of landholders in the Deccan and Southern Maratha Country, were also being gradually deprived of their power and privileges by colonial rule. There had been some rules enacted under the General Regulations of 1827 to deal with inams but a large number of titles were proclaimed to be fraudulent which led to the passing of an India Act XI of 1852 leading to the appointment of Commissioners to enquire into all inam titles. The Inam or Land Commission which investigated into the titles of alienated lands reported in 1857 against the rights of 21 thousand occupiers out of the 35 thousand cases which had been under investigation. The other 14 thousand landowners lived in perpetual terror of ruin. The dispossessed occupants of the estates regarded the action of the government as iniquitous tyranny. In the subsequent year, the newly appointed Political Agent of Nargund, a native state 30 miles east of Dharwar, who was particularly obnoxious in the district from the fact of his having sat on the Land Commission, was murdered.[46] The procedure of enquiry into inam titles proved slow and difficult and after sometimes it was considered better to waive the question of exact proof, and to treat the matter summarily on certain broad principles ; offering reasonable terms to claimants, which if accepted, put an end to troublesome investigations as to title. In 1863, two Bombay Summary Settlement Acts were passed to provide for the final adjustment summarily, of unsettled claims to exemption from the payment of land revenue and to fix the conditions with respect to succession and transfer. The Act II of 1863 was applicable to the districts for which Act XI of 1852 had provided Inam Commissioners, and Act XI of 1863 to those which were under Regulations of 1827. The main principle involved was that the government agreed to forego a special enquiry into the title if the inamdar accepted a summary settlement on the entire estate as made by the collector under the Act. Most of the inamdars accepted summary settlement under the Acts. Initially, the annual revenue alienated amounted to more than Rs. 132.5 lakh. After Summary Settlement under the above Acts Rs. 52.12 lakh had been disallowed, leaving Rs. 80.38 lakh alienated.[47] This implied a considerable curtailment of the power of inamdars. However, the inamdars had not vanished completely as a segment of the landed aristocracy. G. Keatinge noted in 1912 that in the Central Division of the Bombay Presidency, out of a total number of 8000 villages, 1000 were alienated.[48]

In Gujarat, old talukdari estates had survived and remained preserved over 500 villages of Gujarat, out of which about 320 were in Ahmedabad.[49] The holders were declared to be absolute proprietors of their estates under Bombay Act VI of 1862 subject to the payment of a tribute called jama which was fixed for a term of years, and liable to revision.[50] Most of these estates were held in shares on the principles of joint succession. Where there were co-sharers, a manager or *wahiwatdar* was appointed to collect the several shares of the government jama. Legally (section 22 of Bombay Act VI of 1888) the fluctuating jama could be equal to the full survey assessment of all the lands comprised within the estates, but in practice the government demand was generally limited to about 60 per cent of the survey assessment of the cultivated land. The talukdars were exempted from the payment of jama as regards certain classes of land alienated by them before the passing of Bombay Act VI of 1888, and as regards other classes of such lands they were required to pay as jama 50 per cent of the proceeds derived by them.[51] The increased land revenue demand left no margin of profit for talukdars. The arrears of land revenue began to accumulate. Within a decade of survey settlement a significant number of large estates of talukdars and jagirdars in Gujarat and zamindars in Sind were deeply plunged into debt and were threatened with decay, disintegration and dismemberment due to ever-increasing intervention of the usury. The government encroached upon the zamindari rights by issuing a confiscatory order directing the reservation of waste tracts on behalf of the government, and subsequently the Collector of Shikarpur directed to enter such land as government property which was relinquished by the tenants and on which zamindars declined to become responsible for payment of assessment. Earlier all such lands were counted as property of zamindars.[52] As the grip of the usury on talukdari and zamindari estates tightened during the late nineteenth century and their disintegration appeared imminent and inevitable, the state tried to protect them with a view to retain the support of the conservative elements in the countryside through the introduction of the Sind Encumbered Estates Act (Act XIV of 1876) followed by another similar Act after 20 years and Gujarat Talukdari Estates Act (Act VI of 1888). These protective legislations forbade the disintegration and partition of any existing estates without the permission of the government and provided for the state management of such estates till their debts were cleared. In 1901, there were about 620 zamindari estates in Sind under the state protection and another 500 were indirectly relieved by withdrawal of applications by zamindars on the request of their creditors.[53] The relief provided by the legislative measures was very limited. Of the 811 landlords in the Jati taluka in Karachi Collectorate only 8 were found to be free of debts. Of those involved in debts, only 9 zamindars were under the protection of the Encumbered Estates Act.[54] Apart from the burden of debt the endless subdivision of shares among heirs worked towards the decline of zamindari estates. Similarly, a number of bhagdari estates were being broken up owing to the heavy indebtedness and non-payment of land revenue demand. In various districts of Gujarat, the economic condition of landed estates had deteriorated and talukdars were seeking protection under colonial management. Table I shows the number of Talukdari Estates under state protection during 1884 to 1913.

Table I : Landed Estates of Talukdars under State Protection in Gujarat, 1884-1913

Year	Ahmedabad		Kheda		Broach	
	No. of Estates	Total Debt (Rs.)	No. of Estates	Total Debt (Rs.)	No. of Estates	Total Debt (Rs.)
1884-85	40	413443	53	433613	10	504029
1890-91	70	505224	49	430535	7	223152
1894-95	58	464183	34	306189	4	113948
1900-01	37	307072	30	234573	2	22913
1904-05	35	295156	20	234573	2	66913
1912-13	19	196496	18	192699	1	42175

Source: Report on Gujarat Talukdar's Encumbered Estates for the Respective Years.

It was reported that considerable success had been attained by the official agency in providing for consolidation, compromising, and eventually liquidating the debts.

The narvadari and bhagdari tenures had been acknowledged and preserved under Act V of 1862. It restricted alienation of such land and property to non-bhagdars. During 1900 famine, the bhagdars were unable to recover rents from their tenants and could not pay land revenue to the government. So, the bhags were dissolved by government either of their own accord or at the request of bhagdars. With the economic rècovery the bhagdars were anxious to restore the bhagdari tenure. The Bombay Act II of 1910 was passed to empower government to reconstitute such lands into bhags.[55] The Act V of 1886 prohibited alienation of watan rights. The legislative measures had succeeded in retarding the process of decay of the talukdari estates but they could not check it altogether. In 1948, M.B. Desai observed that as the incomes from the estates were dwindling, talukdars were moving towards destitution. Most of the estates were heavily mortgaged to the banias who took the lion's share of the produce by way of interest, dues and repayment of capital. This had resulted in attempts by the talukdars to rack rent the tenants, but the state intervened to check the process and tenancy legislation was passed to protect the tenants restricting talukdar's claim to agrarian surplus.[56]

In Konkan region, especially in Ratnagiri, Kolaba and parts of Thana district, khots occupied the position of privileged landowners. During the initial years of British rule all the khots were treated as absolute proprietors of their villages. During 1851-52, Captain Wingate and Mr. Kambell conducting survey settlement observed that in spite of the vague powers and privileges claimed by the khot his hereditary rights were limited to the office of a village rentier and manager. The government intervened to impose statutory regulation on the status of khots and tenants through the Bombay Act I of 1865 known as Khoti Leases Act. The Survey Settlement Officer was empowered to grant the khot a lease for the full period of 30 years for which a settlement was made in place of the annual agreement. The government had the right to reverse and alter the rates paid by the khots on the expiry of the period of settlement. The khot had the right to settle with the government for the whole village. Also, the tenants had a right to protection against any over-exaction by the khot and the Survey Settlement Officer had the right to fix the demand of the khot on the tenants at the time of the general survey.[57] Ostensibly, the main object of the Act was to set a limit to the exactions of the khot from his tenantry so as to increase the claim of the Colonial State to the agrarian surplus. It was expected to be the *magna charta* of the ryots.[58] The khots saw the legislation as a blow aimed at their tenure. They deeply resented the government's right to fix the demand of the khot on his tenants and protection of tenants from over-exactions. They also opposed the registration of land in the tenant's name.[59] They believed the Act would reduce them to the position of government agents for revenue collection. The khots combined to form an Association for the defence of their rights under the leadership of V.N. Mandlik, himself a khot. They also campaigned through the press and boldly declared that the khots would be satisfied with nothing less than the absolute recognition of their proprietary rights in the soil of their villages. The government cowed down by the agitation of the Khoti Association, appointed a commission in 1874, known as the Khoti Commission.[60] The Report of this Commission formed the basis of the Khoti Settlement Act (Act I of 1880). The Khoti Act did not define the nature and extent of the *khotki* (aggregate of rights of the khot) but merely stated that the khots should continue to hold provided they paid their jama and fulfilled other obligations. It recognized their right as heritable and transferable.[61] The khots were entitled to free state assistance in recovering their rents from defaulters. The khots had a right as against government to resume lands held by privileged occupants in his village which forfeited or lapsed for failure of heirs and those resigned by permanent tenants. He could confer higher rights of a privileged occupant on any or more of his tenants. All miscellaneous land revenue in khoti villages was to go to the khot and all trees in khoti khasgi and khoti nisbat lands belonged to him except those reserved by government. The Act also protected the inferior holders. By this Act, the dharekaris were to pay nothing beyond the government assessment ; the quasi-dharekaris were to pay the assessment plus fixed amount of grain rent. The right of these two classes were heritable and transferable. The tenants, who had occupied the same land continuously from the revenue year 1845-46, were given a right of occupancy, other tenants were declared to be tenants-at-will. The rent payable by the occupancy tenants was the amount agreed upon between both the parties at the time of survey settlement, and if no such agreement was made, the amount was not to exceed one-half of gross produce in the case of rice lands and one-third in the case of varkas land. The khots were given a reciprocal protection in case of neglect of cultivation on the part of the tenants. The Act abolished forced labour under any guise, *phaski, veth, nangarveth,* or *wartala.*[62] On the whole, the Khoti Act of 1880 consolidated the powers of khots considerably throughout the Konkan region. The Act, however, did not resolve the conflict between the khots and the tenants. It declared a large body of long standing tenants to be simply tenants-at-will. Shortly after the Act was passed, a large number of tenants from Chiplun, Khed and Dapoli talukas of Ratnagiri submitted a memorandum asking for the repeal of the Act. Yet, the Government of India approved the Act on the ground that it was an outcome of a long enquiry.[63] From the year 1886, the cause of the tenants was taken up by the Maratha Aikyeehhu Sabha of Bombay and a sustained agitation was launched on behalf of the tenants resulting in some modifications in the Khoti Act.[64] During 1889-90, three khots were murdered and as a result the government appointed the Khoti Enquiry Committee (1890) which warned of serious crisis due to rack-renting and unsatisfactory relations between khots and tenants. Subsequent amendment in Khoti Act (Act I of 1904) aimed at curtailing the excessive powers of khot. It provided for an equitable readjustment of rents where they were deemed to be excessive. In the case of an occupancy tenant, the collector had a discretion to refuse assistance to khots for the recovery of rents exceeding twice the assessment. The amendment also provided for the commutation of the customary crop share rent into cash rent at the prevailing average market prices. Such commutations were likely to undermine the share of khots as prices were continuously rising. They tried to make overstatement of rents, and this created fresh tension in the region. The Act was further amended in 1912 to give some additional right to the occupancy tenants. They could lease out their lands for one year without the consent of khots, and their lands could not be forfeited for non-payment of rent or land revenue until such forfeiture was certified by the collector.[65] By the early twentieth century, khoti system had greatly degenerated leading to the pauperisation of khots and the continued serfdom of the cultivator. The khots had become absentee landlords. Most of the khots had either sold or mortgaged their interests to a *sahukar* who had no concern for the cultivator. The khot had ceased to fulfil any positive administrative function. The collector managed far more villages for the khots than the khots for the collector. From 1920 onwards the agitation against the khots had gathered momentum. The last effort to abolish the khoti system under British rule was made by Dr. B.R. Ambedkar in 1937-38. It was in independent India that the khoti system was finally abolished through the Bombay Khoti Abolition Act in 1949.[66] The powers of the other privileged landowners were abolished through the Tenancy Abolition Act that came into force on first April 1957 and it was known as the 'tillers' day'.

The authority of the village communities and the position of the hereditary revenue officials like patels, kulkarnis, deshmukhs, deshpandes, etc., the so-called service gentry class, was undermined from the onset of the colonial rule. The colonial authorities started maintaining field registers containing the details of area, tenure, rental, etc., of each field in a village in numerical order to enable the revenue authorities to do away with the assistance of the hereditary officers who were the only depositories of such information. The village accountants called kulkarnis in Deccan and Konkan and *talatis* in Gujarat working in conjunction and partly in subordination to the village headmen or patels became salaried servants of the government who had no authority of their own and had to carry out the orders of the district colonial authorities. The chief authority was now vested in the district officials.[67] The village officials were allowed less and less power of interference ; the Company's servants came in closer contact with each individual cultivator under ryotwari system and started fixing land revenue demand on each individual holding. Under the new system, the village communities and village officials lost their traditional powers and function, and also their *raison d'être* and gradually sank into oblivion. Village communities could only be maintained by leaving the task of internal assessment to the village itself. But such an arrangement was against the interests of the colonial rule. The colonial state wanted to deal with individual peasant and extract from him as much land revenue as possible. Under this system the village community and the service gentry became defunct and superfluous. The colonial state by removing the authority of the patel to fix the land revenue on individual ryots and fixing it from above made it more arbitrary because of ignorance of local conditions and individual circumstances. By converting patel into a paid employee of the colonial state it had made him indifferent to extension or improvement in agriculture at the village level. His huks or remunerations were either cut down or drastically reduced. It eroded their authority and limited their power to extract the agrarian surplus. The curtailment or abolition of the village expenses by the village functionaries reduced their power to redistribute the agrarian surplus within the village community. The colonial state considered the village expenses as a pure waste frittered away in foolish spectacles and ceremonies rather than being used for productive public works.

Another noticeable feature of the early colonial rule was the decline of the powerful traditional mercantile class in the big urban centres and flourishing of the petty usury in the countryside. Both these processes were simultaneous and causally inter-connected. As the East India Company acquired monopoly over Indian trade through political conquest, the rival European trading companies and the big indigenous merchants were pushed out of the trade. The native traders survived only as banias, *gomasthas,* agents and subordinate or subservient partners of the English East India Company. The big merchants of India were practically wiped out. Dr. Francis Buchanan wrote about the district of Dinajpur in Bengal in early nineteenth century :

> A great portion of the trade of the District had passed from the hands of the native traders to that of the Company. There were no longer any Saudagars or great native merchants in the District.[68]

Sir Richard Temple, the Governor of Bombay, in his evidence before the Indian Famine Commission of 1880 stated :

> A great many lenders in the principal cities in the interior of India are not so flourishing as they used to be and have not such large concerns as formerly, but the petty moneylenders in the villages in many parts of India has increased, almost multiplied under British rule. For instance, in the Deccan before British rule, the moneylenders were almost entirely Brahmins with a few Marwaris added. Now, after half a century of British rule, the Brahmins mostly remain, and to them has been added a class of Marwaris who are one of the wealthiest and the most powerful and largely ramified classes in the country.[69]

R.N. Gooddine had pointed out in 1845 that the present measures of the land revenue system would make *sahukars* the head of the village, the patel his puppet and the ryots his victim. The prophecy proved strikingly true. As Auckland Colvin remarked before the Deccan Riots Commission in 1876 :

> Under a so-called Ryotwari system it is gradually coming to this, that the ryot is the tenant and the Marwari is the proprietor. It is a Zamindari settlement ; but it is a Zamindari

> settlement stripped of all the safeguards which under such a settlement in upper India are thought indispensable to the tenant. The proprietor is irresponsible ; the tenant unprotected. It promises to become not a Ryotwari, but a Marwari settlement. The settlement in more and more between the government and the Marwari though neither declares the position. While the Marwari has no wish to possess himself of the land but of its produce only, the government so long as the Kunbi is recorded as proprietor, hesitates to look below the surface.[70]

The peasantry was crushed as the entire surplus was drained by the rigid land revenue system of the colonial State and the rapacious demands of the usury. Vaughan Nash visiting India during the great famine of 1900 observed :

> ... the inflexible tribute system is the nether millstone, and the gathering burden of indebtedness is the upper millstone with which we are grinding India.... The British Raj and the Bunya Raj eat up his (cultivator's) crops, and what one leaves, the other devours.[71]

Colonial State and Ideology

The state under colonial conditions was alien to civil society. There was no organic link between the indigenous social classes of the colonies and the state. When the state extended some support and protection to the dominant classes of the colonies, it did so in its own interest. The colonial state was governed by the interest of dominant class or federative of dominant classes in the imperialist countries. Under imperialism, monopoly capital and state organisation were intricately interlocked on a global scale. The colonial state and its legal forms were historically distinct from that of the bourgeois constitutional state. Within Marxist discourse, conception of capitalist state differs considerably among different schools. Whereas the instrumentalists regarded state as an instrument of domination in the hands of the ruling classes over the entire society, the structuralists believed that the state played a crucial role in mediating social contradictions and providing a factor of unity in social formation ; still further, the Frankfurt School considered state as a mystification, that is, a concrete institution which served the interest of dominant class but sought to portray itself as serving the nation as a whole thereby obscuring the basic lines of antagonism.[72] In advanced capitalist societies state had an organic link with dominant classes of society, and hence, mediation and mystification was necessary. In colonial situation, state was external to indigenous society and expressed interests of dominant classes of metropolis. Such mediations or mystifications were neither possible nor considered necessary.

The colonial state was essentially repressive in nature. Unlike the West European Constitutional States which combined domination with consent of the subject people through the hegemonic sphere of ideas and institutions, the colonial state ruled primarily through direct domination based on force and coercion. The consent of the ruled was hardly the concern of the colonial state. The colonial state established its dominance through political and military conquest and consolidated its rule through coercive means. The only legitimacy and justification was force. The educative and formative role of state has relevance for modern states and not for colonies. The colonial state did not exist simply as a politico-juridical organisation in a narrow sense whose functions were limited to the safeguarding of public order and respect for the laws. The so-called nightwatchman state *Veilleur de nuit* (Fr.) or *Stato-Carabiniere* (It.) has historically never existed, not even in the most liberal regimes of industrial capitalism with free trade ideology of *laissez-faire laissez aller,* except in theory as a limiting hypothesis.[73] The colonial state was a *gendarme* state or police state which adorned itself with respectable robes at home but went nude in colonies.

The colonial state was imbued with autocratic ethos. Its governance was not based on the representation of the ruled. The self-governing institutions like village communities were condemned as primitive, barbaric and archaic. It was based on the rule of law, no doubt, but it was the law of the ruler imposed from the above and repressive in nature, a logical consequence of the repressive state. The law did not evolve as an organic formation of the society as it did in the Western Europe. The power and authority of the colonial bureaucracy were virtually unlimited. There were no restrictive elements within the indigenous social structure of the colonies. The indigenous people who occupied the lowest hierarchy in administration had to obey the superior administrators who had reserved the decision-making powers for themselves. The authority of the ruler was undisputed and unquestionable.

Imperialism is akin to parasitism. The colonial state was parasitic in nature. It aimed at the maximum extraction of social surplus by encroaching upon the institutional claimants and ordinary cultivators. The colonial state created a class-structure in which parasitic social classes like landed aristocracy and usury provided instrumentality for internal exploitation in conjunction with external exploitation by the colonial state. This symbiotic relationship sustained colonial rule. Parasites inevitably decay in nature.[74] They flourish on life blood of the host. As the host begins to sicken and die parasite cannot survive for long. The increasing impoverishment and recurrent famines were signals to the impending crisis which awaited imperialism and the parasitic indigenous social classes who were locked together by a cosmic destiny. They perished together. The abolition of landlordism and usury followed the departure of colonial rulers.

The colonial state was not premised upon any fixed definite ideology. As imperialism advanced from mercantile to industrialist and finally to finance capitalist phase, the set of ideas governing colonialism also underwent change. The ideology was a function of the time, of historical circumstances, of changing social conditions in metropolis as well as colonies. No ideology could mask, legitimise or justify imperialist domination over the colonies. They provide some clues towards the governing processes of the colonial state. Excepting those who blindly believe that 'ideas govern the world', it would appear that pragmatist considerations were more important in decision-making than any theory. But the prevailing ideologies constituted a significant component in the social milieu in which these processes were taking shape and could not have remained unaffected by them. It will not be inappropriate to examine the dominant ideas of the age briefly.

Mercantilism was an ideology of the nascent merchant bourgeoisie. It was premised upon the notion that trade, especially foreign trade was the prime source of profit and national wealth. They believed that labour was only productive in those branches of production whose products, when sent abroad, brought back more money than they had cost (or than had to be exported in exchange for them) ; which therefore enabled a country to participate to a greater degree in products of newly opened gold and silver mines. They saw that in these countries there was a rapid growth of wealth and of the middle class. To acquire wealth a country's exports should exceed its imports and balance of payment should remain positive. To maximize trading profits it was necessary to eliminate competition at the point of purchase and at the selling point because competition would reduce margin of profit. It was necessary to acquire monopoly over trade by pushing out the rivals and competitors in the international trade. 'Beggar thy neighbour' policy followed from this. The profits would multiply manifold if a country acquired an exclusive privilege or monopoly in the international trade. Mercantilism also rested on the belief that a nation should export merchandise and import precious metals like gold and silver to become wealthy. It was necessary to conserve bullion supply within the nation and if reverse happened the country will lose its wealth to others. The outflow of bullion to countries like India and China was a constant source of worry as their negative balance of trade had to be met with export of gold and silver from England and Europe. The political and military conquest by trading companies therefore was not incidental. The trading profits could be multiplied if rivals could be excluded from competition and if payment could be arranged at the point or origin itself rather than by exporting gold and silver from England. The State should facilitate international trade and refrain from imposing taxes on trade because that would discourage the trading class and depress the process of formation of national wealth.[75]

The contention was refuted by French Physiocrats who argued that agriculture, and not trade, was the primary source of national wealth. Agricultural labour alone was productive. Industry merely transformed or altered what was produced by agriculture and it created nothing. Trade merely exchanged these products in natural or altered form. Agricultural labour reproduced more than what was absolutely necessary for its subsistence, and that more was rent appropriated by the landowner, the only and true form of wealth. Therefore, wealth appeared as a gift of nature originating from the productivity of land which enabled labour to transform inorganic matter into organic. The other economic activities were merely auxiliary to agriculture. The Physiocrats further argued that rent being the only true form of wealth, it would be appropriate to place all taxes on landed property. Any taxation of other forms of property would ultimately fall on landed property but it would happen in a roundabout way and would be injurious to other economic activities and act as a hindrance to production. It would be more appropriate to tax landed property directly rather than indirectly. A corollary of this proposition was that industry should not be taxed. Taxation and along with it all forms of State intervention were removed from industry itself and latter was freed from all interventions by the state. Since industry created nothing, but only transformed values given by agriculture into another form ; since it added no new value to them, but returned the values supplied to it, though in altered form, as an equivalent, the Physiocrats argued, it was naturally desirable that this process of transformation should proceed without interruptions and in the cheapest way ; and this was only realized through competition. In this form, Physiocracy became the foundation for the ideology of *laissez faire, laissez aller,* of free trade and free competition, the removal from industry and trade of all interference by the state, monopolies, etc.[76]

The permanent settlement or zamindari land revenue system introduced by British in Bengal is seen by Ranjit Guha as a synthesis of ideologies. Dow was a mercantilist, Pattullo and Francis were physiocrats, Law and to a lesser degree Cornwallis were free traders. These divergent intellectual affiliations undoubtedly led to difference of opinion and conflict of individuals. The permanent settlement is seen as a convergence of divergent ideological stances, a slow transition from mercantilism to free trade. This lopsided emphasis on ideologies ignores the real social forces involved in shaping the social processes and realities.[77] Theory meant little to many settlement officers as they struggled to make sense of the complex patterns of landholding they encountered, noted T.R. Metcalf.[78]

As the British rule was established over India, the colonial administrators and others began to probe into the deep past, the language, the manners and customs, and the institutions of the people over whom they had come to rule. They studied and translated the classical texts of oriental languages, the Sanskrit, the Persian, etc. They concluded that India in distant past constituted a great civilization as revealed by their intimate knowledge of its culture, institutions and philosophy. Those who celebrated and glorified India's past or classical oriental past were called Orientalists. They developed a deep respect and sympathetic understanding of Hindu civilisation. They also highlighted that India shared its past with the West. It was reflected in the languages of Indo-European family which had a common origin as revealed by the grammatical structure of classical languages such as Sanskrit, Greek and Latin. Some of the glorious ancient institutions such as village communities also had some common origin in the distant past. Once magnificent, the oriental civilisation had now fallen and relapsed into barbarism. Having reached a high degree of civilisation India began to decline in art, architecture, culture and everything in the middle ages. When British confronted India in the eighteenth century it was in a degenerate condition. They deplored the loss of culture and civilisation. But India could be civilised again with British help who had come here to reform India, on a divine mission, on a 'civilising mission'. There was a veiled ideological justification or legitimisation for political and military conquest of India in the project of Orientalists. It was not a matter of chance but a matter of divine will that they were here to rule over India. The massive projects of reforms which inspired liberals later were an outcome of deep faith in this underlying assumption though they shifted emphasis from divine to human agency.

The historical mission of liberalism was to liberate individuals from age-old bondage to customs and traditions, to priests, nobles and despots so as to make them free, rational and autonomous beings capable of leading a life of conscious deliberation and choice. The liberal ideals had a universal validity. They believed that human nature was intrinsically same everywhere and the essence of history was progress which was also same everywhere. They did not share the orientalist lofty notions of India's golden past, on the contrary they condemned India's past and present, and for that matter they condemned European past as well and called it 'Dark Age' but they were optimistic of change as they saw entire human history as a march from barbarism to civilisation. The wholesale transformation of every society was possible, desirable and inevitable. The agents of this transformation were law, education and free trade. There were differences over urgency and means of reform. Liberalism, in any case, was not a coherent ideology despite many shared assumptions. It was an umbrella term for a vast variety of stances with all the inherent contradictions implicit in it. There were evangelicals, free traders and utilitarians, reformist and radicals with diverse set of opinions. Evangelicism emphasised Christianity as a vehicle of change. To rescue colonial people from ignorance, darkness, tyranny, orthodoxy and barbarism there was no better way than making them good Christians. So, all that was required was to open Churches and schools, to attract indigenous colonial people to them, impart them Christian education and they will become free, happy, and enlightened people. The free traders wanted the State to follow non-interventionist stance and confine itself to good governance. They emphasized *laissez-faire laissez-aller* doctrine as the central one. For utilitarians, the criterion of utility was the measure of social progress. 'Exactly in proportion as utility is the object of every pursuit, may we regard a nation as civilized' they argued. Light taxes and good laws, that was all India needed to free itself from stagnation and make advance towards progress. The representative government was not suited to colonial people. They forgot that there could either be a liberal state or a despotic state but not both. The utilitarian philosophy found its echo in the new political economy developed by David Ricardo who argued that rent was a monopoly value which arose because as an instrument of production land was limited in quantity and variable in quality and because it could be appropriated as private property. With the growth of population and wealth, the same amount of capital and labour gave reduced output. The rate of profit and capital accumulation fell while rent increased. According to Ricardo, the entire production could be absorbed as rent except bare minimum subsistence wages, at least theoretically. The course of economic progress benefited only landlord at the expense of every other class. The landowner contributed nothing to production, while labourer contributed his labour, capitalist his capital. The utility of landowner for production process was zero. Rent was an unearned income acquired due to monopoly of land and hence, the most suitable subject for taxation. Every other tax was open to objection, on the ground that it tended to check production directly or indirectly. On the other hand, rent could be wholly absorbed by taxation without in the smallest degree interfering with profits, wages, or the prices of necessities. Logically, it would be ideal to eliminate the landlord as a social class as it was detrimental to social progress.[79] Was this utilitarianism that inspired the introduction of rayatwari system in western India? We cannot say. If we admit this plea then how do we explain the survival and protection of the privileged parasitic land-owning classes like talukdars, inamdars, khots and zamindars by colonial state through special legislation. Evidently, the ground realities and political expediency had its role in determining the state policies and social processes.

Anyway, attitudes and beliefs may be important but they also change. R.N. Gooddine was contemptuous of the system of village communities which he dismissed as primitive, irrational and archaic institution. This was premised upon the belief that only West European institutions were the enlightened ones and founded upon the principles of perfection and rationality. R.N. Gooddine had observed in 1845 :

> The rude and arbitrary government of a rude people has been supplanted by one of liberal and philanthropic principles.... Oppression has been removed, and the road to improvement lays open before them.

About half a century later another outstanding liberal John Hobson was to dismiss these assumptions contemptuously. He wrote :

> It is now hardly possible for any one who has carefully followed these events to speak of Europe undertaking a "mission of civilisation" in China without his tongue in his cheek. Imperialism in the Far East is stripped nearly bare of all motives and methods save those of distinctively commercial origin.... Nor can it be maintained that the new industrialism of machinery and factories, which we have introduced is civilizing India, or even leading to her material prosperity.... The decay or forcible supersession of the native industrial arts is still more deplorable, for these always constitute the poetry of common life, the free play of the imaginative faculty of a nation in the ordinary work of life.

He further went on to say that

> .... millions of peasants in India are struggling to live on half an acre. Their existence is a constant struggle with starvation, ending too often in defeat. Their difficulty is not to live human lives upto the level of their poor standard of comfort—but to live at all and not die.... We may truly say that in India, except in the irrigated tracts, famine is chronic —endemic.[80]

The taste of pudding is in the eating. This was what constituted the civilizing mission of imperialism.

By the end of the nineteenth century inter-imperialist rivalries were beginning to surface in Western Europe and its accompanying ideology of liberalism was also deep in the throes of crisis. It was being supplanted by a variety of reactionary stances, like racialism, jingoism and social imperialism. In the wake of anti-colonial revolts in the colonies, notably popular uprising of 1857 in India and Jamaican Revolt in 1865, the project of reforms were abandoned. The reforms in colonies were pointless and dangerous. The Afro-Asian colonies comprised of dark and inferior races who were incapable of a civilized order. They were fit to be ruled by white races and imperialism was to rule over them permanently. India was never civilized, India could never be civilized. India was never a nation, India could never become a nation, they asserted. Jingoism openly and blatantly justified and glorified political and military conquest and British imperial expansion. Imperialism was to dominate the world through military means. Social imperialism adopted a more soft and apologetic stance. Social imperialists saw social reform and imperialism as interdependent. To them, a strong and growing empire was vital to Britain's future economic prosperity, which was necessary to pay for social improvements. In turn social reform by generating social cohesion and a healthy and educated population, thereby enhancing Britain's 'national' or 'social' efficiency, was seen as crucial to Britain's survival as a major imperial power. During the early half of the twentieth-century Europe was torn apart by bitter political conflicts and polarised among extreme right wing ideologies of nazism and fascism on the one hand and extreme left wing ideology of communism on the other hand, virtually wiping out the political space earlier occupied by liberalism.

Colonialism–Continuity–Complicity

In some of the neo-imperialist writings, two assumptions have gained currency recently. The first assumption is that there is a continuity in class structure and social institutions from pre-colonial to colonial period. This is ostensibly to dismiss the Nationalists and Marxists argument that there is a discontinuity, disruption or break in the social structure under colonial rule. Both Nationalists and Marxists had argued that colonialism led to underdevelopment, impoverishment and created a social structure that did not allow social progress. This had implied that there was a fundamental contradiction or conflict of interests between the indigenous social classes and imperialism. The second assumption of the neo-imperialists, stressed that there was no such conflict of interests and it is argued that on the contrary there was a complicity of the colonial people in the constitution of the project of imperialism.[81] The neo-imperialist assertions do not stand the scrutiny of the empirical evidence.

The colonial rule was essentially exploitative and parasitic in nature. It aimed at the maximum extraction of social surplus from the colony. To do so it had to undermine the social and economic powers and privileges of the traditional powerful indigenous social classes. At the same time it needed to create an internal mechanism to facilitate this exploitation by promoting certain parasitic social classes which would be instrumental in this process. As the East India Company consolidated its rule by political and military conquest and enforced its monopoly over international and internal trade, the powerful and independent traditional mercantile class of Jagat Seth, Virji Vohra and big saudagars declined and vanished. It was substituted by a new class of petty traders, commission agents, gomasthas, village banias and sahukars who flourished because of their close connections with colonial rule in subservience to the East India Company. The petty-usury thrived by enslaving the petty producers, artisans and cultivators and was strengthened by colonial laws and institutions. In pre-colonial order a moneylender could claim nothing beyond the customary rate of interest and was under the control of village communities and indigenous states. The colonial state removed restrictions on rate of interest and gave moneylender legal powers and support to transfer movable and immovable property of the borrower in case of default leading to expropriation and pauperization of artisans and peasants on a large scale.

The colonial state pushed the land revenue demand to the maximum possible limit. The maximum extraction of agrarian surplus could be possible only by encroaching upon the share of other claimants and the actual cultivator. The land revenue demand was rigid and fixed, often extracted through coercive means including attachment of land and other means. The land revenue under colonial rule had to be paid, crops or no crops. The resilience and flexibility of the pre-colonial order was gone. The powers and privileges of the hereditary revenue officials, the patel and the kulkarni at the village level, and the deshmukh and deshpande at the district level were snatched away. In the new system they had no role in the fixation of land revenue demand as the state proceeded to make direct settlement with the individual cultivator. The powers of the so-called service gentry were assumed by the colonial settlement officers and district collectors. The traditional position of the landed aristocracy declined. A large number of large landowners, including zamindars, talukdars, inamdars and khots were plunged into debt and were involved into deep economic crisis despite colonial intervention through legislation. The independent and small peasantry was losing land and was getting impoverished and gradually sinking into the status of dwarf holding cultivators, tenants and agricultural labourers. The burden of land revenue and usury brought compulsive involvement into the market economy, leading to substitution of food crops for non-food crops like opium, indigo and cotton and where such a shift was under the pressure of state or usury, the cultivator did not benefit but was forced to continue production under degenerating conditions with loss of economic independence. The continuing impoverishment resulted in successive waves of recurrent and intense famines and protracted struggles and revolts against the colonial authority about which neo-imperialist historiography remains silent.

The domain of power is intrinsically interrelated to resistances. The talk of complicity in the colonial situation is absurd. The conflict in the rural society was essentially centred around the appropriation of the agrarian surplus by various agencies. The colonial state extracted surplus through heavy land revenue demand, taxes and fines. An intermediate class of parasites like usurers and landlords also became instrumental in facilitating the colonial exploitation. The colonial rule oppressed all sections of society but not with equal intensity. The oppression was felt unevenly and in stages by various social classes. In the initial stages, the colonial rule severely undermined the traditional position of a section of the landed aristocracy which was uprooted from the estates and forts ; lost its titles, privileges and powers over rural society, and moved towards irrevocable doom and extinction. Consequently, these elements of landed aristocracy came into contradiction with the colonial state and revolted in sporadic and unorganised fashion. Of course, some of the functionaries dealing with local revenue, administration and police matters, like *mamlatdars,* patels and kulkarnis were retained but they lost their hereditary privileges and distinctions and sank into the status of petty paid employees. They expressed their discontent by holding back the necessary information and non-compliance with colonial authority. There were numerous complaints of insubordination in the initial stages of colonial rule. The parasitic classes of usury and landlords which provided instrumentality for colonial exploitation also became targets of attack by peasants, artisans and other oppressed strata of society.

Throughout the colonial rule there were intense uprisings and popular revolts against the colonial authorities and their instrumental parasitic classes.[82] For instance, Bengal Presidency had Sanyasi-Fakir rebellion (1770), Rangpur peasant rebellion (1783), Santhal revolt (1784), Chuar rebellion (1798), Laik rebellion (1806-16), Paik uprising in Orissa (1817-25), Pagalpanthi Revolt in Mymen Singh (1825-27), Wahhabi uprising in 24 Pargana (1831), Kol uprising in Chhotanagpur (1831-32), Farazi Movement (1838-48), Santhal uprising (1855-56), Indigo rebellion (1859-62), Pabna Rent rebellion (1873), and Munda uprising in Chhotanagpur (1899-1900). Similarly, western India also experienced serious outbreaks of violence in Ahmednagar Jail uprising (1821), Kittur uprising in Dharwar (1824-29), Ramoshis revolts in Poona (1826), Koli uprising in Poona (1839-46), Village Headmen's strikes in Nadiad in Gujarat (1813-14), Rajput and Koli revolts in Gujarat (1826-30), Banditti insolence in Kutch (1819-20), Bhil uprising in Ahmednagar (1857), Naikdas uprising in Gujarat (1859, 1868), Vagher rebellion (1858), Koli uprising in Poona (1873), Deccan Peasant uprising (1875), Vasudeo Balwant Phadke revolt (1879), Talavias revolt in Broach (1885) and Bhil uprising in Panch Mahals in Gujarat (1899). In south India, there were Poligar revolts (1799-1801), Moppila uprising in Malabar (1921-22), Rampa rebellion (1922-24) and Telangana uprising (1946-51). In north India, in Punjab there was Kuka rebellion during 1866-72, in Oudh Tenant's revolt in 1921, Chauri-Chaura uprising in 1922. Besides these, of course, the Popular Uprising of 1857 and Gandhian struggles in Champaran (1917), Kheda Satyagraha (1918) and Bardoli Satyagraha (1928) are well known. Towards the end of colonial rule fierce struggles were going on in western India (Warli uprising, 1945), in eastern India (Tebhaga struggle of the cropsharers, 1946-47) and south India (Telangana uprising, 1946-51). Anyone who is remotely aware of these fragments of history of anti-colonial resistances in India will outrightly dismiss the theory of complicity.

NOTES

1. R.N. Gooddine, *Report on Village Communities of the Deccan,* Bombay, 1852 (Part I of the present volume).
2. Henry Sumner Maine, *Village Communities in the East and West,* London, 1876 (rpt., New Delhi, 1985).
3. Marx-Engels, *Pre-Capitalist Socio-Economic Formations,* Moscow, 1979, pp. 234-69, 274-97.
4. B.H. Baden-Powell, *Origin and Growth of Village Communities in India,* London, 1899 ; also, *The Land System of British India,* vol. II, pp. 108-94, London, 1892 (rpt., New Delhi, 1990).
5. Quoted in R.C. Dutt, *The Economic History of India,* vol. I, pp. 239-54 (New Delhi, rpt., 1976).
6. Quoted in T.R. Metcalf, *Ideologies of the Raj,* Cambridge University Press, New Delhi, 1998, p. 70.
7. Bipan Chandra, 'Karl Marx, His Theories of Asian Societies and Colonial Rule'

in *Sociological Theories : Races and Colonialism,* UNESCO, Poole (England), 1980, pp. 383-451.

8. Karl Marx, *Capital,* vol. I, Moscow, 1977, pp. 337-39.
9. D.D. Kosambi, *An Introduction to the Study of Indian History,* Bombay, 1975, Romila Thapar, *The Past and Prejudice,* New Delhi, 1975 ; Irfan Habib, 'Distribution of Landed Property in Pre-British India', in *Enquiry,* vol. II, no. 3, Winter 1965, pp. 21-75 ; also 'An Examination of Wittfogel's Theory of "Oriental Despotism" ', in *Enquiry,* no. 6, pp. 54-73. Bipan Chandra, op. cit.
10. S.N. Mukherjee, 'The Idea of the Village Community and the British Administrators', in *Enquiry* (N.S.), vol. III, no. 3, Winter 1971, pp. 57-67.
11. Louis Dumont, 'The Village Community from Munro to Maine', in *Contributions to Indian Sociology,* vol. 9 (1966), pp. 67-89 ; also his major work, *Homo Hierarchicus : The Caste System and its Implications,* Oxford University Press, New Delhi, 1988.
12. Clive Dewey, 'Images of the Village Community: A Study in Anglo-Indian Ideology', in *Modern Asian Studies,* vol. 6, no. 3 (1972), pp. 291-328.
13. Alexander Gershenkron, 'Agrarian Policies and Industrialisation : Russia 1861-1917', in *The Cambridge Economic History of Europe,* vol. VI, part II, New Delhi, 1979, pp. 706-800.
14. W. Burns (ed.), *Sons of the Soil : Studies of the Indian Cultivator,* Delhi, 1941, p. 24 ; J.B. Shukla, *Life and Labour in a Gujarat Taluka,* Bombay, 1937, p. 129.
15. This appears to be a universal feature of the village communities. See for instance, A.K.S. Lambton, *Landlord and Peasant in Persia,* Oxford University Press, New Delhi, 1969, p. 9.
16. Alexander Mackay, *Western India,* London, 1853, pp. 133-34.
17. L.B. Jagalpure and K.D. Kale, *Sarola Kasar : Study of a Deccan Village in the Famine Zone,* Ahmednagar, 1938, p. 227.
18. *Deccan Riots Commission,* Appendix C, Part IV, pp. 208-11, *Report on Native Newspapers* for the week ending 19 June 1875.
19. V.S. Joshi, *Vasudeo Balvant Phadke : First Indian Rebel Against British Rule* Bombay, 1959, pp. 50-64, 98-100.
20. File No. 263/64B, *'Disturbances at Pilwai Village'* Taluka Vijapur, Kadi Division, 1898, Baroda Record Office, Baroda.
21. Meeta and Rajivlochan, *Farmers Suicide,* Pune, 2006.
22. Karl Marx, *Capital,* vol. III, Moscow, 1974, pp. 333-34, fn. 50.
23. Resolution No. 15-431-1, dated Simla, 11 October 1906 of Department of Revenue and Agriculture (Land Revenue Branch), Govt. of India, *Revenue Department,* vol. 162, *Compilation No. 586 of the year 1906.*

24. *Selection from the Records of Bombay Government, DXXIV Character of Land Tenures and System of Survey and Settlements in the Bombay Presidency,* Bombay, 1914, p. 7, para 27 (Part II of the present volume).

25. *Home Deptt.* (Rev. Br.) No. 135 of 1840, Report on Survey and Assessment (paras 5-10) ; B.H. Baden-Powell, *The Land System of British India,* vol. III, book IV, part II, rpt., New Delhi, 1974, pp. 256-57 ; *Bombay Administration Report for 1882-83,* p. 36.

26. *DXXIV, Character of Land Tenures . . . . ,* op. cit., paras 65-70.

27. *Home Deptt.* (Rev. Br.) No. 135 of 1840. *S.R.B.G. (N.S.) LXX Revision of Assessment in Mawal Taluka (Poona*), Bombay, 1854, para 29.

28. *DXXIV, Character of Land Tenures . . . . ,* paras 29-40.

29. Ibid., paras 42-6.

30. Ibid., paras 47-52.

31. Out of the 1338 village in the Ratnagiri district, 969 were *nival khoti* (purely held by khots), 170 villages were pure *dhara* held by khots, 134 were *khichadi* (mixed dhara and khoti). Thus about 1273 village were managed or manageable by khots. Only 65 village were *khalsa,* held under ryotwari tenure. *S.R.B.G. (N.S.) CCCC XLVI, Proprietary Rights of Khots in the Ratnagiri District,* Bombay, 1907, p. 6.

32. *S.R.B.G. (N.S.) II, Survey and Assessment, Ratnagiri District,* 1852, pp. 8-9, 49-51.

33. *Bombay Presidency Gazetteers,* vol. X, *Ratnagiri District,* Bombay, 1880, p. 209.

34. *S.R.B.G. (N.S.) CXCVII, Captain Dowell's Notes on the Survey of Old Ratnagiri Taluka,* Bombay, 1830.

35. *B.P.G.* vol. X, *Ratnagiri* (1880), op. cit., pp. 209-10.

36. *Revenue Department,* vol. 118, *Compilation 625 of the year 1890.*

37. *S.R.B.G. (N.S.) CXXXIV,* E.T. Candy, *Notes on the Khoti Tenure,* Bombay, 1907 p. 45.

38. *S.R.B.G. (N.S.) II Svy. & Assess. Ratnagiri* (1852), pp. 23, 28 ; *DLIX, Revision Settlement, Sangameshwar Taluka (Ratnagiri*), 1915, p. 9.

39. A.V. Patvardhan, *Serfdom in the Konkan,* Poona, 1925, pp. 9-15 ; *B.P.G.* vol. X, *Ratnagiri* (1880), pp. 212-13.

40. *DXXIV, Character of Land Tenures . . . . ,* op. cit., paras 56-62.

41. Report of J. Pollen on 'Rights of Zamindars in the Province of Sind', in *Rev. Deptt.,* vol. 301, *Compilation No. 1436* of the year 1892, *DXXIV, Character of Land Tenures . . . . ,* op. cit., paras 94-111.

42. A.S. Altekar, *History of the Village Communities in Western India,* Oxford, 1927 ; D.S. Modak, *Bombay Land System and Village Administration,* Poona, 1934.
43. Ravinder Kumar, *Western India in the Nineteenth Century,* London, 1968 ; 'The Rise of Rich Peasantry in Western India', in D.A. Low (ed.), *Soundings in Modern South Asian History,* Berkeley 1968, pp. 25-58.
44. G. Keatinge, *Rural Economy of the Bombay Deccan,* Bombay, 1912, p. 3 ; Alexander Rogers, *The Land Revenues of Bombay,* vol. II, London, 1892, New Delhi, rpt., 1993, p. 79 ; *Proceedings of the Bombay Government on Mirasi Tenure,* Bombay, 1863, pp. 8-9 paras 9-10, p. 49 para 44.
45. *S.R.B.G. CXXIII (N.S.) Papers Relating to Revision of Assessment in Six Talukas of Ahmednagar District,* Bombay, 1870, pp. 16, 52, 86, 107, 126, 143.
46. Evelyn Wood, *The Revolt in Hindustan, 1857-59,* Matheun & Co., London, 1908, pp. 283-90.
47. *S.R.B.G. (N.S.) DXXIV, Character of Land Tenures . . . . ,* op. cit., paras 65-70. Baden-Powell, *The Land System . . . . ,* vol. III, op. cit., pp. 302-04.
48. G. Keatinge, *Rural Economy . . . . ,* op. cit., pp. 30-32.
49. M.B. Desai, *The Rural Economy of Gujarat,* Oxford University Press, New Delhi, 1948, pp. 97-99.
50. Baden-Powell, *The Land System, ... ,* vol III, op. cit., p. 283.
51. R.D. Choksey, *Economic Life in the Bombay Gujarat, 1800-1939,* Asia Pub. House, Bombay, 1968, p. 71.
52. Order No. 176 of 27 January 1865, para 22, in *Rev. Deptt.,* vol. 301, *Compilation 1436 of the year 1892.*
53. *Rev. Deptt.,* vol. 62, *Compilation 1367 Part I of the year 1901.*
54. *Jati Taluka Settlement Reoprt,* Karachi Collectorate, 1899, p. 16 para 39.
55. R.D. Choksey, *Economic Life in Gujarat,* op. cit., p. 77.
56. M.B. Desai, *Rural Economy of Gujarat,* op. cit., p. 99.
57. R.D. Choksey, *Economic Life in the Bombay Konkan, 1818-1939,* Bombay, 1960, pp. 116-17.
58. *S.R.B.G. CXXXIV.* E.T. Candy, *Notes on Khoti Tenure,* Bombay, 1907, Memo. by Mr. Boswell, p. 68.
59. R.D. Choksey, *Konkan . . . . ,* op. cit., pp. 117-18.
60. A.V. Patvardhan, *Serfdom in the Kondan,* op. cit., pp. 34-36.
61. Baden-Powell, *The Land System . . . . ,* vol. III, op. cit., p. 297.
62. The Khoti Settlement Act (Act I of 1880) in *Acts Passed by the Governor of Bombay in Council in the years 1878-80,* Bombay, 1882.

63. *Rev. & Agri. Deptt. (Rev. Br.) Progs.* for Nov. 1880, Nos. 40-41.
64. A.V. Patvardhan, *Serfdom in the Konkan,* op. cit., p. 36.
65. *Deptt. of Rev. & Agl. (Land Rev. Br.) Progs.* Part 'B', Nos. 26-27, Nov. 1898 ; *Legislative Deptt. 'B' Progs.* Nos. 94-95, Nov. 1898 ; *Land Rev. Admn. Reports Bombay Presy. 1907-1908 to 1914-1915* ; A.V. Patvardhan, *Serfdom in the Konkan,* op. cit., pp. 8-16.
66. *Maharashtra Peasant Congress Committee Report,* 1936, p. 58, R.D. Choksey, *Konkan . . . . ,* op. cit., pp. 125-26.
67. D.S. Modak, *Bombay Land System and Village Administration,* Poona, 1934.
68. For details, see Ramakrishna Mukherjee, *The Rise and Fall of the East India Company,* Berlin, 1955, pp. 174-81.
69. *Indian Famine Commission, 1880,* Part II, Appendix II, Selected Evidence, Evidence by Sir Richard Temple, Governor of Bombay, p. 33.
70. 'Confidential Memorandum of the Poona and Ahmednagar Agrarian Riots' by Auckland Colvin, dated 8 November 1875 in *Deccan Riots Commission, Memo., Evidence etc.,* Bombay, 1876.
71. Vaughan Nash, *The Great Famine and its Causes,* London, 1900 (New Delhi, rpt., 1996), p. 92.
72. David A. Gold, Clarence Y.H. Lo & Eric Olin Wright, 'Recent Developments in Marxist Theories of the Capitalist State', in *Monthly Review* (New York), Part I, No. 5, 1975, pp. 29-43 ; and Part II, No. 6, 1975, pp. 36-51.
73. Antonio Gramsci, *Prison Notebooks,* New York, 1978, p. 261 ; S. Bhattacharya, 'Laissez Faire in India' in *Indian Economic and Social History Review,* vol. II, no. 1, Jan. 1966, pp. 1-22.
74. John A. Hobson, *Imperialism : A Study,* London, rpt., 1988 ; V.I. Lenin, *Imperialism, the Highest Stage of Capitalism,* Moscow, 1970.
75. Ramakrishna Mukherjee, *The Rise and Fall of the East India Company,* Berlin, 1955, pp. 15-18.
76. Karl Marx, *Theories of Surplus Value,* Part I, Moscow, 1975, pp. 52-53, 153-54.
77. Ranjit Guha, *A Rule of Property for Bengal : An Essay on the Idea of Permanent Settlement,* New Delhi, 1982.
78. T.R. Metcalf, *Ideologies of the Raj,* Oxford University Press, New Delhi, 2005, p. 36.
79. Eric Stokes, *The English Utilitarians and India,* Oxford University Press, New Delhi, 1992, T.R. Metcalf, *Ideologies . . . . ,* op. cit.
80. John A. Hobson, *Imperialism,* op. cit., pp. 289-90, 307.

81. A major proponent of continuity-complicity argument is C.A. Bayly. His major writings include, *Rulers, Townsmen and Bazaars, 1770-1870,* New Delhi, 1983, *Empire and Information, 1780-1870,* New Delhi, 1996 ; *Origins of Nationality in South Asia*, Oxford University Press, New Delhi, 1998.

82. The literature on this subject is numerous. For a general anthology, see A.R. Desai (ed.), *Peasant Struggles in India*, Oxford University Press, New Delhi, 1979.

PART I

REPORT

ON THE

VILLAGE COMMUNITIES OF THE DECCAN

By Mr. R. N. GOODDINE

Bombay
1852

To

CAPTAIN D. DAVIDSON,

Superintendent of the Ahmednuggur Revenue Survey and Assessment.

SIR,

IN pursuance of your orders, directing me to collect information regarding the Village System generally, but having especial reference to the claims of Village Officers to Purbhara Huks,[1] or remuneration from their villages, exclusive of what they receive from Government, I beg to submit the following Report upon the subject.

2. The villages in which I have carried on the inquiry are the thirty-three which form the Koombharee Purgunna or Mahalkaree's division of the Patoda Talooka ; and as the same usages, with slight modifications, generally prevail throughout the Zilla, the above examples will, I conceive, sufficiently elucidate the question.

3. The nature and amount of the claims of Village Officers principally depend on the position they hold in their villages, and the nature of the tenure of land which prevails in them ; for in some villages the Patel receives no huks on land ; in others Meeras land is exempt, and he only receives them from Gutkoolee or Gairan ; while in others, again, he receives them from every description of land, both Meeras, Gutkoolee, Enam, and Gairan. The above circumstances, together with the numerous collateral ones which it will be necessary to refer to, such as the nature and amount of huks generally, both of village officers and artizans ; the estimation in which they are held by the recipients ; the method in which they are collected ; their effect upon the ryots, agriculture, and trade, will render it necessary to enter into a brief analysis of the Village System. For, I conceive, it will be hopeless to expect to arrive at correct opinions on these subjects, unless we are first masters of the necessary detail, and of the peculiar spirit of the system.

4. As the subject will, therefore, be a lengthy one, for the sake of perspicuity I shall discuss it under the following heads :–

1*st.* The origin, growth, and rights of Village Communities ; the description of the Landed Tenure ; and the rise and progress of the influence, rights and standing of the Village Officers.

2*nd.* The nature of the several Huks : how far their amount is adequate to the support of the several recipients, and how far such amount affects the Ryots ; and what proportion it bears to the Government Assessment.

3*rd.* The nature and amount of Enams, Ready-money Allowances and Sadilwar, the aggregate of which shows the total amount sacrificed by Government in proportion to its revenue, and, together with the amount of Purbhara Huks, the total expense of the system.

4*th.* General observations on the nature and tendency of the system, and suggestions for its improvement,—as the direct remuneration of Village Officers by Government ; the application of Sadilwar, or contingent expenses ; the modification of the Meeras tenure ; the formation of Town Committees ; and the institution of Town Dues in large towns, for their cleanliness and improvement.

Village Communities.

5. Before we can form any just idea of village polity, and the feelings, rights, and customs arising therefrom, it will be necessary to enter into some consideration of its origin. A village, at the first view, would appear as a kind of primitive commonwealth, held together by the individual interests of its inhabitants ; but further investigation would rather show it to be a minor branch of the feudal system of the earlier ages, the natural effect of an unorganized Government. Our data are certainly scanty, but the facts we do possess tend to support such opinion. The most ancient Hindoo law declares the State to be the sole owner of the soil, and the sole paramount power by which the district and village officers were appointed, and to which they were subject.[2] These officers, however, early gained a degree of independence, and inherent right of occupation. Hindoo feeling always acknowledged the right of the children to inherit the livelihood of the parent, from whatever source obtained ; and these offices, in becoming hereditary, became the *de facto* property of their possessors. A village, then, may be termed a self-constituted corporation, organized rather from the primitive necessity of its inhabitants than by design, and

strengthened and perpetuated by the hereditary succession of its office-bearers. The numerous and rapid changes of Government in dissolving all stability, taught men to seek for preservation of name and property within themselves, and conferred a degree of importance upon village communities, which under more stable governments, they might never have attained to. A new and ephemeral ruler could have no inducement to displace village officials, when he had everything to gain from their co-operation ; and the spoiler of a country had only to make himself master of their persons to extort the tribute of the village, their suffering exciting the compassion, and exalting them in the eyes of the people. Though purely the servants of Government, ancient usage had made their office hereditary; and these offices formed the only description, other than personal, of hereditary property in the country, and were coveted by all who possessed wealth or influence : wealth or the service of the State might pass away, but a Wuttun—a sure livelihood and source of respect—always remained. The mere right of settlement in, or of belonging to, a village, was, as a mark of respectability, an indispensable requisite to all classes of people : not only the cultivator, but the poorest artisan must belong to, and possess a house—real property in one. To become *puragunda* was the greatest misfortune, and the surest sign of irremediable poverty. The village thus became the only centre of stability, and the only repository of Civil rights : it was the only institution which the people possessed, and the only object of their national attachment ; yet the rights of the body of people, excepting those of the office-bearers, are vague and undefined ; and it is probable that both municipal organization and landed property, as understood by us, were totally unknown to them ; but so far as they extend, they will, for reasons stated in the 3rd paragraph, require our particular attention ; and, for the proper understanding of them, it will be necessary to enter into a brief analysis of the Village System.

6. These communities are no doubt of the most primitive origin, and are probably coeval with the village themselves, having been formed when society was in its infancy. A few cultivators, assembling together for mutual protection, would be glad to receive among them such artificers as their humble manner of life required the services of ; and, as in all other societies, someone of more influence than the rest would be required to represent them to the paramount power, while that power might be equally

willing to receive a responsible agent from among them. Increased prosperity would increase their wants : a village priest, clerk, astrologer, with a lower description of servants, might soon follow, and the village staff would then be increased to its present form of the Bara Bulootee, viz., 1st, Patel ; 2nd, Coolkurnee ; 3rd, Sootar or Carpenter ; 4th, Lohar or Smith ; 5th, Chambhar or Tanner, and Shoe-maker ; 6th, Khoombhar or Potter ; 7th, Nhawee or Barber ; 8th Pureet or Washerman ; 9th, Joshee, or Bhut, or Astrologer ; 10th, Goorow or Priest ; 11th, Sonar or Goldsmith ; and 12th Muhar.

7. The village being formed, had probably got a wall around it, as a guard against marauders,—a fact of no small importance in those days,—and would thus become a desirable place of residence for those who had not already gained a settlement. But the inhabitants, having been at considerable labour and expense, and feeling their own importance, might not be willing to admit a settler without an equivalent. The usual way of gaining a settlement, it is said, was by making some village improvement, such as digging a well, building a temple, or repairing the wall ; and, perhaps, by feeing the authorities.

8. The village, as thus constituted, would consist of two principal classes of inhabitants,—the cultivators and the office-bearers,—all of whom possessed the freedom of, or right of settlement in it, and were thence termed Gawkurees.[3] But the value of a settlement in a village would increase with the population of the country ; and in the course of time there would arise another class of inhabitants—those who, either from poverty or other causes, could not obtain the right of settlement, but whose presence was either necessary, or who were suffered through charity to remain in the village : these were called Oopree,[4] a name fully expressive of their non-right of residence in the village.

9. Pursuing a similar method of etymological inquiry, it will be advantageous to inquire into the description of the Landed Tenure.

10. Koonbee[5] is the generic name of the agricultural class ; Koonbawa,[6] their occupation, or relation to Government. A tenant is called Sirkar, Koonbawa, or Kool,[7] but they are properly distinguished by the description of their holdings, as —

Thulwaheek,[8] the cultivator of a *Thul.* Thul signifies a place or spot, but, in agricultural language a place or spot in which the holder has dug a well, built a bund, or planted trees, or made such improvement as to entitle him to the uninterrupted possession of such field.

Moondwaheek,[9] the cultivator of a *Moond,* or lot.

Oopree, a person residing in and cultivating land in a village, but one who has not gained a right of settlement in it.

Owundkuree,[10] a person cultivating land in a village, but residing in and belonging to another.

11. Land was also called after its kind, class or tenure : the whole lands of village are collectively called Sewar,[11] being contained within the village sew or boundary ; Wawur,[12] cultivated or culturable land ; Tika,[13] Shet,[14] Purtun,[15] Thul, or Mullaee,[16] a field ; Koorun, preserved grass-land ; Gairan, pasture-land ; Gutkoolee, the Thul or field of an extinct family or cultivator. Other terms, as Meeras, Enam, &c. have since been introduced by the Mahomedans, and will be adverted to hereafter.

Koorun,[17] land preserved for hay or grass, chiefly for the use of the State, or for some Government officer. Its etymon and origin are now unknown : it may have originally been कुराण, bad land ; or कुरण, a bad fight ; or कुऋण, bad debt ; indicating that the village had no participation or share in it.

Gairan,[18] cow's land, i.e. pasture-land ; and indefinite term for all land not brought under cultivation. In summing up the contents of a village, it usually includes all unculturable land, such as beds of rivers, water-courses, and barren patches, as well as such as may have been set aside for grazing. In the latter sense it would appear to correspond to our village commons in England ; but it differs from them, inasmuch as the commons, if I mistake not, are shared by those only who possess the freedom, or other rights, of the village ; whereas Gairan, in being Government property, is common to the whole village—equally so to the occasional sojourner as to the permanent resident. It appears originally to have meant such land as had not been taken up for cultivation, and in some villages all land not entered under the head of Meeras, Enam, or Gutkoolee, is entered under that of Sirkaree Gairan, cultivated or not.

Gutkoolee, the lands of an extinct family, from गत, past कुळ, kool, a family, a debtor, or customer. This term, too, is laxly used, under it frequently being entered all lands not possessed as meeras.

Meeras,[19] heritage, succession patrimony. This word is of Arabic or Hebrew origin, and was introduced by the Mahomedans, the Hindoos have no corresponding term, and it is probable that, under them, land as *bona fide* property was never possessed by the tenant cultivator. It was a distinguished feature of the Mahomedan rule, to endeavour to promote permanent cultivation, the Meerasdar being held responsible for the rent of his land, cultivated or uncultivated. The word may, therefore, have been introduced for the attainment of this object ; or really, as the term implies, inheritance, from the people being considered the hereditary occupiers or proprietors ; but the Emperor Akbar is said to have denied this, and to have claimed all land as the property of the State. Mahomedan law declares all land to be the property of the conqueror, though it is preserved to those who submit. If any of the usage in these districts be different from those in others, the difference, perhaps, arises from this cause, or perhaps from the superior privileges granted by the Nizam and Adilshaee kings in their struggles with Emperors of Hindoostan. The proprietorship of the soil is a question of little importance now, but the uses and abuses of the meeras tenure require some consideration, and must be adverted to accordingly.

Gaw-Nisbut-Meeras,[20] land belonging to the village in its own right ; land which from disagreement among the Patels, or other causes, has not yet been appropriated as meeras ; or perhaps land which the Patels chose to keep under this term, for the purpose of enforcing their dues upon it.

Enam.[21]—This too is an Arabic word, introduced by the Mahomedans, signifying a grant, a gift, the Hindoos do not appear to have any word to denote rent-free land, or free-hold property, except the expressive one of Suwusthan, one's own place[22] ; but this is never found in less quantities than a whole village. Rent-free land under the Hindoos was merely designated by terms signifying the purposes to which devoted, as Dewusthan,[23] an idol's place ; Pasodee,[24] a shawl, the Patel's grant ; Cholee,[25] a bodice or spencer, a grant to the Patel's wife ; Hadola,[26] a row or collection of bones ; Hudkee,[27] a little bone ; Domnee,[28] a dish—these three are grants to the Muhars ;—Dew Shet,[29] a grant to a person who had been successful in a trial by ordeal, such as that of determining the village boundary. Sarwamanya[30] and Jodeemanya[31] are two Hindoo terms for rent-free land : the former signifies grants on which Government takes no quit-rent, the latter those on which it takes one. These terms, however, are said to have been introduced into these districts about the beginning of our rule, by a Canarese Dufturdar of Nuggur.

Sheree[32] may be considered a description of rent-free land : it signifies land appropriated by the State for its own use, from which perhaps, it takes its name, i.e. Sheer, the head, chief, principal. The Mahomedans also designated grants by terms denoting their comparative freedom or alienation from the State, as Sahanuk,[33] a plate, or dish, or the refuse of it, indicating that such grant is irrevocably given. Mokassa,[34] divided or partial grants of villages, in which Government reserves to itself a portion of the revenue.

Suranzam,[35] *Zat-Suranzam*,[36] *Jagheer*, and the like ; but these appertain more to revenue matters than to the present subject.

Gaw-Nisbut-Enam,[37] land granted in enam by the village, for a debt, or some other purpose, the village continuing, by paying the total revenue of such village, to make up the difference, and to ensure Government from loss.

12. As a further introduction to village customs, and the influence possessed by village officials, it will be advantageous to notice as briefly as possible the former system of revenue. It is probable that the earliest assessments would be of the simplest kind, and were, perhaps, those of which some traces still remain under the various names of Aootbundee,[38] Moondbundee,[39] Tikabundee,[40] Tokabundee,[41] and the like ; being assessments by the lump on each plough, field, or holding. Measurements are reported to have been introduced into these districts by the Mahomedans, but the term Beegha,[42] being of Hindee origin, would prove their introduction to have been long anterior to their rule. Both the beegha and its multiples vary in different districts, but in the Deccan thirty beeghas equal one paeen, and four paeens[43] one chahoor[44] of land ; though paeens and chahoors, as nominal quantities regulated for the plough, were perhaps in use long before the beegha. A village spoken of in reference to its size,

is one of so many chahoors. The chahoor being assumed as the standard, fractional parts are deduced and named from it, as rookha $^1/_{12}$, or ten beeghas, paeen ¼, or thirty beeghas. Where the land is good, the measurement of the beegha is generally pretty equal, but where the land is inferior it becomes merely nominal ; for where only one rate of assessment obtained, and that of the highest, adapted to the first class soil only, the inferior lands could not pay it ; and the only remedy in such cases was to throw in more land to make up the difference ; the beegha then became a measure of quality, and not of quantity. These and other causes produced a very lax system of revenue, and threw much into the hands of the district and village officers ; for, in each of the above cases, they became the virtual assessors of the soil : if the assessment were on the plough or on the lump, they were the annual estimators of the amount cultivated ; and if, in measurements, they were allowed to increase or diminish the size of the beegha according to the quality of the land, they were still the virtual assessors. In some districts the Patels, or chiefs of villages, were called Khotes[45] which would imply that in those districts they were the farmers of their villages.

13. The Mahomedan Government appears to have entered somewhat more into detail, but their arrangements, perhaps, tended more to the permanent fixing of the assessment, than to the development of local resources. Villages were measured, and a total assessment, called the Tunkha,[46] put upon them ; that tunkha was to be paid yearly, whether the land was cultivated or not, the Patels or Mokadums,[47] as they were then called, being held responsible for it ; which could not be done unless corresponding immunities were granted them in return. Their perquisites from their villages, under the denomination of huks, were consequently authorized and defined : in some cases they were allowed Mooshaeera,[48] or a percentage on the total revenue ; in others they had a rent-free field granted, which, in these districts, is said to have been five per cent in measurement of the total amount annually cultivated in their respective villages. The sale of their situations, or Wutuns,[49] was also sanctioned, and, as the higher officers had a percentage on such sales, was perhaps encouraged. Where, from sales or other causes, there were two or more Tuksimdar[50] sharers of a Patelship, the village lands were divided between them, and each was held responsible for the amount of assessment on his

share : this was called a Turufbundee[51] assessment. The same principle was extended to the cultivator. The Hindoo Thulwaheeks were termed Meerasdars,[52] and were held responsible for the assessment on their fields cultivated or not. The sale of meeras was also sanctioned. Where village officers were held responsible for the tunkha, or total amount of assessment on their villages, the internal arrangement of them would be, in a great measure, left to themselves. Thus in many villages we find a Kasbundee[53] assessment ; that is, the village was divided into farms or shares—a small piece of bagaeet (garden-land) here, a plot of jeeraeet (dry-crop) there, with an inferior piece of grazing land elsewhere, might compose a farm, kass, or share. One common assessment per beegha was generally fixed upon the whole village, but the number of beeghas in each kass was determined by the quality of the land, and not its quantity. Where two brother or shareholder Patels could not agree, they were sometimes, it appears, allowed to divide the village between them, and to separate. In some instances, a new village was erected by one of the shares in that portion of the lands which had been allotted to him ; in others even the old village site appears to have been divided, and one part called by another name. Each separatist guaranteed the amount of assessment on his share, or rather the tunkha was divided also, and the division was recognized in the Government records.[54]

14. I have observed in para. 11 that Meeras is an Arabic word, introduced by the Mahomedans, corresponding to which the Hindoos have no synonym. Thulwaheek is the ancient name for Meerasdar, but that word conveys no sense of inheritance or of proprietorship ; neither do the negative terms Gutkoolee, Oopree, Sookhwustee and Owundkuree, imply the absence of such meaning ; since the term Gutkool equally signifies a past debtor, or tenant, as a past family ; while the word Oopree would indicate the right to be a municipal rather than an individual one ; and it is this municipal right, with the honors and immunities attached thereto, in which the value of meeras in a great measure consists. The Native accounts of meeras is, that it has generally been obtained from the Patel in troublous times when, from some predatory visitation or pecuniary difficulty, he has been compelled to seek assistance from the villagers, granting them in return honors, and immunities from the Patel's share of huks in kind on their land ; and it is in this sense that it requires

consideration.[55] Exclusive of the Government rent on the land, each individual of the village staff receives from it which in these districts constitutes the real value of meeras, since, should not Meerasdar cultivate his own meeras, he still claims the established impost from the person who does.[56] Besides this impost in kind, the Patel receives several others from the residents of his village, among which is one of a turban, shawl and cocoanut, levied on the marriage of each member of a resident's family, according to his circumstances. The freedom from this is generally stipulated for, in the same manner as that from the land, but sometimes the one and sometimes the other is dispensed with. Patels, however, have occasionally given to poor relation, or members of their families, a nominal meeras, without foregoing any impost. Meeras may, therefore, be of three classes, according to its total, partial, or non-exemption, from impost. The amount of this impost is sufficient to make the freedom from it desirable ; but it is only a secondary object when compared with the other adjuncts of the meeras tenure, the civic honors, and outward means of distinction. What these honors are is to an European as difficult to understand as to describe, but any person conversant with Native character and village economy will readily comprehend the importance attached to them. The priority of place in an assembly, at a festival, or in a procession, and the right of sitting in municipal council, are inestimable marks of distinction to a people among whom there is so little real property, and by whom individual merit and independence of character are so little appreciated. I have been told that in some parts of the Sattara District, a Meerasdar would consider himself insulted were even a private merry meeting to take place without his being at least asked to take *pansooparee* at it. Who am I in the village to be thus slighted ? would be his indignant exclamation ! If, as above stated, the Patel had the privilege of conferring meeras, he could not also confer the right of property in the soil, which privilege belongs to the State alone ; but there could be no obstacle to his relinquishing his own claims, or to the granting of any village distinction which the customs of the country had made desirable. But the practice is fraught with much evil, insomuch as it causes continual quarrels among the cultivators : the Patel, for the purpose of regaining his impost, is induced to take every opportunity of entering meeras land in his own name, or as gutkoolee, or to extort bribes for the restoring of it.

15. The annexed table (No.1) of landed tenure in the village of the Koombharee Purgunna, now reported upon, will further explain what has been stated. In this table the Patel's meeras has been entered in a separate column, and the remainder, belonging to Koonbees and others, has been divided into three classes, as above described, viz. the exempted, the partially exempted, and the not-exempted from the Patel's huk. It will be observed that, in some villages, the whole of the meeras belongs to the Patels, and in most of them the greater part of it : there are exceptions, but they are generally to be accounted for. The village of Rahate, for instance, the Patelship of which is held, and is said to have been seized by force, by the Nimbalkur, an influential Jagheerdar and Sirdar of the late Government, who, it is not too much to presume, having power and influence sufficient to force the payment of his huks, had no occasion to resort to the means of entering the land as meeras in his own name ; or to resist its being entered as non-exempted meeras in the names of its cultivators. Few Patels whatever their difficulties, sell the whole of their Patelships : a half, a third, or a fourth, is about the general amount of the share disposed of ; and its value will of course, depend on the amount of emoluments and meeras conveyed with it. The first column of this table shows the number of these shares. It is true that the Patel in some districts has no huks on land, and is remunerated entirely by Government ; but this can only have happened in districts where the Thulwaheeks or cultivators have, as a body, had sufficient influence to resist such impost and to retain the corporate rights of the village among themselves ; yet they collectively, as the representative of the corporation, have had to hold themselves responsible for every Government due ; or where in later times some powerful Government Officer has had influence enough to rescind them.[57]

16. In such instances there has been no change of system on the part of the Native Government ; the responsibility has merely been shifted to the whole village, instead of resting with Patel—*i.e.* the village collectively is the Patel, and one of their body its representative, who merely enjoys a few forms of precedence, and together with his few huks on the artisans and shop-keepers, his allowances from Government.[58] But in such cases the Native Government, it appears, levied an extra cess[59] upon meeras land, probably to compensate for the extra expense incurred by it in the

remuneration of the Patel, or, probably, as a token of the right of proprietorship still being retained by it. The private right of meeras in such cases did not differ much in the abstract from those already described : the total profits to the holder amounted to about the same, viz. a few annas per beegha above that of Oopree land ; for as Government, in itself remunerating the Patel, had caused him to forego the imposts in kind upon all description of land, it took such remuneration into account in assessing land not meeras, and it paid to Government an extra cess[60] above meeras to compensate such remission.

17. The distinction, then, in these two kinds of meeras tenure, is more apparent then real, the principles of the revenue systems in which they originated being the same. In the one case Government had nominated a sole responsible agent, and had allowed him to remunerate himself by an impost in kind on the land, but from which impost some few of his equals and brotherhood were exempted, and which exemption was in other cases sold by him ; in the other case, the Thulwaheeks of village in a body claimed exemption from such impost, but they were obliged to guarantee every Government claim ; and the Native Government, in sanctioning such exemption, levied, in token of its right of proprietorship, a small extra cess on meeras land entitled to that exemption, and a larger cess, the full value of the exemption, on land not entitled to it.[61] The private rights and advantages of the tenure in both systems were the same, namely, the immunity from the Patel's impost, or from the extra cess levied in lieu of it, as in both instances the holders of meeras, on re-letting their fields, claimed the advantages attendant on such exemption.

18. That the above is the most correct view of meeras, I think, is borne out both by usage and theory. It is a peculiar characteristic of eastern languages, that a name should explain its derivation, or that it should express some property or conditions of the thing named ; and the absence of such name in the vernacular language,—for Meeras is a purely Mahomedan term,—exclusive of Hindoo law, declaring the State to be the sole owner of the soil, affords a fair presumption that this tenure, in the sense understood by us, is not an indigenous one. That each village had its Thulwaheeks, who possessed the freedom of the village, and hereditarily cultivated the same lands, has been already shown, but it is probable that the parallel went no further, and that all other usages of the

meeras originated at a far later period, and are attributable to a different system of revenue management. That a person should possess an hereditary right of occupation, and yet not be the proprietor of the soil, is one of the many anomalies of eastern usages ; but such is the sense, as understood by the people themselves. "The meeras is mine, but the land is the Sirkar's" is the common answer to all inquiries ; that is, meeras, in an abstract sense, is a perpetual lease, or that property resulting from improvement and outlay ; and its value is enhanced by the affection with which men regard their place of birth, and the home of their forefathers : in a general sense, embodies the advantages and profits which are derived from such a property ;— for example, the advantages of village distinction, and the profits derivable from the imposts mentioned above.

19. In this latter or general sense it is liable to many abuses, and perhaps, in many instances, tends to check cultivation, thus frustrating the principal object for which it was encouraged by the Mahomedans. For, if the profits derivable from it act as an inducement for an individual, legally or illegally, to possess himself of more meeras than he can himself cultivate, he, in the event of such being brought under cultivation, becomes a kind of sleeping lessor ; and though the Patel may have sufficient influence to enforce the imposts of his own meeras when cultivated by others, it is not to be expected that individuals of less influence will succeed in obtaining it, without, in many instances, having to struggle for it ; and these quarrels, whether in families or otherwise, always tend to throw such land out of cultivation : the quarrel is ostensible for the field, but in reality it may be for the impost. Besides these interests of the villagers, the higher district officers possess some also : they claim a percentage on all sales, and profess to have the power of disposing of an extinct Patelship, and with it meeras land. They are the referees in quarrels, and it is to be feared not always disinterested ones.

20. The preceding paragraphs will, I hope sufficiently elucidate the fundamental principles of village communities. The inhabitants, it will be observed, are divided into several classes, which result from private interests and conventional forms. The two principal divisions are the cultivators and the office-bearers : the former of these are, again, divided into Thulwaheeks or Meerasdars, and Oopree,—that is, those who belong to village, and those who do not,—a distinction kept

up as a mark of respectability among the cultivators, as well as by the private interests of the office-bearers. The village does not appear to have possessed any recognized, or even definable rights, but all its internal usages not prejudicial to Government interest were tacitly allowed, and seldom interfered with. Its power to punish or to conceal offences depended on the character of the existing Government, and on that of the local authority ; and the settlement within itself of disputes arising among its inhabitants depended on the relative influence of the several parties concerned. If the Patel had been able to maintain his influence, they might be decided in a summary manner by himself, but if he had not attained to or had lost that position they were generally left to the arbitration of friends ; and the decision of that arbitration might be adhered to or not, according to the inclination or influence of the contending parties. In matter immediately connected with the village, the hereditary artisans and office-bearers, with the Patel at their head, were frequently appealed to, as the best informed and most authentic witness of its affairs ; but even their decision might be set at naught by an obstinate and refractory litigant. The most useful and legitimate employment of the artisans was that of labouring for the villagers in the several lines of their craft, but they also held another position, as the village staff and attendants on the Patel, and assistants in the various social and festive ceremonies of the village. An account of these ceremonies, or of the position of the actors in them, is not here required, but some notice of their duties as village servants would appear necessary.

21. The village staff, or Bara Bulootee, was as the name implies, originally twelve in number, but there is some difference of opinion as to who composed it. The most correct and ancient division would appear to be that detailed in the 6th paragraph of this letter ; but others, as the Bheel, Kolee, Moolana, Chowgoolee, &c. have been added in later years, and are now included. The Patels and Coolkurnees, also from their subsequent improved position, assume a higher standing, wishing to be styled zemindars ; but it is the opinion of well-informed persons that in the olden times they were included in the number. The staff is divided into two principal classes, the Bulootee[62] and the Alootee ; as also Karoo-Naroo ;[63] but these are perhaps only instances of that alliterative formation

so prevalent in Muhratee. The former phrase has no definite meaning, but is said to divide the whole into Bulootee, the effective, and Alootee, the non-effective ; while Karoo-Naroo distinguishes the more effective artisans, Karoo, from those less necessary, Naroo as detailed in Table No. 2. They are also divided into three "Olee,"[64] (Kass,[65] according to Mahomedans,) or classes, for the convenience of remuneration ; as 1st Kass—comprising Sootar, Lohar, Chambhar, Muhar ; 2nd Kass—Koombhar, Nhawee, Pureet, Muhar ; 3rd Kass—Bhut, Goorow, Moolana, Muhar ; each division having had, in the event of disputes, a certain remuneration assigned to it, by some former authority : viz. 1st Kass, 30 sheaves per paeen ; 2nd, 25 sheaves ; and 3rd, 20,—this amount to be given by the Patel from the farmer's stack, on the appeal of either party. The duties of the village staff are, in general, so well known, that any enumeration of them would appear unnecessary ; but, for the facility of comparing them with the amount of remuneration received, I shall mention them as briefly as possible, reserving the more immediate Government servants for further consideration.

Sootar.— The Carpenter is at the head of the artisans, his services being most in requisition : he makes up and mends all wooden implements for agricultural purposes, the owners finding the material ; but for any other work, as building a house, or making a cart for other than agricultural purposes, he is paid. His average remuneration is about 6 paeelees per paeen.

Lohar.—The Smith makes and repairs the iron work for all agricultural instruments, the owners finding the material ; but anything apart from these, such as a cart, &c. for other than agricultural purposes, he must be paid for. Remuneration 5½ paeelees per paeen.

Chambhar.—The Shoe-maker makes all leathern halters, whips, ropes, and bands, for agricultural purposes, the owners finding the leather ; but he must find the leather himself for all repairs, such as mending buckets, whips, and ropes, as above mentioned : he also mends the farmers shoes, though they must pay him for new ones. He has also to furnish gratuitously the Deshmookh and Deshpandee of the district, and the Patel and Coolkurnee of his village, with a new pair of shoes each annually. His average remuneration per paeen, as shown in Table No. 2 in the Appendix, is 5½ paeelees.

The above are the three principal artisans of the village, and they possess several perquisites above the others, among which may be mentioned the privilege of sowing in every farmer's field a strip of land each with ralla, each strip consisting of four furrows. The farmer tills the land, and these artisans merely bring each his basket of grain, which is sown by the farmer, and reaped by the recipient when ready.

Koombhar.—The Potter finds all the farmers in pottery of every description : earthen frying-pans, ovens, pitchers, water-pots and jars, are supplied by him according to the casualties and wants of each household ; he generally receiving a cake of bread on the supplying of a fresh article. He also, when the corn begins to shoot into ear, takes a jug and water-vessel to each field, for those engaged watching the crop, receiving in return his nimboor (ears of corn). The artisans, Muhars, and the village staff generally, claim their pottery free also, but the Koombhar stipulates for some service in return. He must also supply any Government servant on his arrival at the village with what vessels he may require, and in this respect is perhaps sometimes hardly used. He finds the several images at the festivals, receiving in return a little grain. His average remuneration, in Table No. 2, is nearly 4 paeelees and a quarter, i.e. 16¾ measured seers.

Nhawee.—The Barber must shave all the farmers and artisans,—to the Muhars he merely lends a razor. He must attend the Patel's wedding, at which he expects to receive a turban. On the occasion of wedding, or other festival, when an inhabitant of one village may send presents to a resident in another, it is the barber's duty to convey them, &c. His average remuneration in nearly 4½ paeelees per paeen.

Pureet.—The Washerman washes the clothes of the farmers (the men's—the women wash their own) at every monthly festival and more frequently, if called upon ; but he is seldom troubled, and is said to be very remiss in his duty, except on the approach of harvest. It is the washerman's duty to spread white clothes as carpets for the passage over of a wedding party, or of some great personage at a festival. His remuneration is about 4½ paeelees per paeen.

Bhut.—The Bhut is the village astrologer, but his duties approach nearer to those of priest. He performs the marriage ceremony, names the children, and reads the muntras over the dead ; casts nativities, explains the almanac to the villagers, predicts favourable times and seasons for any undertaking, keeps the farmers informed of the proper time for sowing and reaping, and performs the ceremony of *pooja* (worship) to the corn when thrashed. His services are required nearly in every undertaking of life, and increase in a direct ratio with superstition of the people. His average remuneration is 2¾ paeelees per paeen ; but this may be said to be only a fraction of his real gains. Each ceremony entails its fee : a pice and a cocoanut the poorest person will bestow, but the opulent must keep up name and character by more substantial donations.

Goorow.—The officiating Priest of the temple, and perhaps the original village teacher and priest, until supplanted by the Brahminical Bhut. Goorows are not Brahmuns, and their duties are confined principally to the temple. The Goorow performs the daily ablution of the idols, anoints them with red paint, and cleans the temple. He performs the ceremony of *ghut* during the nine nights preceding the Dussera, finds the dining leaves for the festivals, and fetches the bride to the house of her husband's parents, on visit to them before having permanently joined her husband. The Goorow's remuneration is 3¼ paeelees per paeen.

Moolana.—This servant was introduced by the Mahomedans, and is to the Mussulman what the Bhut or Goorow is to the Hindoo. Amongst the Mussulmans he may be considered the Kazee's deputy, and performs the various religious rites and ceremonies entrusted to him by the Kazee. His ostensible duty in the village is to prevent the inhabitants of it, Hindoo or Mussulman, eating *moordar,* or any animal not made lawful by the Moolana's ceremony of *hulal.* His average remuneration is 2¾ paeelees per paeen.

Sonar.—The Goldsmith. The above servants compose the Karoo—this and the following the Naroo. The goldsmith's duties were those of Government potedar or assayer : he inspected and assayed all Government revenue, and was answerable for all base coin. During the time of collecting the revenue, it was, after being examined by the goldsmith, sealed up and placed in his charge, until conveyed to the Government treasury ; but these duties are now seldom required from him. He renders similar services to the village, as he assays all coin and jewellery brought for his inspection. If employed to make up jewellery, he is paid for it, and his only other duty is to pierce the children's ears and noses for their ornaments, to make the *mungulsootra,* or marriage string, for the bride, and to adorn her at the wedding. His average remuneration is 2¼ paeelees per paeen.

Bheel.—The Bheel is now the village watchman, but it is perhaps only of late years that he has settled in these districts. He must remain on the alert for the safety of the village ; keep an eye on all suspicious visitants ; trace and find all stolen property, or make it good; watch over the property of any Government officer during his residence in the village ; keep a general watch over the crops when standing on the lands ; and escort the Government revenue to the treasury, &c. He enjoys from our Government an enam generally of about ten beeghas.[66] His huks, which depend entirely upon the pleasure of the donors, vary form 10 to 20 sheaves per paeen, and a small portion from each thrashed heap, called Meer.[67] His average remuneration, as entered in Table No. 2, is 2¾ paeelees per paeen, but I have reason to believe that the villagers have entered somewhat more than he really obtains. His enam is generally cultivated by another, when they divide the produce between them ; and the remainder of his subsistence is made up by hunting, he frequently exchanging a portion of his spoils for corn.

Kolee.—The Kolee does not appear to be an original hukdar in these districts : his duties as a village servant are properly those of Muhar. The duty of the office is to wait upon travellers, or on Government officers, on their arrival in the village ; to procure them water and provisions, and on their departure to convey their things to the next village. The proper designation of the office is Tural, and, when distinct from that of the Muhar, has generally originated in the wants of Government servants in their visits to the village; a man of higher caste being required to perform those little offices that a Muhar, by the lowness of his caste, is incapacitated from. Where the office belongs to the Muhars, they have to find and pay a man of higher caste for the performance of these services, but where it is a distinct one, a separate remuneration is assigned to it, and sometimes an enam, called the Tural Shet. The average remuneration is 3¼ paeelees per paeen.

Mang.—The Mang may or may not be an original hukdar, but he is not found in every village, one Mang frequently performing the duties of four or five villages. He is rope-maker, and sometimes basket-maker ; he makes the muzzles for the oxen ; one broom to each plough ; ropes of hemp for the farmers, they finding the material, and preparing the first strands. He also makes leathern ropes from the raw hide, the Chambar, whose duty it is, refusing to work, except from curried leather. The average remuneration is 2¼ paeelees per paeen.

Muhar.—The Muhar is emphatically called the village eye. He is the watchman and guardian of the village, and the living chronicle of its concerns. His situation or his curiosity makes him acquainted with everybody's affairs, and his evidence is required in every dispute. Should two cultivators quarrel respecting the boundaries or their fields, the Muhar's evidence ought to decide it ; and should a similar quarrel happen between two villages, the Muhars are always the chief actors in it, and to their decision alone it is sometimes referred. The Muhar's duties are so numerous, that complete enumeration of them would be tiresome ;—in short, the Muhar is to the village what peon is to a Government office. In large villages, the duties are generally divided into two or three heads : these are the weskurs, or porters at the village gates ; the khule-weskurs, or guards of the stack-yards ; and the gaow-weskurs, or those Muhars appointed to attend at the Chowree ; and the gaow Muhars, or those for the general duty of the village. The three former offices are generally held year about in turns, their perquisites being something larger, but the office of gaow Muhar is common to the whole Muhars of the village. The porter's duty is to guard the gate, and keep an account of who comes and who goes ; he locks the gate at night, and takes the keys to the Patel. His extra remuneration is the daily collection of bread and broken victuals. The office in some instances is hereditary. The gaow-weskur is supposed to be stationed at the village Chowree : should travellers arrive, he warns Muhars to convey their baggage to the next village ; if they alight for the night, he procures them grass and wood, and gives them general information where their wants may be supplied. If any Government letters arrive at the village, he takes them to the Patel and Coolkurnee, and, if necessary, warns other Muhars to convey them to the next village, or to their destination. On the arrival of a Government officer for the collection of revenue, or other duty, he warns and collects all tenant farmers ; and waits upon that officer during his stay, appointing others to find him fire-wood and grass and to clean his horse. His perquisites are bread and broken victuals, and any chance present he may receive from travellers. The khuleweskur waits upon and guards the stack-yard during harvest time : he keeps a fire burning for the convenience of the workmen, and performs any occasional work required of him—as, on an emergency, the unloading of a gadee, pitching the sheaves on the stack, driving the bullocks in thrashing ; and he makes himself generally useful, receiving in return small presents of broken ears, and handfulls of corn.

Gaow Muhar.—The general duty of the Muhars of the village is to obey the gaow-weskur in finding Muhars for the conveying of the baggage of travellers, Government posts, &c., to next village ; to clean the horses of Government officers to find them grass, firewood, and pickets.[68] Their village duties are to remain generally on the alert ; to furnish a guard of watchmen at night for its protection ; to remove all dead (the skins of which are their perquisites[69]) ; and to run errands as warned by the weskur for the Patels and other Meerasdars. Their remuneration is a Government enam ; a tithe upon everything grown ; present of bread, and other articles begged for services performed, small imposts of oil, sugar, and condiments levied, or rather begged, from the shopkeepers. At some former period each village has had appointed to it a certain number of Muhars,—8, 12, or 16,—according to its size. The Muhar's office in such villages therefore, is divided into 8, 12, or 16 shares, according to the original number appointed ; but from the Muhars in some villages having greatly multiplied each share may be again, subdivided into a number of other shares : thus, if there be three brothers to one share, they take it year about, each performing its services, and enjoying its remuneration, every third year ; the other two, if possible, obtain service as ghorawallas at some Government cantonment, till their turn again arrives, or perhaps they gain a livelihood by selling grass and wood, or by engaging in an occasional pilfering expedition in some neighbouring district. The average remuneration is 14¾ paeelees per paeen, but they are subject to considerable deductions, Government and the zemindars having a claim to their services, which not exacted, a tax, Rabta,[70] is levied instead. Government also exacts a quit-rent from the largest of their enams, called Hudola,[71] the smaller Hudkee being free.

Patel.—I have frequently had occasion in the course of this letter to allude to the situation of village officers, and I hope what I have there stated will afford a general view of their position. They may be considered as the relics of a brighter era of national prosperity ; and they have in most instances profited by the mutability and continual changes of succeeding governments. Their standing in early times is described by Mr. Elphinstone to be purely that of Government servants, and I have endeavoured, in the 12th and 20th paragraphs of this letter, to point out their subsequent progress, and the chief sources of the dignity and profits of their offices. The authority above quoted stated the remuneration of the Patels to have been the provisions and other articles in kind to which the King was entitled from the village, and a glance at Table No. 3 will show that in substance the same system has been continued to the present day though perhaps, materially altered in detail. At that time, it would appear the Patel's impost was levied upon all classes of cultivators, on the Thulwaheek, as on the Oopree ; but, the former class predominating, would form an influential counterbalance to his power, though they *did* contribute to his support. From the advent of the Mahomedans, however, a different bearing and influence may be observed. The placing a total amount of revenue on each village, and holding the Patel responsible for the amount, would as before observed, place much of the internal management of the village in his lands. It made him the feudal lord of his holding, the Zemindar of his village,—to use a revenue phrase, he was the Government Meerasdar, whose every arrangement, having for its object the increase of cultivation, was sanctioned. It would be difficult to follow the internal windings of this system, as it must have varied with the ever-changing circumstances and fortune of the Patel. Were he in affluent circumstances, his system was entirely that of exclusion and self-aggrandizement, and the settlement of a new cultivator, shopkeeper, or artisan, could not be effected without his making considerable concessions : the new cultivator wishing to become a permanent settler must purchase the privilege with a handsome donation, and the occasional Oopree, artisan, or shopkeeper, by submitting to the best terms of impost he could obtain. But fortune sometimes frowned, and the tunkha always remained, and had annually to be met : then indeed, did necessity drive the plough, and a more liberal system was had recourse to. The imposts of the older inhabitants were remitted or sold to them ; the settlement of new cultivators was courted ; meeras was granted ; and every effort made to meet the annually recurring tunkha.[72] Continued adversity necessitated the sale of a portion of the Patelship,—a fourth, a third, or a half, was disposed of, as exigency required ; and should these efforts fail, all must suffer alike, and the deficiency be made up by a collection (wurga, wurgee, or tophir,) from the whole village : hence the many different systems obtaining in different villages—the turufbundee, the kassbundee, &c. But the Patels did not possess imposts in all districts,[73] which could be owing only to the primitive superior position of the ancient Thulwaheeks or Meerasdars of such districts ; but in this case even the revenue principle was the same, though the agency was somewhat different ; that is, the body politic of Meerasdars constituted the Patel, they being in that sense liable for the Government demand ; and the real Patel was merely a Government servant, who had no other remuneration beyond what he derived from Government. It will be evident, from what has been stated, that the position and influence of these officers might vary in every district, and in every village. In those districts where, from the most ancient times, the rest of the tenantry have retained their influence, and have submitted[74] as a body to the demands of Government, and have bound themselves to be answerable for the total revenue of their village, the Patel is little more than a Government servant ; but where, either from the absence of such influence, or from any other cause, the Patel had been the chief responsible agent, he had gained a corresponding degree of influence over the rest of the inhabitants ; and in many instances he exercised rather the functions of a feudal lord than filled the office of a Government servant. But the present change of system has effected a corresponding change in the circumstances of the Patel : each individual ryot being alone responsible for the assessment on his holding, the principle onus is removed from the Patel, and he is deprived of uncontrolled action, and shorn of a great portion of his dignity. In most villages, the Patelship has been divided among a great number of sharers, and the increasing families of these sharers have caused it to be still further subdivided ; and as each individual lays claim to his share in the produce of the Wutun,[75] they collectively present little more than the appearance of a beggarly mob of clamorants, who, by their internal feuds, greatly retard the object of their office. The advantage of the office has in a great measure passed away, while its evil effects remain, so that much careful reform will be necessary before the Patel can efficaciously conduct the duties required of him. I forbear describing the details of this officer's position, as these will be sufficiently understood from what has been already stated. The chief dignity of the office depended on the uncontrolled position of the holder, and was enhanced by the comparative poverty of the people. The Patel of a large village was, indeed, a substantial person, and, compared with the humble inhabitants of his village, occupied an influential and enviable position : his authority was unquestionable, and his will absolute ; while his privileges of precedence on all public and social occasions formed, according to Native taste, an imposing picture of greatness. The profits of his office depended of course on the system of revenue pursued, and on his influence in the village. Under Native Governments his gains were seldom inquired after, as long as he produced the full amount of revenue, and the village appeared generally prosperous. His direct imposts would therefore depend upon his influence over the people, and the perquisites of his office upon the nature of the revenue system, and of the character of its executives. Where, then, this officer had power to enforce his imposts, they were levied upon everything within his village ; upon every description of crop, manufacture and sale. The detail of them would be tedious, but some idea of their extent, even as they existed in the year 1843-44, may be formed from Table No. 3, though this table will give a very imperfect idea of them as they existed in the olden times. The average amount of grain levied by them was something more than 8 paeelees per paeen, but, as the villages of this table are in many instances inhabited chiefly by the Patel's brotherhood, and other Meerasdars, who do not pay the Patel's impost, the average, as shown by it, is only 2¾ paeelees per paeen.

Coolkurnee.[76]—The Village Accountant. A great part of what has been said of the Patel is almost equally applicable to the Coolkurnee, and it is only necessary to point out a few circumstances connected with his present tenor of office. His remuneration, it will be observed from Table No. 4, is, with the exception of enams, more than that of the Patel, while his means of making money from other sources are, under the present Government still greater than those possessed by that officer ; inasmuch as, being less dependent on and responsible to the Patel than he was under a Native Government, his opportunities of illicit gain are more under his own control. Few of the Patels can write, and, in consequence, they frequently hold a very secondary place to that of a designing Brahmun Coolkurnee, who in some instances runs entirely counter to the Patel, and is the cause of severe feuds in the village, the population of which becomes divided into two parties, one headed by the Coolkurnee, and the other by the Patel ; and many are the frauds which from spite or for a bribe, are practised on the records of the village. A whole meeras may be transferred from one person to another, or even a new sharer of the Patelship be entered, with a view to its being discovered when sufficient time may have elapsed to give colour to the claim. There is also another practice of the Coolkurnees, which appears worthy of notice. In small villages, where probably the Coolkurnee and the Wannee are the only persons who can write in it, the poor ryot frequently calls upon the former to inspect his account with the latter. In this duty the Coolkurnee might be of great service to the poor ryot in detecting fraud, but he too often finds it his interest to combine with the Wannee to cheat the ryot. The Coolkurnee's office is in all cases an important one, and, in some of the larger villages, its duties are very onerous ; but although, as with the Patel, in some instances we find his office divided among a number of co-sharers, we more frequently find that one individual holds the office, or is a co-sharer in the offices of three or four villages, a practice which causes much obstruction in the progress of revenue duty. I have heard that in some parts of Goojerat this officer's situation is not hereditary, but it is so in these districts ; and old documents still extant will show it to be of most ancient standing. The Coolkurnee, though second to the Patel, generally possessed much influence, though he exercised it in a quieter manner ; and as it was impossible the Patel could possess any gain or perquisite without the Coolkurnee's connivance, he generally managed to participate in it. His items of impost, therefore do not differ much from those of the Patel ; the average amount per paeen, as shown in Table No. 4, is 8¾ paeelees, which is far more than is possessed by the Patels of the same village ; but the Coolkurnee, unlike the Patels, have no brother cultivators, who refuse to pay them huks, neither is meeras land free from the Coolkurnee's huks,—his imposts, therefore, being levied alike upon all description of land, amount in the aggregate to much more than those of the Patels, which are subject to many remissions.

Deshmookh and Deshpandee.—The duties of these officers are connected more with the revenue of a whole district than of a single village ; but, as they are remunerated by the village, some notice of them would appear necessary. Deshmookh,[77] as the word implies, is the chief of a district ; and Deshpandee[78] the district writer ; so they are to the district what the Patel and Coolkurnee are to the village. The extract from Elphinstone's "History of India"[79] before quoted would show them to be officers of ancient standing, and of some note—probably the lords of a hundred villages ; but the same causes which have changed the position of village officers have had a corresponding effect on them. From ancient records which have come under my notice, it would appear that these officers, in the earlier times of the Mahomedans, were entrusted with considerable power, and formed the chief branch of the executive ; and it is recorded in Grant Duff's "History of the Mahrattas," that they were sometimes of sufficient importance to be treated with much consideration. But these are, perhaps, only solitary instances ; for on other occasions, particularly in later years, they have been treated with much less consideration, when even the whole established right of hereditary succession has been made to yield to the force of superior individual interests. Their duties in ancient times were, perhaps, similar to those of the present Mamlutdars, and even under the earlier Mahomedans they were the principal revenue executive of their districts ; but the introduction of the farming system[80] in the time of the later Peishwas divested them of much of their importance, and under the present rule they have dwindled to little more than district Carcoons. I have never met with any records of their remuneration previous to the advent of the Mahomedans ; but, if we may judge from Hindee names of impost still extant, they were remunerated from their villages. The same system was kept up under the Mahomedan rule, when old manes were either changed or new imposts added. The Hindee names still in use are—Bheeknee,[81] Bhet,[82] and Rabta,[83] &c.; Mussulman names, since added, are Furmas,[84] and Roosoom.[85] Under the term bheeknee is said to have been collected grain in kind, similar to the Patel's adepade, and under that of furmas small internal village imposts, as grass and firewood ; but roosoom is said always to have been a ready-money huk, deducted from the money set aside for village expense. Beside these, there are several others of less importance ; but as, under the present Government, they have in these districts all been done away with, and a ready-money allowance payable from the Government treasury, granted instead, no particular notice of them appears necessary. The old names, however, are still kept up, as will be observed by the Zemindar's Table, No. 6, in which furmas in a permanent sum annually levied upon each village. Bheeknee[86] is levied by a separate rate per cent. For each village on its total revenue, determined from the average of a number of preceding years, and roosoom in this purgunna is two per cent on the jagheer.[87] Their other huks are levied from the chiller, with the exception of rabta, which is levied direct from the Muhars.

The above are the principal officers of the village system ; but, besides these, there are others in large villages, where circumstances or interests have called for them—as Durukhdar, Mahajun, Shete, Chowgoola, Havildar, and other minor servants ; but as none of the villages now reported upon possess them, and as they are only occasionally to be met with, any further consideration of them does not appear necessary. There, however, yet remain the Kazee and Naeekwadee, two district officers appointed by the Mahomedans, and a district Bhut, whose office appears peculiar to this purgunna, as I have not met with it elsewhere.

Kazee.—The Kazee, under the Mahomedans, was the judicial officer of the district : his remuneration was enams in some or all the villages of his district—one rupee from each village, and in some districts ghee and provisions ; besides these, he received fees for registering deeds of sale, and commission of office, none being considered valid unless they bore his and the Zemindar's seals ; he also received fees on marriages, and other religious ceremonies among his own people. His present income is derived from his enams, one rupee paid from the sadilwar of each village, and from several small fees for marriages, &c. among his own people.

Naeekwadee.—The Naeekwadee was a kind of hereditary district police soldier, attached to the Mamlutdar's department, receiving, besides his pay, one rupee from the sadilwar of each village.

Bhut.— In this district there is an Agnehotre Bhut, receiving one rupee from the sadilwar of each village. He is rather a pensioner on the bounty of the villagers than a person possessing any right to this huk ; but, as it is paid to him from the sadilwar and entered in the Government record, it is necessary to include him among the recipients of Government remuneration, though his right to it may be a matter of question.

Nature of Huks, &c.

22. The imposts are of different kinds, and bear different names, according to the kind of crop, and season, or place of collection, and also vary in different districts, both as to designation, kind, and qantity ; they may be divided into two classes, those belonging to the Kalee,[88] or land those of the pandree, or interior of the village. Those of the former consist of a tithe of everything grown, and may be levied either while in the ear, or after thrashing, according to the custom of the village. Both customs are generally in force in the same village, and each may be again subdivided into such a number of items as the various interest and services may have called into existence, some of the principal of which are as follows :—

Goor[89] is the chief huk of the artisans and village servants, and consists of so many sheaves per paeen or chahoor of unthrashed corn, levied at the time of reaping, before it is taken from the field, or before it is thrashed in the stack-yard.[90] The aggregate amount of this huk will vary in proportion to the amount of the other huks received by the artisans, from about 150 to 800 sheaves per paeen. The average of the accompanying tables is 348 sheaves per paeen, and the average amount of grain yielded by them is 48 paeelees per paeen, each hundred sheaves of corn being supposed to yield about 56 seers of grain more or less, according to their size and quality.

Nimboor.—A minor huk, collected by most of the village staff, properly when the corn is in the green ear, but sometimes when in the sheaf. The name varies according to the kind of grain : thus ears of hajree are called nimboor ; of wheat ombiya ; and of jobaree hoorda,[91] &c.: in these tables they have been collectively entered as nimboor.

Wanwula.[92]—Huks or tithes of the various kinds of grain, such as oil plants, &c. which are cultivated in too small quantities to warrant a regular impost ; it is also levied from tobacco, ambarree, hemp, and vegetables. The grains have been entered under this head in the tables ; but tobacco, vegetables, &c. not collectively being capable of weight or measurement, their value has been entered instead.

Adepade.[93]—So much grain per paeen or chahoor, levied by the Patels from each tenant's heap. The average of this huk is about 8 paeelees per paeen.

Aootkee.[94]—So much grain on each plough levied by the Patels of some villages, instead of adepade. It is sometimes synonymous with adepade, and sometimes with Maparkee.

Maparkee,[95] by measure : the Patel's huk in some villages is levied in this manner—that is, for every khundee of grain he receives two or more paeelees, according to the customs of the village. The Muhars also possess this huk, but by them it is generally called Mojun or Pat.

Mooshaheera.[96]—This huk, from its name, appears to have been granted by the Mahomedans as a remuneration to village officers when not remunerated by Government. It may either be a money assessment, or an impost in kind ;—if the former, it was levied as follow : the village officers were allowed to collect the amount of village expenses, so much per cent (in these districts 4 annas per rupee, or 25 per cent) over and above the Government revenue ; out of which sum was paid the Deshmookh's and Despandee's dues, the sadilwar, or village expenses, and the Patel's or Coolkurnee's stipend, as mooshaheera, which either might be a round sum, or so much per cent on the total collection, or so many annas per chahoor on the total amount cultivated ; or it might be levied separately, at so much per chahoor, from the ryots. As a ready-money huk, it was generally allowed to those whose other huks in kind were not a sufficient remuneration for their services. As a huk in kind, it is a misnomer for Ghoogree, and is levied in these districts by the Coolkurnees as the Patels do their adepade.

Sulaee.[97]—When the farmer has thrashed out his corn, and the heap is ready for measurement, the Coolkurnee, in villages where this huk is in force, is called to measure it, and, at each tale of one hundred paeelees, he puts aside a small heap, of one seer or more, according to his influence : on the completion of the measurement these heaps serve to show the number of tales, of one hundred paeelees each, and the aggregate amount of grain; the tale heaps are then collected ; and taken by the Coolkurnee as his huk.

Odha.[98]—A haul ; a huk levied by the Coolkurnee, consisting of as much grain as he can with his clasped hands and circularly extended arms enclose and take away from each tenant's heap.

Bagaeet.[99]—I have found it impossible, in the accompanying tables, to give any correct view of the rate and articles of impost on garden-land, and have, therefore merely entered their value as in jeeraeet. They consist of tithes of everything grown, but except in grain, which may be collected under the heads of adepade, wanwula, &c. they do not admit of any specific rates of collection, and are, if possible, still more vexatious and burdensome to the cultivator. Each individual of the village staff may expect and obtain a handful of fruit, a lap-full of peas or beans, and a wapha (smallbed) of onions, carrots, or other vegetables ; but the voracious claims upon sugar-cane and its produce are insatiable. The reaping of the cane and creaking of the sugar-mill are signals for the collections of a whole bevy of hungry applicants—Muhar, Mang, artisan, Patel, and Brahmin, alike flock to the gathering : a drink of juice, a stick of cane, and lump of sugar, may satisfy their immediate cravings, but their more weighty claims can only be appeased by more substantial gifts. The Patels, Coolkurnees, and Muhars, each, in some villages claim from one to two moulds[100] of sugar per mill, and the rest of the staff in proportion, amounting in the aggregate, perhaps, to seven or eight maunds (of forty seers each) to each mill ; but as the quantity of cane grown to each mill is not uniform, the amount given must vary more or less, according to circumstances.

Pandree.[101]—The Pandree imposts consist of duties and customs collected under the head of Mohoturfa[102] by the Patel and Coolkurnee, as also in a less degree by the Muhars. The principal cesses are tithes of articles in kind from each manufacturer or vender—as a blanket from the Dhungurs ; one weft of cloth woven by each description of loom ; viz. a piece of khadee from the Khutrees, a sarree from the Sallees, a dhotur from the Koostees, and a turban from the Mohmeen, levied each year. In some of the smaller villages, few if any of these classes are to be found ; but in the larger ones they are sometimes numerous, and the huks levied from them are generally commuted into a money assessment. The Wanees are supposed to find the Patel and Coolkurnees with sooparee for daily consumption, and a quantity of sugar at festivals. The same may be said of the oil-man, but his impost is generally commuted into an annual money assessment on each oil-press. There are also imposts levied on several members of the village staff. The shoemaker has to contribute a pair of shoes each to the Patels, Coolkurnees, and Zemindars ; and where there are two or more sharers in the Patelship, each sharer in some instances is entitled to a pair, in others only one sharer ; but as the power to levy the imposts is one of the many instances of dignity, each sharer generally endeavours to force it.[103] The shoemaker also finds leather halters for the Patel's bullocks at the Pola festival. The smith finds iron rings for those halters. The Muhars find firewood at the different festivals for the Patels and Coolkurnees; they also return the skins of any dead cattle belonging to the Patels, for which they are supposed to receive a little grain in return.[104] This privilege is another acknowledgement of dignity, and is rigidly enforced by the Patels. There are other minor imposts, but any minute examination of them does not appear necessary : some of the superior ones are as follows :—

Khureed Khut.[105]—On the sale of any property, the Coolkurnee makes out the deed of sale, and receives a percentage proportionate to his influence or power to exact it, from one to five per cent.

Khoteputra.[106]—Farmers frequently sell their crops by contract, as they stand in the field ; the Coolkurnee makes out the agreement, and receives one rupee from the buyer or seller, as specified in the bargain.

Jukat.[107]—A cess (generally a pice) levied by the Patels and Coolkurnees on each bullock laden with merchandize as it passes through those villages entitled to exact it.

Pewbood.[108]—Corn dealers frequently deposit their grain in underground stores, in the village they purchase it at. The Coolkurnee and Muhars receive a tithe of such grain on the breaking up of the store, the one for keeping the accounts of it, the other for their labour in placing and extracting it.

Lugnamoohoort.[109]—A turban or shawl levied on marriages by the Patel, according to the influence of the parties.

Shewsubjee.[110]—Tithes in kind on vegetable vendors, levied by the Patels of market villages on market days.

Dhungurs.[111]—A caste who either follow the vocation of shepherds, or of blanket-weavers, or both. In the former capacity they pay to the Patel one or more sheep per flock at the Dussera, and a little wool to the Coolkurnee ; in the latter they give a blanket for each loom to both officers.

Sallee Koshtee.[112]—Under this head are entered the imposts on the different descriptions of weavers, as above described, each contributing one piece of cloth per loom of the kind woven by him.

The above are the principal huks of this district, but besides these there are others, and many variations in the rate and method of collection. It is difficult to describe, with any degree of method, customs which are totally devoid of all order and regularity. Had these imposts originated in, or been controlled ay any superior authority, some degree of regularity in the levying of them might have been expected ; but where, on the one hand, they depend on the power of the recipients to exact, and, on the other, on the power of the contributors to resist that exaction, much identity in the articles taxed, and in the rate of taxation, cannot be expected. The accompanying tables have been drawn up with the intention of affording as broad a view of these imposts as the nature of the subject will admit of ; but, from the difficulties already mentioned, great exactness in the definition of rates and quantities has—particularly under those headed pandree—been found impossible ; and too nice an inquiry into them would only have excited suspicion, and ensured their falsification. They have been drawn up with as much minuteness as possible, but, for want of room, several distinct and minor imposts have been entered in one column, as the noticing of each separately would have increased the length of the table, without any advantage being derived from it.

23. The preceding description will, I hope sufficiently explain the nature of huks, and the services for which they are given, it has been my wish to give as comprehensive and correct a view of them as possible, by entering in a tabular form each individual's income, under their several heads, and I have pursued this plan as far as possible, but, for reasons before stated, I have only partially succeeded. There is a table for each description of recipient for the thirty-three villages of the purgunna, which with the help of the description contained in the preceding paragraph, will, I hope, be sufficiently perspicuous. Those of the Patels, Coolkurnees and Zemindars, have been prepared from the records in the Mamlutdar's office, as annually given in by recipients, and checked by others from themselves ; those for the artisans and Muhars have been prepared from reports called for by me from the Patels and Coolkurnees of the several villages, and I believe them all to be as correct as, under existing circumstances, it is possible to obtain. It is probable that motives may exist to induce the village officers to give in false statements of their purbhara huks, but, after a careful consideration of the subject, I am unable

to say whether they would be led to exaggerate or to diminish the true amount. For the purpose of obtaining increased enam, or other Government allowance, it has always been their interest to represent them lower than the truth ; but, on the other hand, as for some years past they have been aware that it is the wish of the present Government to give them compensation in lieu of these huks, it would appear now to be their interest, for the purpose of obtaining a greater amount of such compensation, to represent them to be above what they really receive. It is possible that the Patels, as possessing enam, have been actuated by the former motive, and have entered a trifle less, or at all events no more than they receive ; while the Coolkurnees, as possessing no enam, and being fully alive to present circumstances, may have entered all they could lawfully lay claim to : but whether or not in some instances the Patels have entered somewhat less,—as many of these villages are inhabited principally by Patels who do not pay each other huks,—the total and average amount of them will not be much affected. With respect to the lower artisans and village servants, the probability appears in favour of the village officers giving in a lower rate of remuneration than the correct one, because they, as well as the ryots, feel it rather heavy, and document of the kind given in to Government may at any future period be called upon by either party as proof of the correct rate of remuneration. The pandree imposts do not admit of the same definite rate of collection as whose of the kalee, and it will be observed, that though there are a number of columns in each table for the different heads and items liable to impost, few of them are entered. The articles of subsistence derived by the Muhars and other village servants from the pandree, being bread, and other articles, begged, rather than levied, cannot properly be called imposts : but those of the village officers assume the form of customs ; and, with respect to them, we naturally look for more specific rates of collection. But many of these villages do not contain a single Bunya's shop, or artisan, other than those of the Bara Bulootee, and in other villages, where they do exist, they have been considered worthy of being entered. There are villages, however, such as Kopergaon, Rahatee, and Puntambee, not liable to this disadvantage ; and where, in such instances, there are none specified, it must be presumed that recipients either have not deemed it advisable to enter them, or that they are of so mixed and indeterminable a description as not to admit of specification. The few that are entered, together with the description of some of those entered under their several names is paragraph 22, will, I hope, convey some idea of what they would amount to in such towns as Yowila, Sungumneer, or Nassick. They are mentioned here because they existed in year 1253, A.D. 1843-44, now reported upon ; but they have since been done away with, and have lost their importance : their connection, however, with the income, and the sacrifices of village officers, required notice.

24. Allowing, then, that with regard to the kalee, or land imposts, these tables are correct, the rates and averages derived from them will afford dara for determining two principal facts of the village system—1st, the sufficiency or otherwise of the remuneration to each individual of the village staff, as compared with the services rendered by him ; and 2nd, the burden which the total amount of these imposts place upon the land.

25. The average amount (throwing out the minor fractions) of each individual's huk, has been entered under their separate heads in paragraph 21, and it is only necessary to multiply this average by an assumed average of cultivated land, in order to obtain each individual's total amount of remuneration in a moderate sized village.

Statement showing the average Amount of Huks received by the Village Officers and Artisans of any Village in which there may be 80 paeens of Cultivation, also the sufficiency of those Huks for their support.[113]

Names of Hukdars.	Average remuneration per paeen.		Total Cultivation.	Amount per annum.	No. of days in the year.	Average Subsistence per diem.		Amounts in Bushels per annum.	
	Paeelees.	Seers.	Paeens.	Seers.	Days.	Seers.	Dec.	Bushels.	Dec.
Patel	2	3¼		900		2.	4	34	4
Coolkurnee	8	3½		2840		7.	7	108.	8
Sootar	6	1		2000		5.	4	76.	6
Lohar	5	2½		1800		4.	9	68.	9
Chambhar	5	2½		1800		4.	9	68.	9
Koombhar	4	0¾		1340		3.	6	51.	3
Nhawee	4	0¾		1340		3.	6	51.	3
Pureet	4	2¾		1500		4.	1	57.	4
Bhut	2	3¼	× 80 =	900	÷ 365=	2.	4	34.	4
Goorow	3	1		1040		2.	8	39.	8
Moolana	2	3¼		900		2.	4	34.	4
Sonar	2	1¼		740		2.	0	28.	3
Bheel	2	3¼		900		2.	4	34.	4
Kolee	3	1		1040		2.	8	39.	8
Mang	2	1¼		740		2.	8	28.	3
Muhar	14	2¾		4700		12.	8	180.	1

26. The second column of the above Statement exhibits each individual's average amount of huk per paeen, as derived from the accompanying tables, which average, being multiplied by 80 paeens, a fair amount of cultivation for moderate sized village, will give each individual's total amount of huk for a year, as shown in the 3rd column, and which, again, divided by 365, will give his daily average of subsistence, as per 4th column. The last column of this table exhibits their total amount of huk for the year (vidė column 3) converted into English bushels, assuming the seer to contain 85 cubic inches, as before stated. From 2½ to 3 seers is considered a sufficient quantity for a day's subsistence for a family of five persons, adults and children, while the above table shows each individual member of the Bulootee is amply provided for. It is true that all villages do not contain 80 paeens of cultivated land, some being much smaller ; but in that case one artisan is generally the hukdar of two or more villages. How far each individual is rewarded according to his services depends upon how those services are relatively estimated by the villagers. The Muhars, according to their number, have apparently the lowest rate of remuneration : as in a village of this size there should at least be eight Muhars, with their families ; the above average, therefore, of 12.8 (twelve, decimal eight) seers, will give only 1½ seers to each family per diem ; but they have also a Government enam, and various other means of subsistence.

27. The above table comprehends merely the imposts on the land, and has nothing to do with those derived from the pandree, or interior of the village ; it also refers to the imposts, and to the system, so far only as they relate to the adequate remuneration of the recipients, their bearing upon the ryots having still to be considered. Confining ourselves to the imposts in kind on the land, and referring to the tables, we find that the total amount of cultivation in this purgunna for the year which these tables were prepared was 68,977 beeghas, and that the total amount of grain collected as imposts by each class of recipients was as follows :—

Vide Statement No. 9, column 3,

Statement showing the Total Amount and Value of Purbhara Huks, as collected from the Kalee, or Land, in Purgunna Koombharee, for the Year 1253 Fuslee.

	State.	Col.		Aamount of Grain.				Value.			Sundries.			Total.		
				Khun.	Mds.	Pls.	Seers.	Rs.	a.	p.	Rs.	a.	p.	Rs.	a.	p.
Vide No.	3	13	Patels	11	17	8	1½	354	12	6	30	2	0	384	14	6
"	4	15	Koolkurnees.	65	16	13	1	1993	4	3	179	6	0	2172	10	3
			Total	77	14	5	2½	2348	0	9	209	8	0	2557	8	9
"	5	23	Muhars	101	0	11	3½	3213	13	3	53	12	0	3267	9	3
"	2	41	Artisans	356	13	11	1½	11274	8	0	178	11	6	11453	3	6
			Total	457	14	7	1	14488	5	3	232	7	6	14720	12	9
"	9	30	Grand Total.	535	8	12	3½	16836	6	0	441	15	6	17278	5	6

I have kept the village officers separate from the rest, for the convenience of comparison, in a future paragraph. The amount of grain here stated if five hundred and thirty-five khundees, eight muns, eleven paeelees, and three and a half seers ; which, reduced to seers, equal 6,85,359 seers ÷ 68,977 beeghas, the total amount of cultivation gives nearly ten seers to the beegha. The value of the above grain, as estimated by the Natives themselves, is Rs. 16,836-6-0 ; but, besides the grain, there are sundries, of which the value only could be entered, viz. Wanwula, Rs. 13-20-0 ; Bagaeet, Rs. 281-14-6 ; and Coolkurnee's Nugde Mooshaheera, collected from the ryots, Rs. 146-15-0 ; Total Rs. 17,278-5-6 ; which also, divided by 68,977, gives Rs. 0-4-0 (four annas) per beegha—a large sum when contrasted with the low rates introduced by the survey. This is the amount, according to the present value of grain ; but, as the price of grain is continually fluctuating, this cannot be considered a permanent average of the expense borne by the ryot, for, were grain half as dear again as it is valued at in these tables, the average would then be six, instead of four annas, per beegha ; and when, during the Native rule, the price of grain varied from 5 to 7 paeelees per rupee, it would approach nearly to eight annas per beegha. Four annas per beegha, however, I believe, is considered by the Natives themselves to be a fair estimate of the average expense borne by the cultivator on account of huks.

28. The above, as remarked in the last paragraph, relates to the land imposts alone, and is compiled from statements, the correctness of which there appears no sufficient reason to question. But, whatever error may exist in the individual rates of remuneration there appears to have been no design to exaggerate their total value ; for the value of the grain as here entered is, perhaps, somewhat below the market price which then prevailed, and in valuing this grain no account has been taken of 8,01,503 sheaves of straw received with it.

Ready-Money Grants, Enams, &c.

29. Before summing up the total village expenditure, in order to show the expense of the system, it will be necessary to notice that part of it which comes under the head of Ready-money Grants, Sadilwar and Enams. The former in these districts appear to have been very rarely conferred on the Patels ; and when such instances do occur, they appear to have been merely given as an occasional reward for the prosperous state of the village, as Seerpa, Pagota, and Tushreefee. Under the tunkha system, the Patels, being the farmers of their villages, probably had no regular assignment, either of land or money, but remunerated themselves from the surplus revenue of their villages ; and the origin of many of these grants may, perhaps, be dated from the breaking up of that system. When the assignment was regular, it was called either Nemnookh,[114] or Mooshaheera,[115] and might be collected either over or above the Government revenue, or paid from it. The Coolkurnees, in some instances, it appears, possess both a Government and village Mooshaheera. The total grants to Patels and Coolkurnees in this district for the year reported upon are as follows :—

Statement showing the Amount of Ready-Money Allowances paid to Village Officers is Fuslee 1253.

	State.	Col.		Government. Nemnookh. or Mooshaheera.			Village. Seerpa.			Village. Mooshaheera.			Total [116]		
				Rs.	a.	p.	Rs.	a.	p.	Rs.	a.	p.	Rs.	a.	p.
Vide No.	3	3, 4	Patels	130	4	0	31	0	0	0	0	0	161	4	0
"	4	1, 5	Coolkurnees.	327	0	0	0	0	0	135	4	0	462	4	0
			Total Rupees	457	4	0	31	0	0	135	4	0	623	8	0

30. *Sadilwar.*—It was stated in paragraph 22 that the village officers were allowed to collect 25 per cent, or four annas to the rupee, in excess of the Government revenue, for the purpose of paying the Jemadar's dues and village expenses. On the accession of the present Government this was done away with, and in these districts 6 per cent on the total collections payable from the Government treasury was allowed instead, the village authorities still being allowed the control over it with a view of forming some idea of the actual application of this money, I called upon the village officers to furnish me with a memorandum of the several heads under which it had been expended in the preceding year, and the accompanying Statement (No. 8), it will be observed gives a total expenditure of Rs. 2,439-3-0, being 6 per cent.[117] on Rs. 40,687-12-6, the total collection of revenue for that year. Under the word Hukdars is entered the sums paid to the Kazee, Zemindars, and Naeekwadees. Dewusthan comprehends the expenses of religious festivals, presents to officiating Brahmins, and oil and pigments, &c. for the temples. Dhurmadaee,—sums expended in charity to village pensioners, or to religious mendicants, &c. and contingencies,—includes pens, ink and paper required for the village, oil for the Chowdee, and travelling expenses for the Patels and Coolkurnees, when proceeding to a distance on Government duty.

31. *Enams.*—The practice of granting rent-free lands, either as a subsistence, or a remuneration for services appears, by the Hindoo names used to denote such grants to have been of very ancient origin ; but the absence of any general or abstract term for them would not lead us to suppose that the practice had been very general. If, under the tunkha or other early system, the village officers were answerable for one uniform annual assessment, which in the first place had been fixed sufficiently low to leave them a profit, they, perhaps, received neither enam nor other remuneration from Government, and the lands which these officers might grant for the subsistence of other servants of the village would either be at the expense of the contracting Patels, or of the whole village ; such lands, therefore, when granted, would be designated by names, specifying their application, (as we find them to be,) without any general term denoting their freedom from the State, because the State might not have given them. Subsequently, however, on the breaking up of the tunkha

system, Khairat[118] and other grants were, perhaps, conferred in the latter years of the Mahomedan Government, under the name of enam, and which name soon became applied to all classes of rent-free land. The following abstract of Table No. 7 will show the total enams of this district :—

Abstract of the different classes of Rent-free Lands in Purgunna Koombharee.

		Description of Grant.	Under what Government obtained. Unknown.	Mogul.	Peishwa.	Scindia.	British.	Total.	Possessing Sunnuds	Not possessing Sunnuds.
	Cols.		Beeghas.	Beeghas.	Beeghas.	Beeghas.	Beeghas.	Beeghas.		
	2	Kazee	415	1006	90	....	....	1511	1065	446
	1	Zemindar	....	1622	....	....	....	1622	1622	
	3	Patel	....	3285	....	120	....	3405	120	3285
	4	Coolkurnee	30	....	7	....	....	37	7	30
	10	Muhar	3485	....	....	....	....	3485	....	3485
	7	Bheel	191	....	....	....	260	451	260	191
Vide Statement	6	Halwutee	....	180	....	....	....	180	....	180
No. 7	5	Taroo	....	....	54	....	....	54	....	54
	14	Khairat	10	577	....	....	....	587	....	587
	12	Dewusthan	209	97	210	30	....	546	106	440
	13	Dhurmadaee	....	250	60	....	....	310	40	270
	15	Bukshish	25	600	854	580	40	2099	1505	594
	17	Total	4365	7617	1275	730	300	14287	4725	9562

Out of fourteen thousand two hundred and eighty-seven beeghas of rent-free land, only four thousand seven hundred and twenty-five beeghas have sunnuds : in fact, a careful perusal of this table will, I think, abundantly confirm the opinion that *bonâ fide* rent-free grants confirmed by sunnuds are comparatively of recent date, and that probably all the earlier, and many of the later grants have been bestowed by the village alone ; some under the then existing system of revenue, with the tacit permission of the State, and others without either its authority or knowledge ; but all of which, on the accession of our Government, the district and village officers took care to get confirmed.

32. Having now described the several customs relating to the position and influence of the village officials, and the sources of their emoluments, I may proceed to enumerate the total amount of village expenses, and to show how they bear on Government and the ryots. The total area of the Koombharee Purgunna is, as before stated, 220,247 beeghas, out of which

must be deducted 56,760 beeghas of waste, leaving 163,487[119] beeghas of culturable land, rated according to the old kumall, at Rupees 176,694 ; the immediate expense of collecting which may be noted under two heads namely, grants by enams, and ready-money grants, of so much per cent on the collections, and may be stated as follows :—

	Total Arable Land.	Enams	Per cent.	Estimated Ready-money Allowance.	Total per cent.
Beeghas	163,487	14,287	8.73		
Assessment .... Rupees	1,76,694	15,469	8.75	10 per cent	18.73

Showing the immediate expense of collection to be about 19 per cent of the whole kumall, that is 9 per cent of enam, and 10 per cent of ready-money grants. But, with respect to the enams, to strike the percentage on the old kumall does not give a correct impression, because that kumall was never realized. I have, therefore, framed the following table, striking the percentages from the collection for Fuslee 1253, namely Rs. 40,687-12-6 :—

Statement showing the Total Amount of Village Expenditure in the Koomharee Purgunna, for the year 1253 Fuslee.

			Names of Recipents.	Enams.			Ready-money Payment.			Total Government.			Purbhara Kalee Huks.			Total		
	No.	Cols.		Rs.	a.	p.	Rs.	a.	p.	Rs.	a.	p.	Rs.	a.	p.	Rs.	a.	p.
Vide Statement	7	2	Kazee	1733	6	3				1733	6	3				1733	6	3
,,	6	1, 5	Zemindars	1814	1	0	1133	14	6	2947	15	6				2947	15	6
,,	3	5, 13	Patels	3426	13	0	161	4	0	3588	1	0	384	14	6	3972	15	6
,,	7	3																
,,	4,	1, 3.15																
,,	7	4	Coolkurnees	35	4	3	327	0	0	362	4	3	2172	10	3	2534	14	6
,,	5	4. 23	Muhar	3663	12	6				3663	12	6	3267	9	3	6931	5	9
,,	2	31, 32	Bheel	460	13	3				460	13	3	716	13	9	1177	11	0
,,	7	5	Taroo	63	0	6				63	0	6				63	0	6
,,	7	6	Halwutee	204	6	0				204	6	0				204	6	0
,,	8	11	Sadilwar				2439	3	0	2439	3	0				2439	3	0
			Total	11401	8	9	4061	5	6	15462	14	3	6541	15	9	22004	14	0
			Per cent	28	0	4	9	15	8	38	0	0	16	1	3	54	1	3
,,	9	28	Bukshish	4067	9	9				4067	9	9				4067	9	9
,,	7	16	Artisans										10736	5	9	10736	5	9
			Total	4067	9	9				4067	9	9	10736	5	9	14803	15	6
			Per cent	9	15	11				9	15	11	26	6	2	36	6	1
,,	7	17	Grand Total	15469	2	4	4061	5	6	19530	8	0	17278	5	6	36808	13	0
			Total percentage.	38	0	5	9	15	8	48	0	1	42	7	4	90	7	5

To make the total of this Statement agree with the total of statement No. 9, the Muhars, rabta, &c. should be deducted, and the pandree huks should be added—thus :—

			Total, Rupee	36,808	13	6
Vide Statement	5	9	Deduct as per column 9, Statement 5	468	15	9
			Remainder, Rupees	36,339	13	9
"	9	31	Add, as above, pandree huks	2,323	11	0
				38,663	8	9

The ready-money payments are of course disbursed with reference to the amount of revenue collections, and are, as shown in the table, 10 per cent of the revenue ; but the enam, being a fixed allowance, its proportion to the amount of Government realizations will vary with goodness or badness of the season. Thus, in the above Statement, it is 38 per cent of the year's collections, which, together with the 10 per cent in the form of money grants, makes a total expense to Government of 48 per cent of its collections for that year. The huks paid by the ryots amount to 42 per cent, so that the total sum paid by Government and the ryots for the year in question is 90 per cent of the collections. It is proper here to mention that Fuslee 1253 does not afford a fair specimen of the average collections of the purgunna ; but even should the average collections be taken at double the sum realized that year, this would only affect the enam percentage, reducing it from 38 to 19, and would still give a total expenditure on account of the village system of 70 per cent.

General Observations.

33. In giving the above details of the village system, I have confined myself to those which bear immediately upon the question of huks, and the remuneration of village officers ; and there are many points appertaining to revenue and police arrangements, as well as the internal customs of the village, which I have purposely omitted to notice, as it was my object merely to show the general tendency of the village systems, as bearing upon the subject under discussion.

34. Opinions may vary with regard to the inherent merits and efficacy of the system ; but its indisputable primitive origin, and indestructible

permanence, have, I believe, disposed most to regard it as an emanation of the wisdom and forethought of the patriarchal times. This view of it is certainly imposing, and, if correct, would go far to prove the inalienable right of the village and its office-bearers ; but my own inquiries have led me to a different conclusion, and to consider the system as having naturally arisen out of the wants of the people in a very early stage of society ; and that it has been maintained by the self-interest of its office-bearers, and by its adaptation not only to the genius of people, but to the views of their arbitrary rulers. On reviewing it, we find no particular right or privileges possessed by the body of the people not office-bearers ; no independence or equality ; no civil rights, such as the freedom of election ; no principle of progressive liberty. The privileges of the people were confined to the freedom of their village, and to the hereditarily occupying the same lands ; but the advantages of immunities and pecuniary gain were enjoyed by the office-bearers alone. The necessities of a very early stage of society caused the villagers to encourage certain mechanics and servants permanently to settle in their villages, whom they remunerated by a payment in kind, which settlement and remuneration became, in course of time, an hereditary right, and increased in value, perhaps, by the increase of mechanical knowledge and competition. The same, to a certain extent, may be said of the village officers. Originally appointed by Government and remunerated, perhaps solely, by an impost in kind on the land—constant changes of government, and of the revenue system, eventually converted them into hereditary farmers of their villages, the entire control and management of which were thrown into their hands. Thus the village officers and artisans were the persons by whose interests the system was upheld, the remainder of the inhabitants not possessing any particular interest, save the natural pride arising from the degrees of respectability attached to the two divisions of Thulwaheek and Oopree. The system, then, was one of exclusion and official aggrandizement, but it was not without merit, as it formed a strong safeguard against destructive changes, and afforded a ready and cheap method of collecting the Government revenue. With the spirit of government then in force, it was inseparable, but the great change that has now taken place has entirely altered the position of the chief actors. Old interests are destroyed, and new ones generated, the various circumstances of which cannot be too much borne in mind, whether as regards the amelioration of those who may have suffered, the iradication of any noxious principle still extant, or the calling forth of other principles which may conduce to the well-being of the people.

35. The working of any system of revenue must depend in a great measure on the character of the subordinate agency employed on it, which, again, must depend on the nature of their remuneration and on the character of the system. To ensure the fidelity and zeal of Native subordinates, it is necessary that their interests should be so bound up with those of Government, that injury or success may be reciprocal. It was, perhaps, on this principle that the Mahomedans acted, when they acknowledged the hereditary rights of the Patel, and made him the superior head of his village, who, being, as it were, the hereditary proprietor of those rights, possessed the strongest motives for its improvement. But this principle would appear to be either wrong, or its object impracticable, since the system has, perhaps, never been found to fulfil the ends for which it was intended. If the principle were correct, but failed in execution, it could only be from the misconduct of the subordinate agency ; if its object were impracticable, it must have failed from causes in direct antagonism with the principle. In a financial point of view, the chief advantage and support of the system were its supposed immutability of operation, and the bringing into the Government treasury a specified amount of revenue with the least possible expense and trouble ; but it is possible that the very means taken to ensure these effect were the chief cause of its failure. The Patel was liable for the demands of the district and Government officers, who were remunerated from the village, and whom it was necessary for him to conciliate. If the season were a bad one, he was the direct and chief loser ; and if a good one, all claimed the privilege of participating in his gains. He was thus ostensibly liable for the greatest amount of revenue the village was capable of paying, and he had also to meet the rapacious demands of the district officials claiming remuneration from it ; but he had no voice in the fixing of that amount, or of altering it to meet the exigencies of the season ; and under these conflicting interests he too often found it expedient to make the most he could of the present, and to join in the general scramble for the spoil, seizing every feasible opportunity of establishing a new huk or item of gain. A system, therefore, which looks so well in theory, and which, with an agency of fewer interests, and higher

moral qualification might have answered the expectations formed of it, was marred by the latitude of its operation, and the conflicting interests engaged in it. Whether or not I am right in attributing its failure to the causes here mentioned, it is certain that from the very earliest times there has been great confusion in its working, and that, with a general sense on the part of the ryots of the insecurity of property, there exists a still greater spirit of extortion among the officials ; while this spirit has become so habitual to them, that any attempt at once to eradicate it must be hopeless ; but the peculiar circumstances which have fostered it must be borne in mind, ere we can efficaciously introduce any new measure of improvement.

36. But should it be inferred, that as under the present improved system of revenue these cause do not exist,—that in removing the adverse interests of district and Government officials, Government have also removed all obstacles to the correct working of the system, and that the Patel may be safely entrusted with his legitimate duties,—I would observe that Government have not only removed the causes, but, in removing them, they have also changed the position of that officer. Government, in correctly defining, measuring, and assessing its lands, have removed the occasion for the services of the Patel in the particular channel they were before required ; for if those lands be correctly and truly valued, so as to yield a sufficient profit to the cultivator, and all adverse official interests be also removed, private or individual interests will always be sufficiently strong to ensure their cultivation, without the assistance of the Patel ; and if the cultivation of such lands be not sufficiently remunerative, any system of forcing cultivation must always be injurious. But if it be urged that the Patels might be legitimately and advantageously allowed to farm their respective villages, it should be borne in mind that we have not sufficiently advanced in reform to admit of this. We may have shut the door upon corruption, but she still waits without, and any return to such a system would only be the re-opening it to her ravages. Both the moral principle of the officials, and the worldly condition of the people, must be changed, ere we can think of it. The adoption of such a measure under the present condition of the people would make some Sowcar the head of the village, the Patel his puppet, and the ryots his victims. The legitimate duties of the Patel, I conceive, should be purely those of a Government servant—those of a police officer and Government agent ; and these in a large

village will be sufficiently onerous to exercise all his zeal and ability. But as he is now situated, he possesses no inducement to the exercise of either : his huks on the land are generally mortgaged or swallowed up in grants of meeras, and his brotherhood claim the privilege of sharing with him the enam, leaving them a very paltry remuneration for his services, as will be observed from the following Table :—

Statement showing the Average Value of the Remuneration received by each Patel in the Koombharee Purgunna, for Fuslee 1253.

		No.	Government Remuneration.	Purbhara Huks.		Total.	Average per family.
No. Cols.			Rs. a. p.	Kalee.	Pandree.	Rs. a. p.	Rs. a. p.
Vide Statement. 3 5,13,30,31	Patels	284	3,588 1 0	384 14 6	234 6 0	4,207 5 6	14 13 0

It will be seen from the above Statement, that although the total emolument received by the Patels is very considerable, being on an average Rupees 128 per village, the average amount enjoyed by each family is very small being only Rupees 14-13-0.

37. Two plans, I am aware, have been proposed for the remuneration of village officers, any criticism of which on my part would be presumptuous ; but I hope, after endeavouring to explain the tendency of the system, I may be allowed to point out a few principles, which I conceive, should guide us in any endeavour to improve it : namely, to abstain as much as possible from changing, against the general wish of the people, any old custom not positively injurious ; that whatever extra remuneration it may be thought fit to give, should be given in the direct name of pugar, and not on the principle of a huk or bab, thereby precluding all possibility of such remuneration being claimed as a right, rather than as a reward for services ; that this remuneration should be granted to, and enjoyed by, the working official alone, and the rest of the Bhaoobund be debarred from it ; and that in fixing any new scale of remuneration, special attention be paid to the leading features of the old.

38. Enam in these districts is considered rather as a present from Government than a remuneration for services—it is therefore claimed as the common property of the whole of the Patels, and is shared by them accordingly ; but the number of sharers is in most instances so great, that

it only gives a trifle to each. The mooshaheera and purbhara huks are supposed to be enjoyed by the seniors of each tuksim share, but even these, when divided among the number of tuksims, will afford only a small sum to each, (as will appear in most of the villages in Table No. 3,) and is by no means sufficient to encourage a working Patel to a zealous performance of his duties. Government already pays away a large and ample portion of its revenues to district and village officers ; but, with respect to the Patels, it must either declare the enam and other allowances to be the remuneration of those in office only, or it must grant them others in lieu of them.

39. The chief official marks of the dignity of the Patel's office are his enam, and the power of levying huks : the general effect of huks, if judiciously exacted, may not be positively bad, but they open a wide field for extortion on the part of the village officers, and tend to keep up principles inimical to the improvement of the people. A village artisan, being remunerated by huks, is sure of a livelihood, and, not being liable to competition, has no inducement to improve himself in his art, and a ryot, being annually subject to the payment of them, earned or not, is not thereby encouraged to preserve his implements. Irrespective of the channel which they open to extortion, they in some measure tend to give the village officer another position, and other interests, than those of a Government servant ; they retard mechanical improvement, and promote quarrels between the recipient and the donor,—quarrels which will become more frequent and virulent as the ryot becomes more enlightened, and is enabled to procure cheaper and better labour. But at present it is neither possible nor advisable to abolish the whole of these huks, and the Patel's and Coolkurnee's shares being only a small proportion of the whole, (vide Statement para 32, in which the proportion of huks of village officers to the remainder is about 14 per cent of the whole) the abolishment of them alone would not afford much relief to the ryot, and perhaps no immediate beneficial effect might accrue ; but if the tendency of the custom be such as I have described it to be, the abolition even of these would be the commencement of an amended principle, and an opening for future improvement.

40. These huks, as privileges of the olden times, are much esteemed by their holders, and are preserved (if only in name) not merely for present profit, but as openings for future increase. Any forcible abolition of them

would, therefore, be extremely unpopular ; yet, what from force or compulsion would be unpopular, might, if backed by a positive advantage, and left to the free choice of the people, gradually work its way into favour. The adoption of the measure for the Coolkurnees of the Poona district has, I have heard, much improved their condition, and I would infer, has given general satisfaction. If, therefore, the extension of the measure be deemed advisable, and although here the Patels and Coolkurnees are much better off, I am inclined to think it might be carried into effect with their entire concurrence I would not, however, promulgate it as an order, but, after fixing a scale of remuneration, leave it to their free choice ; and though, in some instances, it might not be accepted at first, a positive good would not be long rejected. There are districts into which its introduction would be comparatively easy ; the village officers of Ankola, Newassee, and Parneer, I am told, with few exceptions possess neither enams nor huks, but are remunerated almost entirely by Government mooshaheera, and the introduction of the measure into these districts would not be a change of custom, but a remodelling of the old one. The senior Patels of Jamkher and several other districts, also, I am told, after becoming answerable for their father's debts, are the sole enjoyers of the Patel's enam, and other Government allowances,—a circumstance which would materially facilitate the settlement of these districts.

41. The remuneration in lieu of huks should be on a sufficiently liberal scale to induce the village officers to forego them. Table No. 10 will show the amount and average of these huks for the last four years, from which may be made an estimate for the allowance of each officer whom it may be desirable to remunerate : the following is the abstract total of this Table, from which will be seen the proportion of the several items of remuneration now received :—

Abstract of Table No. 10 showing the Average of Renumeration received for the last four years by the Patels and Coolkurnees of Purgunna Koombharee.

	No.	Col.		Government.						Purbhara						Total[120]		
				Enam.			Mooshaheera.			Kalee.			Pandree.					
				Rs.	a.	p.	Rs.	a.	p.	Rs.	a.	p.	Rs.	a.	p.	Rs.	a.	p.
Vide State.	10	4	Patels	3,426	13	0	187	13	3	386	8	10	226	10	0	4,227	13	1
	10	6	Coolkurnees	35	4	3	384	8	0	2,362	13	9	33	5	3	2,815	15	3
			Total	3,462	1	3	472	5	3	2,749	6	7	259	15	3	7,043	12	4*

42. The above, it will be observed, corresponds with the rest of the tables, showing the Patel to be remunerated chiefly by his enam, and the Coolkurnee by his purbhara huks. Thc pandree huks, it may here be mentioned, have been done away with by the late Government order respecting moturfa. The amount of enam is of course the same, whether the whole or a part of the village be cultivated, but the purbhara huks will vary with the amount cultivated. Owing to the number of Meerasdars not paying huks to the Patel, it is impossible correctly to ascertain what would be his total income were the whole of his village cultivated, but the difficulty does not appertain to the Coolkurnee, as he receives alike from all : the total amount for each is shown in Table No. 9, as estimated from what they receive for the proportion already cultivated.

43. Should you deem it expedient to form a scale of remuneration for either of these officers, similar to that in the Poona district, I would beg to call your attention to the suggestion contained in a former paragraph, that whatever be given may be given under the direct name of pugar, and not as a huk or bab. That which is given in Poona and Guzerat may, to all intents and purposes, be pay, but, unless it bear the name, it is not considered as such : more depends on the signification of a word than may at first be apparent, the truth of which is exemplified by the very subject in question. The Mahomedans were, perhaps, the first who granted a ready-money allowance, and that they granted it as pay, and not as huk, is evident from the denomination (mooshaheera) under which they gave it, مشاہرا pay, or wages ; but as they gave it the name it bore in their own language, and not in that of the country, its meaning was misunderstood, and its effect perverted, as mooshaheera is to this day universally considered as a huk, and not as pay. I have before explained the tendency of the village officers to pervert and make the most of a measure as here shown ; and as in making this arrangement the chief object would be to break up that tendency, and not to add to the intricacies of the system, I conceive too much care cannot be taken to avoid the error in question. It is difficult to determine what method of remuneration is best calculated to insure a correct performance of duty, without pressing too heavily on the ryots. The advocates of the old system say, that if the village officer be remunerated by the ryots, he, being, as it were, their servant, would be the more likely to labour for their interest ; but by this supposition it is

incorrectly inferred that the interest of Government and the ryots are at variance, and that the village officer is the protector of the ryot from the avarice and oppression of Government.

44. Remuneration from percentages upon Government revenue would appear to be best calculated to insure Government interests : but it lies under the objection of partaking more of the nature of a huk or bab than of pay ; and it is possible that in some instances it might tend rather to produce a superficial prosperity than solid improvement. Under the old system, it was one of the principal duties of the Patel to encourage cultivation by procuring loans from the Sowcar for the ryots, and by assisting them to procure bullocks and other necessaries ; but this plan tended only to enrich the Sowcars, and was always inimical to the true interests of the village. The Mahomedans, in granting mooshaheera, frequently assigned a lumped allowance to the Patel or Coolkurnee, according to the size of the village, and other sources of remuneration, a plan which, under proper modification, might be adopted in future. The pay of both Patel and Coolkurnee, for instance, might be fixed on a fair estimate of the average amount of collections on the new rates—say three-fourths of the new kumall. Pay fixed with care on this principle would, in a number of years, vary very little from the correctness of a percentage allowance, while any reduction, as a punishment, or increase as a reward, would then have its due effect. Take, for instance a village the new kumall of which is Rupees 1,600, and in which village the Patel has neither enam nor purbhara huks. After a careful consideration of the circumstances of such village, let us endeavour to estimate the probable average of its future collections, say Rupees 1,200 and in consideration of the Patel having no other sources of income, say it is determined to fix the pay of that village at (about 5 per cent of its probable average collections) a round sum of Rupees 60 per annum, under the direct vernacular name of pugar. If the estimate of the probable average collections were made with sufficient care, the average deviation in a number of years would, I imagine, be very small, and an occasional reward of a pair of bullocks or Europe plough for diligence, or fine for negligence, would then have its due effect, and would considerably tend to diminish that professional spirit so injurious to Government interests, which is so prevalent among Patels, and which spirit all huks and percentages tend to foster.

45. As far as my limited space would allow me to examine so vast a subject, I have endeavoured to show that the present system of remuneration has solely grown out of the different revenue systems that have prevailed. I have first noticed the ancient Hindoo system when the assessment was paid in kind, and the village officers were remunerated in kind also. Next, the advent of the Mahomedans and the introduction of the tunkha system, under which the Patel, being the farmer of his village was his own master, and *remunerated himself.* After this, the introduction by the Mahomedans of the Bheeghownee system, which would appear to have early failed to fulfil the expectations of its projectors ; hence the kassbundee, turrufbundee, and other modifications of it, together with the various methods of remuneration appertaining to them, viz. remuneration by purbhara huks only, by enam, by mooshaheera, or by two or more of these combined. And after the Mahomedan, I have noticed the Native Muratthee Government, under which prevailed the farming system, and under which the remuneration depended on the strength of the several parties, and on circumstances. The Patel, having contracted with farmer to produce a certain amount of revenue, was, for the purpose of increasing cultivation, frequently compelled to forego his purbhara huks, trusting for his remuneration chiefly to the chilher expenses, and to other surreptitious means. A nominal enam, if not enjoyed, both from inquiry and from examination of the various methods of remuneration now in force in different districts, that the method of remuneration has continually been changed, either in accordance with the changes of the revenue system, or according to the wisdom or caprice of succeeding Native revenue officers. And this being the case, there appears no sufficient reason for Government to hesitate in introducing any new method more adapted to its present system of revenue. But the introduction of a measure so important as the revision of the method of remunerating district and village officers, should, I conceive, be based upon as broad a foundation as possible both with the view of its application to any particular district, and to the extension of the same plan throughout the Deccan. For instance, the districts in which enams are enjoyed by the Patels, or in which they are shared by the whole Patel's brotherhood, may be so few as to warrant Government in abolishing the Patel's enam altogether, or at least in awarding it as remuneration to the working Patel alone. I would, therefore, respectfully suggest, that a Return similar to the following should be called for from

every district throughout the Zilla, and from Poona, and other Zillas, if possible :—

Return showing the nature of Remuneration received by the Patels of the Nuggur Zilla.

Name of District.	No. of Arable Beeghas	No. of Villages	No. of Patels.		Remuneration.				Total.	Remarks
			No. of Tuksims	Total No. of Sharers	Enam.		Adverage of Last 4 years.			
							Ready-Money Allowances.	Purbhara Huks last 4 years.		
					Beeghas.	Rs. a. p.	Rs. a. p.	Rs. a. p.	Rs. a. p.	
Koombharee	16487	33	76	284	34053	3,426 1 3	187 13 0	613 1 10½	4,227 13 1½	
Jamkeir	...	...	...	...	...	... ...	... ...	... ...	... ...	
Ankola	...	...	...	...	...	... ...	... ...	... ...	... ...	

Returns similar to the above, from as many Zillas as possible, would show at one view the nature of the different methods of remuneration which prevail in their several districts, and would greatly aid us in the formation of a new and general plan.

46. The Jemadar's remuneration in these districts would appear to have been previously revised ; and as they are now remunerated entirely from the Government treasury, no further revision appears necessary, unless it be intended to grant them compensation for their purbhara huks, which are now rescinded.

47. In the 14th and 19th paragraph of this letter I entered somewhat largely into the nature of the meeras tenure, and I would now beg to call your attention to the injury to cultivation which may arise from it. I described meeras as that property arising from long occupation and improvement ; but I endeavoured to show that present usages have converted it into a nominal property, the value of which consists in the freedom from the Patel's impost, and which property is contained in every description of culturable land, either on the part of the Patel who has retained his impost, or on the part of the Meerasdar who has purchased the freedom from it. In villages where the greater part of meeras land belongs to the Patels, and where it has not yet been divided by them, there are continual quarrels for possession. Where, also, an

individual has more meeras than he can cultivate, he, by various means, endeavours to maintain a control over it, so that he may obtain possession of it when required, or that he may receive some profit upon it. There can be no doubt that meeras in small portions is beneficial, as it affords an inducement to improve agriculture, and encourages the digging of wells ; but in large quantities it would appear to have an opposite effect. It was encouraged by the Mahomedans for the purpose of increasing cultivation, it being a matter of little consequence to them whether the owner himself cultivated it, or re-let it to another ; but as we do not now hold him responsible for its cultivation, nor subject him to any loss on its laying waste, it would not be unreasonable to deprive him of the power of injurious interference. Any direct abrogation of the meeras privileges would, of course, be extremely unpopular, neither is it required. Government has already forbidden the cultivator of another's meeras to be ejected, which was the first grand blow to the evil ; and it now only appears necessary to allow as little sub-letting as possible. It, therefore, seems advisable to do away with the ambiguous term Gaow-Nisbet-Meeras, and to require the division of the Patel's Sumaeek Meeras, which might be effected by the aid of the district establishment previous to the commencement of the survey ; and to take care, when letting land on the new rates, not to allow a Meerasdar or other individual to take up land for the purpose of re-letting, a practice which, however it may temporarily increase cultivation, is, under the present state of the agricultural class, exceedingly pernicious. A few precautions like these, together with the commutation of the Patel's huks, would, I conceive, remove most of the evils to which the meeras tenure is subject. That these evils are similar to what I have stated, will readily be apprehended from the fact that so few ryots avail themselves of the permission of Government for new meeras being granted to them : no doubt the Patels, for the purpose of retaining their huks, offer every opposition, and a meeras paying huks is little more valuable than Oopree land, where land is so plentiful.

48. In paragraph 30 I gave an account of the chilher expenses, and it now appears necessary to consider how far this money is expended for the good of the village. Under Native Government the chilher expenditure was sanctioned, ostensibly for the support of Government officials during

their visits to the village, as well as for its other contingent expenses. The Patels and Coolkurnees had charge of this allowance, but, as in other cases of the ancient revenue system, there were too many adverse interests engaged to admit of the money being expended for the real good of the village. The fact of the expenditure of a portion of it being authorized for the support of Government officers in their visits to the village, enabled those people to lay claim to all they could obtain ; and the Patels too often found it necessary to purchase their pretended services in higher quarters, or their forbearance from hostility. Under these circumstances, the chilher expenditure was perhaps never inquired after, and the village officers were tacitly recognized as the uncontrolled disbursers of it. They might, from the example set them by the higher officials, endeavour to appropriate a portion of it to their own use ; but religious Brahmins, and other mendicants, being aware of the large sum allowed, have generally, it appears, managed to obtain a share. A sum of money, therefore, which, under proper management, was amply sufficient for the erection of public works, and the improvement of the village, became the prey of official and religious plunderers, or was frittered away in foolish spectacles and ceremonies.

49. Such was its application under the Native Government : the present Government, however, though it curtailed the amount, expected it to be applied in a proper manner, and various arrangements have been made to prevent peculation ; but, excepting bribes to Government officers, the original object of its application would appear to be nearly the same. The average amount expended in charity (dhurmadee) is about one-tenth ; on religious ceremonies (dewusthan) one-fourth ; and for paper, and other contingencies, and the expenses of village officers in their journeys to and from the district cutcherry, more than one-half of the whole chilher, there being no rules whereby to restrict or check the expenditure in charity, it is difficult to form an opinion whether the sums recorded under that head have been laid out in the manner specified, but the paper and travelling expenses are in some measure open to investigation, and may be tested by assuming any averaged size village as a specimen, and allowing a liberal sum for each item. Take, then, a village the amount of the collections of which in any one year is Rupees 2,000 : this, at 6 per cent, gives chilher Rupees 120.

ESTIMATED EXPENDITURE

	Days.				Rs.	a.	p.
Kazee and other Hukdars					5	0	0
Paper for 5 Account Books, and Sundries					10	0	0
Oil for Village Chowdee					2	0	0
Travelling Erpenses.							
For 2 Patels, 1 Coolkurnee, and 2 Muhars at Jummabundy days	30						
Ditto conveying Revenue Treasure by instalments	8						
Ditto Police and other duties.	15						
Total for 5 individuals, at 6 annas per day	53 =	19	14	0			
1 Patel, 1 Coolkurnee, giving in Accounts at the end of the year, days 15 – at 3 annas per diem		2	13	0			
Coolkurnee for various miscellaneous duties, days 15, at 1 anna per diem		0	15	0			
Total Travelling Expenses				Rs.	23	10	10
Total Contingent Expenditure				Rs.	40	10	0

And leaving Rupees 80 at the disposal of the village.

50. The above calculation would show that, on a most liberal scale of allowance, the legitimate expenses might be much curtailed, though it is only fair to add, that under the head of Pot-Khurch is frequently entered the expenses of the several tomashas (spectacles) at the festivals, and other minor items. In villages where the working Patel and Coolkurnee have sufficient influence to lead, or address to deceive, their fellow-sharers, it is possible they may save and appropriate to their own use a part of the sum entrusted to them ; but in cases where they are not so successful, they must spend a portion of it according to the prevailing taste, and find the village with the usual festive entertainments. Considering frequencies of the journeys of village officers to the district cutcherry on Government duty, and their right to defray the expenses of such journeys from the public purse, together with the other claims upon the sadilwar, peculation to any serious amount may not be carried on in small villages. Instances however, may occur in large village near the district cutcherry, where they have a greater amount at their disposal, and, having a less distance to go, have less in proportion to do with it than in the case of a small

village. And it may be admitted as a general rule, that small villages are much worse off in this respect than large ones, and that they have little to spare if their officers are allowed to defray their travelling expenses from it. Take, for instance, two villages from the accompanying table, one a small one, "Gharee," whose amount of contingent expenses is Rupees 20, and the other a large one, " Kokumthan," whose contingent expenses is Rupees 219, and it will readily be perceived that the former can have barely met its expenses, while the latter may have had a large surplus. (Vide Statement No. 8.)

51. Admitting, however, that those sums have been expended in the manner there detailed, the question still suggests itself—Is this expenditure necessary—and might not the money be more usefully employed ? If we direct out attention to the villages themselves, we can be at no loss to determine where it might be beneficially expended. Ruined chowdees, bundaras, and wells ; broken down gateways, and dilapidated walls, most impressively point out the legitimate but neglected object of its application. But as these have usually been repaired by Government, or by the Patels from their profits, and as the village have been accustomed to some little expenditure in the manner now applied, and which is perhaps necessary, it is to be feared that few opportunities would be found of introducing such application. Still much might be effected by changing the supervision of this money, by placing it at the disposal of the whole village, instead of its officers, and by endeavouring to excite a little of that public spirit of which the Natives are so void. The Meerasdars might be required to meet and determine how they wished the money to be applied previous to its being issued from the treasury ; and though in many instances this arrangement might be productive of little apparent benefit, it would give rise to a principle which hereafter, would lead to great results.

52. The subject of the preceding paragraph forcibly brings to our notice the utter incapacity of the village to renovate or improve itself : that it possesses the quality of permanence cannot be denied, but that very permanence would appear to be the mere effect of its torpidity. In how many instances would an active and self-progressive agency be of benefit—but how utterly incapable of originating or carrying into effect any schemes of improvement is the present one ! Whether we examine the smallest village or the largest city, we are sure to find that, if anything

be required for the good of the people, it must either be effected by Government, or by the charity of private individual ; and that as sôon as the influence or protection of either be removed, the structure which it had raised will moulder to decay. As a case in point, I may mention one of many that has come to my notice. Yewla is a thriving market town of some note, which was founded about the commencement of the last century by the exertions of an ancestor of the present Patel, who having money at his disposal, and being desirous of increasing the value of his patrimony, encouraged the settlement of merchants, shopkeepers, and artisans, by advancing them money, or giving them ground to build upon, but at the same time stipulating for his right to levy the usual imposts for himself and for Government. These fostering arrangements, together with the happy adaptation of its saline waters to the dyeing of silk, soon collected a number of silk-weavers, dyers, sowcars and others, and converted it into a rising market town. Yewla thus prospered ; but it suffered from scarcity of water during the hot season. The town is built on the side of a slightly elevated plateau declining from the hills, with a rivulet on each side, but these rivulets are at such a distance as not to be available for supplying the town with water : the wells are deep, and generally dry in summer. The munificence of some individual in bygone days had formed a tank, but it has since become choked with mud, and is consequently useless. As usual in such cases, the Patel might have afforded some assistance from his profits, but he had become involved, and lacked the means ; or he might, in virtue of his office, (by forming a subscription, or what not,) have made the necessary arrangements ; but this was contrary to the regulations of the present Government. During the last few years, several efforts, I understand, have been made to induce the present Government to form an aqueduct, and it had consented to defray half the expense, if the inhabitants would defray the rest. A subscription list was set on foot, but the amount of promised subscriptions fell short of the sum required, and the measure failed, through the dissension or disunion of its promoters. Government subsequently rescinded the mohoturfa, or town dues. A petition was again made for an aqueduct, and Government again professed its willingness to bear half the expense, if the town would bear the remainder, urging at the same time that, as it had relieved the people from so great an amount of taxes, they ought cordially to cooperate in effecting an object entirely for their own benefit. Another attempt was made at a subscription, but seemed again likely to fail from want of unity among the inhabitants; they stating that they would gladly continue to pay the mohoturfa tax, if Government would supply the town with water. How the matter has since ended I have not heard, but it is probable that nearly one-half the less opulent inhabitants will have to leave the town this season for want of water.

53. I have been thus explicit, because this instance affords an excellent illustration of the system in reference to our present mode of government. From this statement we gather the following facts :—

1*st.* That a rising manufacturing town is much distressed for want of water, and its improvement thereby impeded.

2*nd.* That under the former system of government the Patel, or some other influential person, most probably, would have made the necessary arrangement for supplying it, but which arrangement is incompatible with the present system.

3*rd.* That if the ancient town taxes were still in force, they might be applied to the object in question, but that having been abolished, they are now not available.

4*th.* That present Government might have made the necessary improvement, and that it offered to find one-half of the sum required ; but that, owing to the disunion of the people, the measure is in danger of falling to the ground, and the improvement of the town being sacrificed. These facts are not peculiar to this town alone, but, with slight modifications, are equally applicable to most of the large towns of the Deccan ; for they almost all want some assistance, but possess no principle of action within themselves to carry it out ; and we may infer that the system is unequal to the maintaining any community beyond that of a village, and that, even in this limited sphere, by cutting the gains of its officers, illegal and injurious though they were, we deprived them of the little power of doing good they once possessed, without providing any adequate substitute.

54. It may be found necessary, for the sake of good government, to bring the village and district officers, as much as possible, within the limits of Government servants, but it is next to impossible that Government

can attend to those minor local improvements, which can only come under the eye of interested local residents. These officers, from a long course of corruption, have incapacitated themselves from exercising the original functions of their office for the good of the people ; and the effect of this is, that the people themselves cease to take an interest in, and are incapable of, conducting public affairs. The trouble of Europe in the twelfth and thirteenth centuries taught her people, in framing their municipal corporations, to resist tyranny, and to lay a sure foundation of freedom and prosperity ; but the oppression of ages has failed to stimulate those of Asia to raise a single bulwark in their defence. The cause of this is their hereditary village or patriarchal Governments ; the effect is, that the people have no aptness or capacity to conduct the smallest operation which may be requisite for their improvement. But still, with a right use of the knowledge thus conveyed to us, much may be done ; and I would beg to bring to your notice the propriety of endeavouring to form some local fund, or means of carrying out those measure which are so vitally requisite for the well-being of the people.

55. In the instance I have given, it would seem to have been advisable to have kept on the mohoturfa tax, allowing its proceeds to go towards the construction of the aqueduct ; and this suggest the idea, that in abolishing the tax it would have been well to have kept on a part of it to form a fund for city and village improvements. Government, I believe, in rescinding the tax, had it in contemplation to devise means for the improvement of villages, the repair of their walls, &c. I am not aware whether it was intended to levy a new cess for this object, or to devote a part of its present revenues to it ; some assignment, however, is required, and it perhaps might be necessary in large towns to levy an assessment for the purpose ; but were Government sufficiently to remunerate village officers, so as to remove their claims upon the chilher, it might form a fund sufficient for the purposes in view. With respect to the merits of levying an assessment in large towns for this object, it does not appear necessary for me to give an opinion, but I may mention that there are a great number of Brahmins, Sowcars, Wannees, and other, who pay no assessment beyond that of trifling excise ; and it appears nothing but fair that wealthy residents and traders should contribute to the prosperity of the place in which they live.

56. Some assessment or assignment having been provided for the purposes before mentioned, there would still be great difficulty in securing its legitimate application. Village and district officers are not to be trusted ; other minor Government officers would not have leisure, and if they had, it would only be subjecting them to temptation ; and it might be difficult to induce a respectable Native to labour for the public good, or to subject himself, *as they conceive,* to the danger of disgrace, in being falsely charged with, and punished for, malpractices, at the design of some rival. The fact is, that district and village officials have always endeavoured to impress the people with this feeling, and to prevent their assuming functions which they consider to be peculiarly their own, and any infringement of which they conceive lowers their dignity, and weakens their authority. A measure of this kind would, therefore, meet with the most strenuous opposition on the part of these officials ; but the benefit to be derived from it is sufficient to make its attainment worth a trial. That respectable Natives are fully alive to the honor of being called to consult upon public affairs, may be inferred from the fact of the importance they attach to the privilege of occasionally being called upon by Moonsiffs and Mamlutdars, as juries, to determine any doubtful or knotty point under investigation. And I conceive that this feeling, with a little fostering care, might be turned to the public good : it would be too much to expect them to originate or to carry through any measure without assistance, and it would be necessary for Government both to collect the assessment, and to have some control over its application ; but a town council, elected annually, might be found to deliberate upon measures required for the public good, and their sanction should be required to the expenditure.

57. That some such measure is requisite, is evident form the present state of all large towns throughout the Presidency, and the utter impossibility of Government directing its attention to, or becoming acquainted with, the various local arrangements so requisite for their prosperity. Could Natives, particularly in manufacturing towns, be induced to take an interest in their local government, the improvement to manufactures and commerce might be immense ; and, it is to be hoped, the moral effect on the people would be equally great ; but is must be confessed that the introduction of such a system would be a work of time, labour, and difficulty : the opposition of interested officials, and the

indolence and apathy of the people themselves, would all have to be overcome.

58. In conclusion, I must apologize for the unusual length of this Report. In its preparation I was desirous, for the proper understanding of the subject, to portray the characteristics and tendency of the system, and to distinguish between its adaptation to the spirit of the present and of former Governments. The present subject appears to me to be an important one,—one in which there are two methods of procedure, diametrically opposite to each other : the first is, by continuing the former method of remuneration, to preserve the spirit of the ancient system, and the influence of its officials ; the second is, by making these officials purely Government servants, and throwing more of the domestic management of a community into the hands of its members, to teach the people to think and to act for themselves, and to lay the foundation of those domestic institutions so necessary for their improvement. That the former method is fully compatible with good government, there cannot be a doubt—if by good government be meant the mere subjection of the people ; but is it conducive to their intellectual or moral improvement ? Let the past history and the present state of Asia answer the question. Not only the history of Asia, but that of the world, will show that the domestic political institutions of a country form the basis of its moral and national prosperity. It is true that the spirit of free institutions has sometimes tended to anarchy, but it is for the statesman, in framing these institutions, to adapt them to the wants and to the temperament of the people. India though the land of ages, and the cradle of the arts and of learning, has never been able to rise above mediocrity. Subject from the earliest time to an arbitrary system of government, she has naturally partaken of the evil as well as of the good of that system. A munificent Prince, or wise local Governor, might raise his immediate neighbourhood to opulence and prosperity ; but for one such life there have been ages of misrule and oppression ; and, owing to the peculiar system of hereditary village government, the people have never been able to institute a single measure for their relief : broken and disunited, they have necessarily been dependent on their arbitrary rulers. Still the system had some merit : if it did not promote the improvement of the people, it preserved them in that medial state the best adapted to the system ; and the surplus wealth of its officials, either from charity or

self-interest, was generally expended in works for the people's benefit. But a great change has now taken place : the rude and arbitrary Government of a rude people has been supplanted by one of liberal and philanthropic principles, which seeks to raise its subjects to its own intellectual and moral standard. Oppression has been removed, and the road to improvement lays open before them ; but they have too long been subject to an helpless dependence on their rulers, and are still subject to too many adverse interests, to admit of their accepting of the boon which is held out to them ; and they are thus deprived of the advantages of the old Government, while they are unable to receive the full benefits of the new. Government, in its anxiety to deprive its Native officials of the power to oppress, has been compelled also to deprive them of the power of doing the little good they were once capable of, while its own supervision is too limited to admit of its becoming acquainted with the domestic wants of the people ; and, however anxious it may be for their improvement, as yet it has prepared no adequate domestic government as a substitute for the one which it has removed. I sincerely hope that in calling your attention to this subject I may be the remote, the humble means of originating a measure so vitally necessary for the improvement of the country.

I have the honor to be, &c.

(Signed) R.N. GOODDINE,

Sub-Assistant Superintendent
Ahmednuggur Revenue Survey and Assessment.

Nassick, 10th October 1845.

NOTES

1. परभारा, by intermediate, or other than the direct way ; and حق right, due, claim.
2. "Munoo states there is to be a lord of a single village ; a lord of ten ; a lord of one hundred ; and a lord of a thousand towns—all to be appointed by the king. Each is to report all offences, &c. to his immediate superior. The compensation for a lord of one town is the provisions and other articles to which the king is entitled to from that town. That of a lord of ten villages, two ploughs of land. The lord of a hundred villages is to have the land of a small village ; and of a thousand, that of a large town."—Vide *Elphinstone's History of India,* Chap. II. page 39.
3. गाव, village, and करी, an agent, a doer, a possessor.
4. उपरी ; from उपर, upon. A sojourner, a temporary resident ; one who does not possess the freedom of the village.
5. कुणबी ; an individual of the agricultural order or class ; कुणबीकी agriculture, tillage.
6. कुणबावा, agricultural occupancy.
7. कुळ, a debtor, a customer.
8. थळवाहिक, or थळकरी ; from थल, a place, वाहणे, to cultivate, and करी, an agent, a doer,
9. मुंडवाहिक ; from मुंड, head, principal ; stipulated sum or quantity ; वाहणे, to cultivate.
10. वोवंडकरी, ओवंडकरी, आवंडकरी ; from वलांडणे, to cross over ; as a road, or boundary.
11. शिवार ; from शिव, or सीमा, a boundary, border, limit.
12. बाबर ; from बाहणे, to cultivate.
13. ठिके, a parcel, patch of ground ; a mole, a field, a spot.
14. शेत, a field, cultivated piece of ground.
15. परतन turning ; from परतणे, to turn ; such a length as the bullocks will conveniently drag ploughs without tiring ; a field of convenient length for such turning being by metonomy, a field.
16. मळई, the rich ground along the banks of some rivers, formed by alluvial depositions ; a field of garden or meadow land.
17. From कु, bad, राण, land, रण, fight, and ऋण, debt.
18. From गाय, a cow, and राण land.

19. ميراث heritage, succession, patrimony.

20. गावनिसबतमिरास ; from, गाव a village, and نسبت belonging to or in the charge of, and ميراث heritage , &c.

21. إنعام a present, gift, reward.

22. संस्थान from स्व, own, proper स्थान a place.

23. देवस्थान from देव, a deity, and स्थान, a place.

24. पासोडी, a shawl.

25. चोली, a spencer, bodice.

26. हडोळा from हड, a bone, and बोळ, a line ; or perhaps course, fashion, line, (of deportment, or procedure,) having reference to the Muhar's occupation of clearing the village of dead cattle.

27. हडकी, a little bone ; a smaller enam held by the Muhar's.

28. टोमणी ; from टोमणा, a dish ; a wooden bowl or platter, so-called by the Muhars; more generally the name of another small enam sometimes possessed by them.

29. देवशेत ; from दिव्य a deity, an idol, and शेत, a field.

30. सर्वमान्य ; from सर्व, all, every, and मानणे, to allow.

31. जोडीमान्य from जोडी, a pair, and मानणे, to allow.

32. शेरी ; from शोर, the head, or from शेर subsistence, شير chief, that has come off superior.

33. معنك a dish, a means of subsistence.

34. موقاسه past participle of قوس قيس قاس measurement, comparing one thing with another, *i.e.* sharing, division ; or from خاس (Hebrew) to cut, to divide, to appropriate. Vide قاس para 13. Grants in enam, being commonly granted to artisans, village officers, and religious mendicants, person of distinction among the Marathas affected to consider that a grant of mokassa or jagheer, however small, entitled them to be included in the list of Government officials or nobles.

35. سرانجام utensils, furniture ; remuneration for feudal services.

36. ذات سرانجام from ذات self, possessed of, and سرانجام in contradistinction to that for the support of troops.

37. गावनीसुबत इनाम ; from गाव, village نسبت belonging to, and إنعام a gift.

38. आउतबंदी from आउत, an implement, a tool of husbandry, a plough harrow, &c., and बंदी, from بستن to bind. An assessment fixed on each plough of two or four bullocks. Compound words, derived, the one from Hindee, and the other from

Persian or Arabic, are not uncommon : this may have originally been **बंधी**, from बंधणे, but which orthography is now obsolete.

39. मुंडबंदी ; from मुंड, a lot, and बंदी.

40. टिकेबंदी ; from टिके, a field and बंदी.

41. ठोकेबंदी, agreement by the lump ; from ठोकणे, to strike.

42. बिघा ; from विघ्रा battle, fight ; the body. Vide *Shakespear's Hindoostanee Dictionary, and Molesworth's Murathee.*

43. पाईण; from पाय, fourth.

44. चाहूर ; probably from चार, four, four-fold : thus, four bullocks, or four pairs, are called a chahoor team—hence as much land as can be cultivated by them.

45. खोत, a farmer of land revenue, a contractor ; also a contract.

46. تنخواه from تن the body, and خواستن to desire. An assignment on lands and their revenue. The above in the text is the most popular interpretation of the Tunkha system, but it occurs to me that this system was merely the first rough settlement of the Mahomedans, before they found themselves strong enough to enter into details, and that measurements and a more regular system were introduced by subsequent Mogul emperors. The kumall کمال perfection, completion, accomplishment, as the name implies, would appear to have been such subsequent settlement from actual measurement.

47. مُقدم antecedent, prior, chief.

48. مشاہرا pay, wages.

49. وطن one's native place.

50. تقسیم دار from تقسیم dividing, separating a share, and دار from داشتن to have, to hold.

51. طرفبندي from طرف side, margin, quarter, بستن to bind.

52. میراث and دار—vide note to para 11.

53. قاسبندي from قاس measuring, comparing one thing with another.—Vide note to Mokassa, para 11.

54. Such divisions are numerous, and are to be met within almost every district, of which many of the villages bearing the affixes Boodrookh, greater, and Koord, less are instances.

55. Even up to the later years of the Peishwa's rule, the Patel had the power of disposing of land in meeras ; indeed, it was not only tacitly sanctioned by Government, but the Patel in many cases was enjoined to sell it for the purpose

of increasing cultivation. The value of such meeras depended upon the benefits conveyed with it. Thus a nominal meeras, or one which merely conveyed the freedom of the village, was not so valuable as one which conveyed the freedom from the Patel's impost also. It is true that in some few districts the Patels had no huks on land, but this appears only to have happened where there had been a sufficiently influential Government agent, who, by instituting a different system of revenue, had the power ot prevent the Patels from exacting them.

56. I have frequently found this to be admitted up to present day, though it is generally attempted to conceal it. If the Meerasdar enter the meeras in his own name, and re-let it, he easily succeeds, but if Gonvernment let another person's meeras, he does not always obtain the impost.

57. The Newassee and Parneer Talookas were for long time under the charge of Naroo Babajee and his dependents, relatives of the late Peishwa's and in these districts the Zemindars and Patels have less remuneration than those of any others : there are few or no enams and huks, which, it is said, is owing to the arrangements of this officer.

58. In later times, however, under the farming system, he generally managed to obtain a good haul from the surplus revenue, collected to remunerate the Zemindars, and to defray the expenses of the village.

59. Meeras Puttee, levied every three years.

60. Land not meeras in many districts paid four annas per beegha more than meeras.

61. This appears the most probable reason of the origin of those two singular cesses, the meeras puttee, and the extra cess upon gutkool land. But so many revenue systems have prevailed,—and these usages are purely the offspring of those systems, that few can give an authentic account of their origin.

62. बलूते ; perhaps from बलुवंत, strong, *i.e.* the village strength or staff.

63. कारू, an artisan.

64. ओळ a row, a line, a rank.

65. قس a division, class, share ; measuring one thing with another. Vide note 26 to para 11, page 5.

66. And this enam is generally cultivated by the Patel, or some other resident of the village, who pays the Bheel a portion of its produce as rent.

67. The name of the post to which bullocks are tied in the operation of treading out the corn.

68. The Muhars find the wood—it is the Sootar's duty to form it into pegs.

69. The Patels, as a mark of dignity, do not alow the Muhars the skins of cattle their own property ; but they give them a small quantity of grain for their

trouble in skinning them : this huk the Muhars call *hat dhone,* हातधुनो washing hands.

70. राबता from राबणे, to labour.
71. हाडोळा, or स्लामी, a lumped assessment on each hudola.

[Vide Table No. 5, column "Government Deductions".]

72. The reason for the sale of a portion of a Patelship, as generally stated in the deed of sale, is the seller's inability to meet the Government demand ; and whether the tunkha system were continued or not, all Governments held the Patel responsible for the greatest amount of revenue his village could possibly pay.
73. Instance Ankola, and some others.
74. Vide paras 14 and 17. Whether or not the Meerasdars came forward, they were held responsible by Government.
75. In some few districts the eldest son, or heir to the Wutun, alone enjoys the usufruct, but he alone is responsible for his father's debts, and not the brotherhood.
76. कुळकर्णी from कुळ, a debtor, or tenant, and कर्णी, a doer, an agent.
77. देशमुख from देश, a country, district, and मुख्य chief.
78. देशपाद्या from देश, and पांच, a writer.
79. Vide note to para 5.
80. The farming system was one continued struggle between the Zemindars and the farmers of their district. Their interests being incompatible, it was difficult for them to act in concert. If the farmer attempted to look too closely into, or to diminish their gains, they invariably endeavoured to oust him, by representing to Government that the district could pay more, or that the farmer was oppressing the ryots ; had he sufficient influence at Court, he might laugh at their efforts, but if he had no friends there, he was generally obliged to succumb. Jemadars of districts, therefore, which had been farmed for a considerable time by the same influential personage, have generally far less income than those of other districts : as instances of this, I may mention those of Nawassee and Parneer, which were farmed for a long time by relatives of the late Peishwa, and where the Jemadar's remuneration is less than in any other districts I have visited.
81. भीकणी ; from भीकणे, to beg.
82. भेट, meeting, interview.
83. राबता ; from राबणे, to labour ; a cess upon the Muhars in lieu of their services, to which the Jemadars were entitled.

84. فرماش from فرمايش an order, command ; that which has been ordered, commanded.

85. رسوم dues, taxes, fees.

86. These arrangements have been made by the present Government.

87. As the various items into which the revenue of the Peishwa's Government was divided is well known, any enumeration of them would appear unnecessary : the Jagheer in this district was cent per cent.

88. काळी, black, *i.e.* the land, from its dark colour ; in opposition to पांढरी, white, *i.e.* the village, because it is generally built of white earth, from its superior power of resisting rain.

89. गूड ; corn in the sheaf.

90. The former method is the most general, but the latter may sometimes be met with.

91. निबूंर ; वेंब्या ओब्यां ; हुर्डा.

92. वानवळा ; from वान, sylvan, wild, ओळ, moist, green.

93. आडेपाडे ; an alliterative formation आड, of interjacency ; intervention minor, that is perquisites from the several ryots, or perhaps from आड, as above, and पाड, price current, rate.

94. आउटकी ; from आउट, a team, yoke of oxen ; and by metonymy a plough, or other agricultural implement.

95. मापारकी ; from माप, a measure, and आर and की, affixes.

96. मुशारा ; from مشاہرا pay wages. It is properly a money assessment, and when used to denote a huk in kind, it is through ignorance.

97. सळइ, the tale ; the marker.

98. ओढा ; from ओढणे, to pull.

99. Very few of the villages reported upon contain graden-land.

100. The sizes of the moulds vary in different districts : in this, they are generally about 20 seers (40 lbs. avoirdupois). The aggregate claims of the whole staff on sugarcane will therefore vary. In some villages it is as high as 200 seers or 400 lbs. per mill : in others, perhaps, not much more than half that amount; but as the amount cultivated to each mill varies much, its rates per beegha will vary also. If we average five beeghas to each mill, the above amount will show the aggregate amount of this huk to be from 20 to 40 seers of gool, or

coarse sugar per beegha ; and, averaging the price of gool at about 15 seers per rupee, it will give a rate of from 1¼ to 2½ rupees per beegha in excess of the Government assessment.

101. Vide note to commencement of para 22.

102. مروطرنه purchased, purchaseable.

103. The rescinding of the Moturpha dues has done away with this huk.

104. Called हातधुनो washing hands. Vide note 69 to para 21.

105. खरीद्खत from خريدن to purchase, and خط a writing.

106. खोतपत्र ; from खोत, a contract, and पत्र, a letter, writing, deed.

107. زكراة customs, duties, taxes or exports or imports.

108. पेवबुड ; from पेव, a subterranean place to hold grain, and बुडणे, to sink, to be immersed ; or from बुड, the bottom, *i.e.* the lowest or inferior grain, in which this huk is generally paid.

109. लग्रमुहुर्त from लग्र, a first marriage, and मुहुर्त, a second marriage.

110. سيوسبزي from سيو business, trade, and سبزي green.

111. धनगर a caste ; shepherds and blanket-weavers.

112. सालीकोष्टी, two classes of weavers. Under that head are entered all classes of weavers from whom huks are received.

113. For the proper understanding of the accompanying table, it will be necessary to state that Native dry measure of this district is computed as follows, viz : 4 seers equal one paeelee ; 16 paeelees one mun ; and 20 muns one khundee. The seer varies in almost every district, but the Naggur seer is now being gradually introduced. The seer in use in the villages now reported upon is, I believe nearly twice as large as that of Bombay, and one-fourth less than that of the adjoining district of Patoda. Its cubical contents, up-heaped measure, which is always used, is about 85 cubic inches.

114. नेमणुक from नेमणे to appoint ; an appointed sum, provision.

115. مشاهرا pay, wages.

116. This does not include the ready-money payments to Jemadars, because, being paid from the Government Treasury, their stipends do not come under this head of village expenditure.

117. Throwing off fractions for each village.

118. خيرات alms, charity.

119. The above details are derived from the records of the Mamlutdar's office, which either from boundary disputes, or other causes, differ by 370 beeghas 11 pands from Statement No. 1, as given in by the village officers.

120. The average of cultivation and collection for these years :—

Average	of cultivation	Beeghas	72,655
,,	of assessment	Rupees	74,156
,,	of remissions	,,	21,574
,,	of collections	,,	52,582

PART II

SELECTIONS FROM THE RECORDS OF THE BOMBAY GOVERNMENT.

No. DXXIV – New Series
(As Revised in 1914)

CHARACTER OF LAND TENURES

AND

SYSTEM OF SURVEY AND SETTLEMENT

In the

BOMBAY PRESIDENCY

such an important element in the determination of the assessment and which had been prepared in the most elaborate manner, were so erroneous as to be worse than worthless. But meanwhile the settlement had been introduced, and with the result of aggravating the evils it had been designed to remove. From the outset it was found impossible to collect anything approaching to the full revenue. In some districts not one-half could be realized. Things now went rapidly from bad to worse. Every year brought its addition to the accumulated arrears of revenue and the necessity for remissions or modifications of the accumulated arrears of revenue and the necessity for remissions or modifications of rates. The state of confusion in the accounts, engendered by these expedients, was taken advantage of by the native officials to levy contributions for themselves.

Measures taken in 1835.

4. It was when matters had reached this crisis that, at the end of 1835, an examination and correction of the operations of Mr. Pringle's survey in the Indapur Taluka of the Poona Collectorate were ordered in view to a revision of the settlement in that district. The duty of conducting the work was entrusted to Mr. Goldsmid, of the Civil Service, then an Assistant Collector, and Lieutenant Wingate,* of the Engineers. With these gentlemen Lieutenant Nash, of the Engineers, was subsequently associated. This was the real commencement of the revenue survey in the Bombay Presidency.

New method of Classification adopted : Founded on the capability of the land and the general circumstances of the districts.

5. As the new operations progressed, the extremely defective character of the original survey became apparent. Much of the measurement had to be undertaken *de novo,* but when areas were not faulty to any great extent they were accepted as the basis of the new assessment. An entirely new method of classification was adopted. Abandoning all attempts to arrive at a theoretical ideal of assessment by endeavouring to discover the yield of different soils, and assigning a certain proportion of this as the Government demand, the survey officers adopted the simple expedient of ascertaining the average productive capability and depth of soil in each field, and classing it accordingly—no more than nine gradations of valuation being employed for the purpose. In fixing the rates of assessment

they were guided by purely practical considerations as to the capability of the land and the general circumstances of the district. The more intelligent among the agricultural class were even taken into consultation on the subject, and their opinion allowed due weight. No safe standard of assessment existed. The rates in force in the prosperous times of the district had, through the continuous depreciation in the value of money, long ceased to represent any moderate share of the produce of the land, and the ruinous consequences of the first settlement forbade any reliance being placed on the system of fixing the Government demand on estimates of the yield of the land.

Satisfactory results of the change.

6. The result showed the wisdom of the course taken. In the second year of the Indapur settlement the Revenue Commissioner reported to Government that "the sum *actually collected has never been so great* except during the first four years of our occupation, when it is generally acknowledged our demands were much too high"; and, again, "the outstanding balances *have never yet been so low at the end of the official year as they were last year.*" A marked extension of cultivation was one of the immediate results of the settlement, nearly 68,000 acres of waste land having been brought under the plough by the end of the second year, besides more than 3,000 acres reclaimed by immigrants from other districts attracted to Indapur by the revived prosperity of the taluka.

Extension of Survey operations into other districts.

7. The Indapur experiment having proved thus signally successful, the survey operations were rapidly extended to other districts, the same results following everywhere. In the course of a few years separate surveys were organized for the Poona and Ahmednagar Collectorates and for the Southern Maratha Country. As experience was gained, improvements were introduced in the methods of procedure, the end in view always being to render them as simple and susceptible of thorough check and control as possible, as well as to adapt them to the varying circumstances of the districts which successively came under the survey. But it was not till 1847 that a definite and permanent form was given to the system of survey operations. In that year, in accordance with the orders of Government, the Superintendents of the three surveys met at Poona, and

drew up a joint report setting forth what they considered to be "the best means for bringing the somewhat diversified operations of the several revenue surveys of the Presidency into conformity as far as practicable, and also for ensuring the results of the surveys being turned to the best account, and maintained in their original integrity in the future management of the districts." The Superintendents, besides defining the objects of a revenue survey, and the general principles on which the assessment of land should, in their opinion, be conducted, submitted a body of rules for definition and demarcation of fields, the settlement of boundary disputes, the classification of soils, the interior regulation of surveys and the administration of settlements, which, having received the approval of Government, became an authoritative manual for the conduct of all future survey operations. Up to this period, though there had been a general adherence to the main principles by which the work was governed from its beginning, some diversity of practice had prevailed in the different surveys. A greater degree of uniformity and completeness was now given to it.

Sketch of the system.

8. At this point it seems desirable to sketch briefly the general features of the revenue survey system as then defined under official sanction with the modifications which the progress of the survey has since required, though indeed very little modification was made till the survey was completed and till more or less partial revision of the original survey was found necessary.

Organization of the Department.

9. First, with regard to the interior regulation of the different surveys. Each survey was under the direction of a Superintendent, subordinate to whom were several officers designated Assistant Superintendents, having charge of parties or establishments of measurers or classers. The operations of measuring and classing were conducted, as a rule, by separate establishments, and generally the classification of a district followed the measurement at an interval of one season. Every detail of the survey operations was closely supervised by the Assistants. The work in the field was subjected to regular test by them and none was accepted as trustworthy unless it had stood such test satisfactorily. On the Superintendent devolved,

besides the general control of the survey, the duty of determining the relative valuation of fields, and submitting proposals for settlement to Government, and introducing the settlement when sanctioned. In this last operation an officer of the Revenue Department was usually associated with him.

Commissioner of Survey and Settlement.

10. In the year 1863-64 two Commissioners of Survey and Settlement were appointed. The office indeed, had been created at an earlier period in the progress of the survey, when Major Wingate was entrusted with the chief control of the department for the entire Presidency. On his retirement from the service in 1853 it was abolished, but was revived some years later by the appointment of Colonel Anderson as Commissioner of the Southern Division, and soon afterwards of Colonel Francis as Commissioner of the Northern Division of the Presidency. These officers were charged with the direction in chief of the survey operations and with the control of expenditure. The office of the Survey Commissioner was the channel of communication between the Superintendents and Government, more particularly as regards the settlement proposals sent up by the former. On the retirement of Colonel Francis in 1877 Colonel Anderson was placed in charge of both the Southern and Northern Divisions, and thereafter, though a nominal distinction between these two offices was for some years retained, they were in practice amalgamated into one. When, however, Colonel Anderson signified his intention to retire, an opportunity was taken to give effect to the wishes of the Secretary of State for India to appoint a member of the Civil Service to the office. This was done in 1881 by appointing Mr. Stewart to be Survey Commissioner of the whole Presidency, except Sind, the control of the Survey of which province was given to the Commissioner in Sind. The control of the Mysore Survey, which hitherto had been under the Survey Commissioner of the Southern Division, who was also Inam Commissioner of that province, was withdrawn, owing to the assumption of the administration of the State by His Highness the Maharaja.

11. In 1884 the post of Director of Land Records was created and steps taken to organize a Land Records staff who were destined eventually to succeed the Survey Department and maintain its completed work and traditions. The first holder of the post of Director of Land Records was

Mr. Ozanne who had also been appointed head of the Department of Agriculture created in 1883. Meanwhile the work of the Survey Department went on under the supervision of Mr. Stewart, until 1891, when he retired and was succeeded by Mr. Ozanne who shortly after assumed the title of Survey Commissioner and Director of Land Records and Agriculture. In 1901 the Survey Department as such was definitely declared to be abolished, and the words "Survey Commissioner" were directed to be omitted from the designation.

12. The two offices of the Director of Land Records and the Director of Agriculture remained combined under one officer till the year 1905, when, owing partly to the great development of the Agricultural Department under the orders of the Government of India, and partly to the inception of the Record of Rights, they were placed under separate officers styled the Director of Agriculture and the Director of Land Records. In 1907 the later officer, being mainly responsible for Settlement work, was given the higher status of Settlement Commissioner.

13. Before leaving the subject the following extract from a Government Resolution reviewing the last progress report of the Survey Commissioner may be read with interest :—

> The value of the services rendered to the State by the Survey Department can hardly be exaggerated. At the time when the existing system was introduced, that is to say, about 60 years ago, Government were still confronted with the formidable problem of settling upon an equitable and workable basis the revenue demand for a vast number of small holdings. Several modes of settlement, based on pre-existing practice, had been tried ; some of them, such as the Pringle Settlement had disastrously failed. Out of the prevailing confusion the principles of the existing system of survey settlement were evolved by the genius of Messrs. Wingate and Goldsmid, the authors of the celebrated Joint Report. Upon the principles laid down in that report has been founded a system of land tenure and assessment admirably adapted to the requirements of the widely varying conditions of the different parts of the Presidency. Under the system of measurement and classification by subordinate agency, subject to the test of technically trained and skilled supervising officers, methods were

employed by which the area of every one of these small holdings could be measured, and the relative productive capacity of the soil estimated with scientific accuracy. By the system of grouping the relative economic and climatic advantages of different tracts were duly taken into account. In this manner the equitable distribution of the assessment was secured. The rates charged at the original settlement per acre of land occupied were in many instances extraordinarily low as compared with those previously levied. But as anticipated by the framers of the system the effect of the fixed tenure and of a certain and moderate assessment was at once seen in a rapid expansion of cultivation, which even at the low rates of assessment sanctioned yielded a large increase of revenue. The extensive areas of waste land existing at the time when the system was introduced have been employed largely for the growth of crops valuable for export purposes. Despite the check occasioned by many bad seasons and several disastrous famines and notwithstanding the heavy burden of indebtedness with which the agricultural population was saddled from the first, the value of land and the prosperity of the country, and with them the revenue have steadily increased. When the first leases of 30 years expired, it was found possible to increase the assessment by very substantial amounts ; but the enhancements have with rare exceptions been borne without difficulty. The Survey Department has cost the State from first to last many lakhs of rupees. But the outlay has been repaid over and over again. One peculiar merit of the system deserves mention. By the division of the whole culturable area into what may be called units of assessment, the extension of cultivation was made to carry with it an increase of revenue, while the revenue payer was placed in a position to ease his burden by giving up the occupation of lands unprofitable to him. The extensions of cultivation which have occurred have thus been profitable to the State no less than to the individual ; whereas under a zamindari or kindred system, the State would have gained nothing however much cultivation had extended throughout the whole of 30 years' leases. But it has not been only as a revenue producing instrument that the Survey Department has proved its unsefulness. The system to which the valuation of soils has been reduced is in many respects unique, and has resulted in a record of that valuation complete for innumerable small parcels of land. Probably no other province or country is possessed of any similar record. Its chief and immediate value for administrative purposes is that it enables field operations to be entirely dispensed with in all future settlements. This change of assessment can be decided for a whole tract on a review of its economic conditions and revenue history and the people are saved from all the uncertainty and harassment consequent upon inquiry into the circumstances of individual holdings. The greatest credit attaches to the founders of this system, which has stood the test of experience and practical application in the most satisfactory manner. Developments have been introduced, but in no particular have the principles, and in very few have even the individual rules and directions laid down in the Joint Report been widely departed from. For the intelligent and sound application of the rules to innumerable varieties of climate, soil and agriculture, the Government has had to depend on the integrity, skill and intelligence of the officers and subordinates of the Department who deserve the warmest acknowledgment for the untiring devotion and zeal which they have displayed in the performance of their laborious duties. The technical knowledge and the intimate acquaintance with the rural economy of the country acquired by the principal officers of the Survey Department have been of the greatest advantage to Government. Several of the Heads of the Department, besides its famous founders, Colonel Francis, Colonel Anderson, Mr. Theodore Stewart and Mr. Ozanne, have shown administrative ability and judgment of an exceedingly high order. Other officers, such as Major Preston, Mr. Pedder and Mr. Beyts, of the older generation, Mr. Fletcher, Colonel Godfrey and Mr. Hearn of more recent years, have left on record reports of high value regarding the economic condition and productive capacity of the various parts of the Presidency in which they served. Among the native subordinates not a few attained a high degree of skill in the valuation of soils. Mr. Symonds has the credit of guiding the operations to a satisfactory close. While recognizing that the work for which the Department was constituted has been completed, the Governor in Council cannot but regret that the technical knowledge and skill which the members of it had acquired to the great advantage of the administration will be no longer available.

14. With regard to the general principles on which Survey operations were conducted, the unit adopted, at the outset at any rate, was the survey number or a field capable of being cultivated by one pair of oxen. When the Survey was first started no attempt was made to indicate holdings belonging to different persons, but after a time a practice arose of demarcating sub-divisions of survey numbers in accordance with the rights of private persons in the land and clubbing two or more of these sub-divisions (which in Survey parlance were known as *pot* numbers) together so as to form one survey number. This practice, however, led to the entry in the revenue accounts of a large number of minute holdings and for the convenience of revenue administration it was found necessary to check it. Accordingly in 1868 orders were issued by Government directing that sub-divisions below a certain limit (which varied in different tracts and different classes of land) should not be recognized, except with the special sanction of the Survey Commissioner, and these orders have remained in force until the present day. The result is that at present the survey number is a unit for mapping and account purposes only and there exist many rights in the land included in a survey number which it is not attempted to show on the map or in the village accounts. In fact registration in the village accounts is evidence of liability for assessment but not necessarily of proprietary or other rights in the land. Information regarding the latter is shown in the Record of Rights (*vide* Paragraph 25 *infra*).

Survey at first for purely revenue purposes.

15. Up to the period (1867) when operations preparatory to the introduction of revised settlements were begun in the Poona and Nasik Collectorates, it was never attempted to give anything of scientific precision to the survey, or to ensure accurate topographical results. The survey was instituted, as has been shown, for purely revenue purposes, and at an emergent crisis questions of geographical utility could be allowed no place in presence of the paramount consideration of how to afford the means of improving the land revenue administration, and ameliorating the condition of the agricultural classes in the shortest time, and at the least cost. In its early years the work was of the roughest description ; but as it advanced,

and a stricter supervision was exercised, some degree of excellence was attained even from a topographical point of view. At the present day the village map is constructed with much accuracy, and, besides presenting a thoroughly correct delineation of field boundaries (its chief object), shows village sites, roads, paths, tanks and the physical features of the country within its limits with considerable fidelity. In the districts in which the revenue survey followed the Imperial Topographical Survey, the character of the work was greatly improved by taking the great trigonometrical triangulation as a basis of survey, and adopting the system of village traversing. The plan of working in connection with the Imperial Topographical Survey proved successful.[1]

16. As revision operations by degrees became more and more restricted and partial, because the work of the old survey, as it progressed, naturally became more and more correct, at later revisions that work was found good enough to be accepted as final, and the utilization of the work of the trigonometrical survey became unnecessary. One limitation was necessarily observed. A cadastral survey map for revenue purposes cannot in rugged country be also a correct topographical map.

Method of classification of fields.

17. The method of classification or valuation of the fertility of the soil which is peculiar to the Bombay Survey was originally introduced by Mr. Goldsmid and Lieutenant Wingate in Indapur and as described in the rules attached to the Joint Report it continued with modifications suggested by experience until the close of the Survey. The system postulated a minute examination of each holding, field by field, a careful record of the results of the examination in accordance with certain fixed principles and close supervision by skilled European officers to ensure that a uniform standard of valuation was preserved. In course of time these principles became so well understood and the native members of the staff so expert in their application that the maximum difference between the results arrived at by them and those finally accepted as correct after test by skilled supervising agency did not exceed 3 or 4 per cent. It may be noted here that comparative variations in the fertility of soils were expressed for convenience of handling in parts of a rupee, 16 annas representing the valuation of a perfect field,

from which deductions were made for faults, such as slope or irregularity of surface, excess of lime or moisture, or inferiority in the character or depths of the soil. This at least was the arrangement introduced under the Joint Rules. As time went on, experience showed the advisability of making allowance for advantages by making additions to the scale which carried the maximum above 16 annas. One or two of these advantages may be mentioned so that the character of this improvement in valuation may be more clearly understood.

As excess of moisture from surface springs lowers the agricultural value of land, so the advantage of position raises this value. If, for instance, by its position a field derives a beneficial flooding from a river through a deposit of fine silt after a flood subsides, or if by position a field is near enough to a running stream to enable the cultivator to irrigate his land by erecting a well on the bank of the stream, an increment in classification is justified and indeed is called for to ensure a fair distribution of the assessment.

Another instance may be specified. The ordinary classification does not deal with any depth beyond three feet. As a rule that is sufficient for the approximate valuation required, but with this classification two fields may be valued alike which may be of diverse value in that in the one irrigation water may be found at short depth and in the other at a very great depth ; or in the one if wells are dug sweet water will be found and the other salt water unfit for irrigation. Hence again a differentiation was needed which was not provided for in the "Joint Rules."

The application of advantages was regulated by prescribed scales. Some of these advantages have been elaborated into large measures of extensive application, such as the "sub-soil water advantage," the "general position class." To correct a common misunderstanding it may be added that, whatever be the application of such methods of making the relative valuation more correct than it was, it can have no effect on the actual assessment imposed on a tract as a whole.

18. When the classification was completed, the Superintendent, having before him full information as to the measurement of the different map units and their comparative classification according to a well-understood scale, was in a position to submit proposals for the application of definite

rates to each village. For the purpose of these proposals it was generally (and still is) the practice not to deal with a larger area than a single taluka at one time. This enables the officer proposing the settlement to give the most minute consideration to the condition and requirements of the tract of country with which he has to deal, and at the same time permits close scrutiny of his proposals by the reviewing authorities and by Government. A further advantage of this method of proceeding is that it affords an opportunity of observing the working of a settlement on a small scale and judging of the suitability of rates applied to a limited extent of country before imposing them over a large area.

Term of Settlements.

19. The maximum term of settlements is thirty years, except in the province of Sind, where, owing to the still imperfect condition of irrigation, it has been thought desirable to adopt the shorter period of ten years.

20. Such are the general principles on which revenue survey operations were conducted in this Presidency, the whole of which except some alienated villages has now been brought under the survey settlement.

Necessity of legalizing Survey operations. (Act I of 1865, Bombay)

21. These operation had been in progress many years before any question arose as to the expediency of giving them legal sanction. A revenue survey was a measure for which there were sufficient precedents, the whole of the Deccan having been surveyed by direction of the celebrated Malik Amber, and partial surveys having been executed under the Maratha Government. The survey now under description had, therefore, all the legality that consonance with previous usage could give it. But with the progress of British administration the value attached to rights in the land, and the inclination to resist any attempt to encroach on them, were constantly increasing. The survey itself had largely contributed to this result, and as it advanced and valuable interests became affected by it, a disposition to question the legality of its proceedings began to be manifested. It became, therefore, imperatively necessary to confer on these proceedings a validity which could not be disputed. Accordingly, in the year 1864 a bill was introduced in the Legislative Council "to provide for

the survey, demarcation, assessment and administration of lands held under Government in the districts belonging to the Bombay Presidency, and for the registration of the rights and interests of the occupants of the same." This became law in the following year under the title of the "Bombay Survey and Settlement Act" (Act I of 1865). This Act confirmed previous settlements, empowered Government to "direct the extension of the survey to any part of the Presidency," defined the powers and duties of survey officers, provided for the demarcation of field and village boundaries and the settlement by the survey officers of disputes connected with them, and for the erection and repair of boundary marks. It empowered the officer in charge of survey to assess Government and alienated lands and required him, when making settlements of land revenue, to prepare a record showing all rights and interests in the land, and giving all other necessary information. It also provided for the administration of survey settlements, and empowered Government to direct a fresh survey, and to revise assessments on the expiration of a term of settlement. Shortly after the passing of the Act of settlement leases of the earliest settled talukas began to fall in and in these field operations preliminary to the introduction of revision survey rates had to be undertaken. Indapur was the first taluka in which revision field operations were commenced, these operations were conducted on the same general principles which guided similar operations in the original survey and which are described above. The policy of this Government was from the beginning opposed to entire re-measurement and re-classification, but as in the tracts settled during the infancy of the department the work of the original survey was found to be too faulty and imperfect to be adopted as the basis for revision of rates, a general re-examination and revision of the old measurements and classification were found at first to be necessary. Gradually, however, as the tracts latterly dealt with by the original survey came up for revision the fieldwork became more and more partial until in the talukas last dealt with the fieldwork of the original survey was found to be sufficiently correct to be adopted for the purposes of revision settlements without any detailed test or re-examination. Advantage was taken at revision to improve the old valuation with due caution that such improvement should not in any degree be a virtual tax on improvements carried out during the currency of a lease by the expenditure of private capital.

Land Revenue Code : Limitation of enhancements and non-taxation of private improvement.

22. Until 1879 the law which governed these operations was contained in Act I of 1865. In this year Bombay Act I of 1865 was repealed and the provisions therein contained were re-enacted in the Bombay Land Revenue Code (Act V of 1879). In this Code, while all the provisions of Bombay Act I of 1865 relating to assessments in revision were re-enacted without any change, a new provision was inserted whereby a right was reserved to Government to take into consideration in fixing revised rates certain classes of improvements effected by the owners or occupants from private capital. This provision was opposed to the fundamental principles of the Bombay settlement system, and further as it was considered likely to discourage the application of private enterprise and capital to agriculture, Government in 1884 issued an executive order giving a general assurance that all improvements effected by occupants from private capital should be exempt from taxation in revision and further restricting the enhancements in revision settlements to the limits prescribed in the following rules :—

1st.—The increase of revenue in the case of a taluka or group of villages brought under the same maximum dry-crop rate shall not exceed 33 per cent.

2nd.—No increase exceeding 66 per cent shall in like manner be imposed on a single village without the circumstances of the case being specially reported for the orders of Government.

3rd.—No increase exceeding 100 per cent shall in like manner be imposed on an individual holding.

Amendment of Land Revenue Code.

23. Notwithstanding this assurance it was considered inadvisable to retain the objectionable provision above referred to in the statute book and it was accordingly amended by Act IV of 1886, whereby the following two principles have been laid down for the guidance of settlement officers in fixing rates in future revision settlements :—

(1) That assessments will be revised on consideration of the value of land and the profits of agriculture, and

(2) That assessments will not be increased at revision on account of

increase to such value and profits due to improvements effected on any land during the currency of any previous settlement by or at the cost of the holder thereof.

24. In course of time the periods of guarantee granted to talukas in which revision settlements had been introduced came to an end and second revision settlements had to be introduced into them. Indapur Taluka was the first of these and similar second revision settlements have been and are being introduced as they fall due under the supervision of the Land Records Department. No fresh classification or measurement operations are undertaken at these second revision settlements.

The Record of Rights.

25. Before explaining the various tenures, two important improvements which have in recent years been introduced into revenue administration of this Presidency may be described. The first is the introduction of the Record of Rights in this Presidency by Bombay Act IV of 1903. The record prepared by the Survey Department was necessarily a fiscal record the object of which was to show from whom the assessment was due and what that assessment was. It was not a record of rights or title. In course of time it was found that a Record of Rights based on possession, if not on title, was indispensable for the needs of the administration, especially because the occupants in this Presidency, unlike tenants elsewhere, to whom in status they correspond, had an unrestricted right of transfer. The necessity of having such a record was pressed upon this Government by the Government of India and after a great deal of discussion regarding its suitability to this Presidency it was resolved in 1901 to prepare an initial record designed to show in accurate detail exactly how the land was held, because the revenue records gave only partial and in some respects misleading information on the point. The record was intended to show every right from that of a registered occupant to an annual tenant at will. The experiment so started in selected talukas was found to be successful, showing as it did that the preparation of a Record, to compel persons acquiring new rights to give information of it to the revenue authorities, and to require the Civil Courts to insist on the production of extracts from the Record in Civil Suits tried by them, which relate to land, Act IV of 1903 was passed. This Act requires that a complete initial record

showing all varieties of right in the land should be prepared by the Village Accountants, examined and checked by officers of the Revenue and Land Records Departments and announced to the rayat. Provision has been made in the Act and the rules under it that the Record after its completion and announcement should be accurately maintained by what is called the Mutation Resister. The Record has now been prepared in all Government villages and some alienated villages of the Presidency, and is being maintained and kept up to date by Mutation Registers. Its preparation has placed at our disposal a large amount of important information regarding the various rights in land and the profits of cultivation, and has proved extremely useful.

26. The second important feature that has been imported into the revenue system of this Presidency is a regular system of suspensions and remissions of land revenue when the crops fall below a certain standard or when the water supply on irrigated lands fails. The assessment fixed under Survey Settlement is a fixed demand and represents the revenue payable on an average in a series of years, the original idea being that on an average the rayat saves in a good year sufficient to enable him to pay the assessment without borrowing in a bad year. Experience, however, showed that among the smaller land-holders and in tracts subject to frequent vicissitudes of the season this idea was fallacious, and in 1906-1907 a regular system of suspensions and remissions was introduced. The system authorizes the Collector, when he has ascertained by local inquiries that owing to a partial or total failure or destruction of crops throughout any tract, suspension of the collection of land revenue is necessary, to grant suspensions according to a scale to all occupants, agriculturists and non-agriculturists alike, without inquiry into the circumstances of individuals. As regards remission, the grant of them depends on the character of three seasons following that in which the assessment is suspended. Ordinarily suspended arrears which are more than three years old are to be remitted by the Collector. The remissions are to be granted to occupants cultivating their own holdings and also to non-cultivating occupants, provided that when land is cultivated by tenants, corresponding remission is granted by the superior holder or landlord to the inferior holder or tenant.

THE SURVEY TENURE.

Definition of the Survey Tenure.

27. The ordinary survey tenure may be described as the right of occupancy of Government land continuable in perpetuity on payment of the Government demand and transferable by inheritance, sale, gift or mortgage without other restriction than the requirement to give notice to the authorities. This is the tenure as defined in the original Bombay Land Revenue Code. Act V of 1879. There is, however, another variety created under the amending Act VI of 1901. Under this Act the Collector is authorized to grant the occupancy of lands for limited periods or on such conditions as he may think necessary, the principle of them being that the occupant cannot alienate his land without the previous permission of the Collector. This tenure is known as the restricted or non-transferable tenure.

Area held under Different Tenures.

	Nature of Tenure.		No. of estates or holdings.	No. of villages.	Area in acres. *
1.	Rayatwari Khalsa surveyed ...	(A) Peasant Proprietors paying separately.	1,191,729	23,161	28,675,980
		(B) Peasant Proprietors holding lands at privileged rates.	213,429		4,434,682
2.	Talukdari		497	497	1,363,986
3.	Mehwasi		62	62	12,375
4.	Udhad Jamabandi		40	40	58,717
5.	Khoti		3,317	3,317	2,352,107
6.	Izafat		30	30	36,338
7.	On lease		40	40	62,336
8.	Revenue free, that is Inams and jaghirs		2,242	2,212	5,224,601
	Total		1,411,386	29,389	42,329,172

* In the Rayatwari area the acreage is for occupied land only. The area of other estates is given in the gross and include unarable and unoccupied land.

TENURES IN THE DECCAN.

The Miras Tenure.

28. Previous to the survey settlement all land in the Deccan, not alienated, was held by two classes of occupants. The first was the mirasdar, or tenant with right of occupancy ; the second was the upri, or tenant-at-will. The mirasdar was the freeman of the village, his

land was heritable and transferable, and he held at a fixed assessment, though under the Maratha Government he was liable to demands on account of extra cess. In former times the name of mirasdar carried some degree of distinction with it, and the position was regarded as an enviable one. It could be acquired by simply consenting to pay the Government demand on the entire area in occupation, whether cultivated or not—an essential condition of the miras tenure—and by the payment of a fine. The most remarkable incident of the tenure was that it was nominally at any rate not subject to forfeiture for default of revenue payment or even for the abandonment of his village by the mirasdar, unless he was absent for a longer period than thirty years. If in this respect, however, he enjoyed an apparent advantage unknown to the survey tenure, there were counterbalancing circumstances in his position which rendered it greatly inferior to that of the occupant under the survey settlement. For he was not only liable to extra and arbitrary impositions, but was required to make good the claims of the Government on defaulting brother mirasdars. The assessment also was so high as to leave an unimproved land absolutely no margin of rent to the mirasdar. The privilege of re-entry within a period of 30 years after relinquishment or failure to pay was subject to the obligation of reimbursing all arrears due and expenses incurred during the period of absence. This condition was regarded by Mr. Chaplin as rendering virtually nugatory the privilege in question. According to the same authority a mirasdar could also be compelled at any time to give in a deed of renunciation, if he declined to sow his lands or pay the Government dues. There is no practical distinction between this penalty and forfeiture for contumacy in withholding Government revenue.

The Upri Tenure.

29. The "upri" had no status in the village in which, as the name imports, he was regarded as a stranger. He cultivated the common lands of the village or those of absentee mirasdars, but had no proprietary interest of any kind in either. On the other hand, he could not be called on to pay revenue on any larger area than that actually under crop, nor be held liable for the default of other cultivators. The assessment of his land was also lighter ordinarily than that of the mirasdar. In the case of the "upri", then, fixity of tenures has been substituted for tenancy-at-will, but coupled

with the greater responsibility necessarily attaching to a settlement leased in definite areas.

TENURES IN GUJARAT.

The Talukdari Tenure.

30. The Talukdari tenure is one of the most important in Gujarat. It prevails in the districts of Ahmedabad, Kaira, Broach and Panch Mahals, the greater number of estates held under this tenure being situated in the Western talukas of Ahmedabad adjoining Kathiawar, viz., Dhandhuka, Dholka, Gogha and Viramgam.

Talukdars defined.

31. The leading characteristic of Talukdari tenure is that Talukdari estate is held neither in gift from the Crown (i.e., 'alienated') nor in occupancy (i.e., 'unalienated'), but with full proprietary rights antedating the advent of British Rule and including ownership of mines, minerals and trees. Exceptions to this rule are the Naiks of the Dohad Taluka in the Panch Mahals District and the Kasbatis of the Viramgam Taluka in Ahmedabad, who though included in the definition of Talukdar (Section 2 of Bombay Act VI of 1888) are considered to hold their estates as permanent lessees under certain conditions.

Position of a Talukdar under Act VI 1862 and system under which Government demand is levied.

32. All Talukdari estates are held subject to the payment of Jama (land revenue) to Government which may either be *udhad* (fixed in perpetuity) or fluctuating. The estates in Kaira and Broach are mostly held on *udhad jama* or quit-rent fixed under the Summary Settlement Act, while those in Ahmedabad pay *Jama* which is liable to revision on expiry of a term of settlement not exceeding 30 years. Legally (section 22 of Bombay Act VI of 1888) the fluctuating *jama* may be equal to the full survey assessment of all the lands comprised within the estate, but in practice the Government demand is generally limited to about 60 per cent of the survey assessment of the cultivated lands. The Talukdars are exempted from the payment of Jama as regards certain classes of land alienated by them before the passing of Bombay

Act VI of 1888, and as regards other classes of such lands they are required to pay as Jama 50 per cent of the proceeds derived by them therefrom. The Talukdari estates of Ahmedabad (except those of the Parantij Taluka) have been surveyed twice (in 1864 and 1889) for the purpose of fixing the Government demand ; and a detailed survey is now in progress, which has been extended to Broach, Kaira and Panch Mahals estates also.

Settlement Registers.

33. An important operation undertaken in connection with the survey is the preparation under section 5 of Bombay Act VI of 1888 of the Settlement Register which is intended to serve the purpose of a Record of Rights in Talukdari estates, which have been exempted from the operation of the Record of Rights Act.

Liability of the estates to Local Fund Cess.

34. All Talukdari estates (except the villages held on a fixed Jama by the Thakor Saheb of Limbdi in the Dhandhuka Taluka) are liable to Local Fund Cess at the usual rate, but during the current settlement the liability has been limited to an increase of 25 per cent over the amount formerly due.

Origin of Talukdars.

35. The Talukdars of Gujarat are historically identical with the ruling families of Kathiawar and other Agencies and their loss of political power is generally ascribed to the geographical accident of their estates being situated in the *rasti* (settled) potion of the Province which was brought under the direct rule of the Paramount Power, while their kinsmen in the *mulkgirt* (unsettled) portion continued to be treated as tributaries. The Talukdars comprise men of varying position, ranging from Jurisdictional Chiefs holding Talukdari villages in British districts and the holders of recognised Chieftainships such as Sanand, Gamph, etc., to the holders of a frew acres in a coparcenary estate, who are fast being converted into yeomen cultivators. With the exception of a few Mahomedans, Kathis and Charans, they are all of pure or mixed Rajput descent, embracing Vaghelas, Chudasmas, Zalas, Parmars and others. The lower strata include the Koli Thakardas of Viramgam and Parantij. Molesalams, the descendants

of Rajput converts to Islam of the Broach and Kaira Districts and of Ranpur in the Ahmedabad District, retain their status and rights as Talukdars.

System of recovering rents.

36. Nearly all the more important estates such as Sanand, Gamph Gangad, etc., observed the rule of primogeniture, but the bulk of smaller estates are held by co-sharers whose increasing number threaten the estates with rapid disruption. Except where repeated sub-division of shares has forced the Talukdar to the plough, he lives upon the rent of the land and regards manual labour as degrading. The rents are taken in kind or cash, the levy of the former being generally fixed by *dharo* (customs) of the village which is recorded in every case. The division of landlords and tenants' share is made either by *makhal,* i.e., actual weighing out of the crop in the common grain-yard, or by *dhal,* i.e., appraisement of the standing crop. The rent levied by the Talukdars in kind or cash varies in different estates and even in different villages of the same estate within very wide limits. In some cases it is less even than the Government assessment, and in others it may be as much as two or even three times the assessment. Probably the general average would be from 1¼ to 1½ times the assessment.

Rents are levied in cash in all the estates of the Kaira and Broach Districts, but the crop-share system prevails in most of the estates of Ahmedabad. Cash rents based on the survey assessment are being gradually substituted for crop-share in estates brought under Government management.

The tenants are invariably tenants-at-will, but eviction is rare and in many cases the tenants retain the same holding for generations.

Alienations.

37. Talukdari estates contain large areas of land given to cadets, widows of the family and other relatives for maintenance and to village servants and others either in reward for past services or as remuneration for services still being performed. Service lands falling within the last category are resumable at will, and in other cases the Talukdar has a right of reversion on the failure of male heirs. These inferior holders generally

contribute little to the estate though in some cases a small quit-rent is chargeable.

Some important features of the Talukdari Tenure and extent of Government interference in the management of Talukdari villages.

38. Other distinctive features of estates held on the Talukdari tenure are the following :—

(1) under section 31 of the Gujarat Talukdars Act, Bombay VI of 1888, a Talukdar cannot encumber his estate beyond his own lifetime without the permission of the Talukdari Settlement Officer, and cannot alienate the same without the sanction of Government.

(2) A Talukdar is liable for the cost of the village police-force employed in his village.

(3) No Civil Court can entertain a suit for the partition of Talukdari estates, such applications being tried by the Talukdari Settlement Officer subject in certain cases to appeal to the District Judge.

(4) Government do not interfere in the internal management of the estates, but the latter may be taken under management under the following conditions :—

(a) For apprehended injury to the well-being of inferior holders or breach of the peace ;

(b) while partition is being effected ;

(c) on the application of the Talukdars ;

(d) under the operation of the Land Revenue Code, Court of Wards Act, Civil Procedure Code and other enactments enabling public officers to assume charge of private estates.

In the case of (a) and (c) the managing officer is entitled to call upon all creditors of the Talukdar to submit their claims with accounts within the period of six months and to negotiate for a settlement.

Vanta Tenure and its Origin.

39. The *vanta* (divided) tenure (in contradistinction to *talpad,* paying full assessment) prevails more or less in certain villages all over Gujarat north of the river Tapti. *Vantas* held by Talukdars differ in no way from

whole villages owned by that class. The origin of the *vanta* is generally ascribed to the action of the Mahomedan invaders of Gujarat who deprived the original chiefs of all but one-fourth of their possessions which took the name of *vanta* (divided). In some cases the *vantas* were held free, but in the majority of cases a quit-rent was imposed sooner or later by the Paramount Power. No holder of *vanta* land has any documentary evidence to prove his title before the enactment of the Summary Settlement Act (VII of 1863) under which some of the vanta holders accepted *sanads* and converted their former lump quit-rent into a *numbervar salami* under Act VII of 1863. Other vantas still continue to pay *udhad jama.* A few villages exist in which the lands are divided into two portions, called respectively *vanta* and *talpad* separated by some fixed boundary, a river, road or stream, the village site itself being also divided. Vanta holders are generally but not invariably Talukdars.

40. *Senja*—undivided, in contradistinction to *narvadari*, *bhagdari,* and others divided villages—is the ordinary *rayatwari* or Government tenure of the province, the assessment being placed on each revenue survey number, and the settlement made by Government directly with the occupant.

Narvadari and Bhagdari Tenures.

41. The peculiarity of the *narvadari* and *bhagdari* tenures is that they involve joint responsibility for the payment of the Government revenue. The first-named tenure prevails chiefly in the district of Kaira, a few villages being also found in Ahmedabad and Surat while the latter is confined to the Broach Collectorate. There is one *khalsa* or Government village in the Panch Mahals which is held and has been settled on the *bhagdari* tenure.

The Narvadari Tenure.

42. The lands of *narva* villages consist of certain main divisions (*muksh bhag*), containing sub-shares (*peta-bhag*), which, in their turn, are up to a fixed limit divided into fractional parts. The head of each estate or main division is called a *muksh bhagdar*, and is responsible for the payment to Government of the assessment leviable on the whole share. Similarly the holders of sub-shares of a main division (the *peta bhagdars*) are collectively responsible for that portion of the assessment which has been allotted to their several sub-shares. All sub-sharers have equal rights,

are called *patidars*, and are descendants of the old proprietary cultivators. The shares or divisions, great and small are sometimes of equal and sometimes of unequal amounts, but always in well-known and recognized proportion, so that the assessment due by the whole village is exactly apportioned among them. As the *narvadari* and *bhagdari* tenures had been acknowledged and preserved under Act V of 1862, special arrangements were required for the settlement of villages in which these tenures existed.

Settlement of common (Majmun) land.

43. The register of existing shares was accepted and the lump sum due from the village [with the exception of the assessment on certain common (*majmun*) land which was excluded from the *narva*] was apportioned among the different shareholders according to the rules entered in the register of *phalavni* or rate of apportionment. It is seldom that the whole of he land of a *narva* village is included in the *narva*. There is almost always a portion of *vighotia* lands, i.e., survey numbers on which the assessment is levied individually and not in the lump as in the case of *narva* lands.

Land common to the whole *narva* is known as *gao majmun* and land common to one or more *bhags* is known as *bhag majmun*. The assessment on *majmun* lands is distributed among the various shares in proportion to the amount of assessment for which they are liable on account of the numbers included in their respective shares.

Varieties of Narva Tenure.

44. The *narva* villages are not all constituted precisely alike ; there is, for example—

(1) The perfect *patidari,* in which all the lands are held in severalty by different proprietors each person managing his own land and paying his fixed share of the assessment, the whole being jointly responsible if one sharer cannot fulfil his engagements. This is ordinary *narvadari* and *bhagdari* tenure which exists in a large majority of the villages.

(2) The imperfect *patidari,* in which part of the land is held in common and part in severalty, the profits from the common land being first appropriated to payment of the Government revenue made up

according to rate on the several holdings. The peculiarities of each have been upheld by the new settlement.

Under the survey system many *narva* village communities have been allowed, at their own wish, to divide their respective responsibilities for the revenue, according to the assessment of their respective shares, instead of according to the old symbolical division (*phalavni*) of the lump assessment responsibility originally entered in the register of the *narva.*

Position of tenants in Narva and in Bhagdari villages.

45. In *narvadari* and *bhagdari* villages all persons cultivating *narva* or *bhagdari* lands, whatever rights they may have, are tenants, not of Government, but of the *bhagdars*, who are alone responsible for the renvenue. They are—

(1) Tenants-at-will, holding at the pleasure of the *narvadars*, who can eject them, or increase their rents at discretion.

(2) Customary tenants who cannot be ejected so long as they pay the customary rental, which is either a fixed share of the produce or more commonly the customary *bighoti* rates, which are generally recorded in the village books.

Soon after the introduction of the survey settlement a "record" is prepared, setting forth the respective rights of the superior and inferior holders. These records have not, however, the force of judicial decisions.

Difference between the Bhagdari and Narvadari Tenures.

46. The *bhagdari* tenure differs from the *narvadari* in one important particular only, viz., that in the former there was always a fixed *bighoti* assessment on each field ; and although the assessment of each share (*bhag*) was not the aggregate of the assessments of the several fields which the share comprised, it was the amount of the total field assessment of all *bhagdari* lands, divided according to the register (*phalavni*). In the *narvadari* tenure, on the other hand, there was never a separate field assessment, the revenue being fixed in the lump. It will be seen that, although the *narva* and *bhagdari* tenures have been preserved in their integrity by the survey, yet the amount of revenue to be paid in the lump

has been ascertained by a field assessment ; so in the event of a contingency arising, such as is contemplated by clause 2 of section 8 of Regulation XVII of 1827 (reversion to Government on account of non-payment of revenue), the survey rates could at once be introduced in exactly the same way as in ordinary Government (*senja*) villages.

Mehwasi Tenure.

47. In some parts of Gujarat, viz., on the banks of the river Mahi in the Kaira district and the Parantij Taluka and Modasa Mahal in the Ahmedabad district, certain villages known as Mehwasi villages are held by the descendants of Mehwasi Koli or Rajput Chiefs, once great freebooters and the terror of the country. In Parantij and Modasa their tenure is exactly similar to the tenure of the Talukdari vaillges of the Ahmedabad district : that is to say, the *jama* is subject to revision and the holders are considered proprietors. The villages on the Mahi in the Kaira district are held on the *udhad jama* tenure, that is to say, the *jama* is fixed and is not liable to revision. The principal shareholders are generally Thakors, and are called *muksh bhagdars,*[2] the sub-sharers being known as *peta bhagdars,* as in villages held on the *narva* tenure. Most of these villages were originally held rent-free, or subject to a small tribute. Conditions were generally attached to the tenure, such as the police management of a small portion of the country, the keeping open of certain roads infested by robbers, or forbearance from plundering on the part of the holders and their fraternity. Under British rule and a better system of police these conditions are, of course, unncessary, and the villages are held subject to the payment of the *jama* only. Of late years, *talatis* (village accountants) have been introduced into some attached mehwasi villages, and the *jama* collected from the shareholders, who sublet their lands either on cash or grain rents. The steps which were taken in 1877 to introduce the revenue survey into these villages were rendered futile by the destruction by fire of the survey records at Surat in 1887, but some of the villages have recently been resurveyed and they are to be treated in the same way as Talukdari villages as regards the imposition and levy of a *jama*, which will be proportioned to their survey assessment and will be liable to revision at the end of a term of years.

In the Kalol Taluka the headmen of 23 villages with their shares under the name of Mehwasi *patels* claim certain privileges amounting to a distinct tenure. It was decided (1887) that this tenure did not correspond exactly with the *narvadari* or *bhagdari,* but more nearly approached that of the Talukdari villages in the Ahmedabad Collectorate, and that the villages undoubtedly fell within the category of those described in section 8 of Regulation XVII of 1827 as held by shareholders setting hereditarily, and under certain terms, were at the same time offered to the *patels,* but it was not until 1887 that a settlement was arrived at. The tenure has now been recognized in 21 villages, and its more important conditions are that the *patels* have a lien on their waste lands on condition that they limit their demands on their tenants to the survey assessments and pay as *jama* certain proportions of the assessments of the cultivated lands held by themselves and their tenants. The proportion varies according to the area of forests reserved in the villages, and the forest rights of Government in the waste lands have been maintained, though liberal privileges have been conceded. The *patels* (headmen) employ their own *talatis* (accountants), but are under obligation to keep accounts and furnish statistics.

Maleki Tenure.

48. In the Thasra Taluka of the Kaira Collectorate is a clan of Mahomedan yeomen known as the "Maleks," who hold their villages on a special tenure, the origin of which is as follows :–

Nearly four centuries ago Mahomed Begada, Sultan of Ahmedabad, granted as a reward for military services, at the taking of Pavagad (a celebrated hill-fort near Champaner), 12 villages to certain Musalman families, known as Malekjadas. On the introduction of British rule these 12 villages had, by the founding of new hamlets, increased to 17. They are now 27 in number, into all of which the new settlement has been introduced. These villages seem to have been originally rent-free, and so continued for 2½ centuries. About 150 years ago the Maleks were compelled by the Marathas to pay a fixed tribute (*udhad jamabandi*) on their villages. Soon after (about 1769) the *Mulkgiri* army of the Gaikwar levied an additional tribute, called *ghasdana,*[3] which was continued till the introduction of British rule, when this exaction was commuted and paid by the British Government to that of the Gaikwar. Besides this, several Maleki villages were subjected to a tribute payable to the Babi of Balasinor, which was also commuted and paid by the British Government to the Babi. To meet the Maratha tribute (*udhad jamabandi*) demand the Maleks levied from their cultivators a poll-tax (*karam vero*) and a tax in kind (*waje*), amounting to one-third of the produce of the land.

Present Settlement.

49. In 1865 the Maleki villages were measured and valued by the revenue survey, and a settlement introduced, which has since been confirmed by the grant of sanads to the different Maleks. Under the Settlement the management of the villages is in the hands of Government. The Maleks nominate the *talatis* who are appointed by Government. The revenue of the villages is shared between the Government and the Maleks whose shares vary from 7 to 9 annas. Besides the Maleks hold rent-free "Gharkhed" lands.

Udhad Jamabandi Tenure.

50. In some whole villages, or parts of villages, *vanta* lands entered as *sarkari* or Government are held on *udhad jamabandi* tenure, which means that they are liable to a fixed cess (*jama*) only, such *jama* remaining intact even at a general revision of assessment, there being a "right on the part of the occupants in limitation of the right of Government in consequence of a specific limit to the assessment having been established and preserved." Other villages, not *vanta,* are also held on this tenure. These villages have been surveyed in the lump only, and the fixed assessment has remained intact. A few, however, in the Kaira Collectorate, which have been under the management of the Collector and of the Talukdari Settlement Officer as embarrassed estates, have had and are now having their lands surveyed and classed in detail, with a view to the survey settlement being introduced.

Sarakati Tenure.

51. A few villages in different parts of the province are held on what is called *sarakati* tenure. The term *sarakati* is derived from the Arabic, meaning a partner. In these villages Government is entitled to certain proportion of revenue, and the holders to the balance ; the

proportion of the respective shares varies from 10 to 6 annas. It is not unlike what the Maleki tenure has now merged into, the holders having in both cases the right of occupying and subletting all their lands subject to the payment of the fixed proportion of revenue due to Government.

Alienated Lands.

52. The wholly or partially alienated lands in Gujarat are extensive, and of various denominations, the principal being—

Chakariat of all denominations (lands held for service) ;

Pasaita (land given in charity or to artificers, Bhats, Charans, or others) ;

Haria (the price of blood or reward for defence) ;

Wazifa (an alienation to religious persons of the faith of Islam).

These may be *nakra* (rent-free) or *salamia* (liable to quit-rent). These again may be *vechania* (sold) or *garania* (mortgaged), and are then described and known as *pasaita-salamia, pasaita-vechan-salamia, pasaita-vechania-nakra, haria-garania-salamia* and so on.

All the lands, with the exception of *chakariat,* are now *sanadia* or held by *sanads* under the Summary Settlement Act, and are entered in the accounts under the one distinctive title of *jat inam sanadia,* the old denominations of *pasaita vechania, garania nakra* and so on, not being retained. Lands granted to temples and religious corporations as distinct from individuals (called *devasthan* or *dharmadaya*) are also excluded from those under the title of *jat inam sanadia. Sanads* have not been issued for *chakariat* lands, including those held by district officers who have elected to do service for them.

Tenures in the Konkan

I Northern Konkan.

The Survey Tenure.

53. Land in the Thana Collectorate is held almost wholly on the survey tenure, the occupier having in general had no right so good as that

conferred by the survey. There is no *miras* properly so called, but a considerable quantity of land was previously called *suti* and held on a tenure analogous to that of *miras,* but not so advantageous. This tenure has, however, been merged in the survey tenure, which is in fact scarcely, if at all, less valuable than the old *miras.*

Other Tenures.

54. The exceptions to the survey tenure in the Northern Konkan are as follows :–

1st.—A considerable number of *khoti* villages chiefly in the Salsette Taluka.

2nd.—A number of *izafat* villages scattered over the different talukas.

3rd.—Lands known as *shilotri* lying either along the coast or along the larger creeks.

There are, of course, a number of villages held in ordinary *inam,* and also the usual service *vatans,* but these differ in no way from the same tenures in the rest of the Presidency.

Khoti Tenure.

55. It is necessary to distinguish clearly between the *khots* of the Northern and those of the Southern Konkan. Those of the Northern Konkan are, in fact, leaseholders (though more commonly called farmers) of a certain number of villages, several being generally held in one family, and they obtained their land in all cases from the British Government, though at an early period. They have never claimed to be the proprietors of the soil, and the title and rights of those who hold land under them are in no way affected by the fact of these *khots* having their villages in lease. Most of the *khoti* villages have been measured and the survey settlement introduced, and, therefore, in all such villages the survey tenure is in force. The former rights of the tenants, which are distinguished as *suti* (described above) and *chikli* or *gatkuli* are only in force now in the few villages not yet surveyed.

Izafat Tenure.

56. The *izafat* tenure is a variety of service tenure, of hereditary district officers chiefly Deshmukhs and Deshpandes. At the introduction

of British rule there were 124 villages under this tenure. They were resumed and managed by Government as the duties of the hereditary district officers had become useless during the continuance of the Maratha farming system. When it was decided to restore villages to their former holders, most declined to resume charge, and the number remaining on *izafat* tenure fell to 16. When the *izafat* villages of the Karjat Taluka were surveyed, it was decided that the holders were liable to pay the full survey assessment, but as no assessment was placed on any but rice land, the holders enjoyed under the thirty years' lease the profits of *warkas* (dry crop) cultivation. In the villages of other talukas the survey tenure was introduced but the izafatdar was allowed 10 per cent of the revenue as remuneration for the collection of the assessment. The lease of the Karjat Izafat villages having expired, a similar remuneration has been allowed to the holders, the full assessment on *warkas* as well as rice being leived. They were further allowed the privilege of occupying land belonging to persons dying or disappearing whiout known heirs according to previous practice. *Izafat* villages are in fact now held on the survey tenure, the izafatdars holding a position analogous to that of superior holders.

Shilotri Tenure

Shilotri lands are lands that have been embanked and reclaimed from the sea, and the permanence of which is dependent on the embankments being kept up. These reclamations are commonly known as *khars*. The tenure is of three varieties—first, *shilotri* proper under which the *khar* belongs to the person by whom it was reclaimed or his representatives. The *shilotars* are considered to have a proprietary right, they let out these lands at will, and according to old custom levy a maund of rice per bigha, in addition to the assessment, for the repair of the outer embankments. These lands were surveyed and re-assessed at the survey in the same way as Government lands. The second class of *shilotri* lands is that in which either Government reclaimed the *khars*, or became possessed of them by lapse. The cultivators of these *khars* hold their land just as other survey tenants do ; but an extra assessment, which is supposed to represent the *shilotri maund* mentioned above, is appropriated to the repairs of the embankments. The third class *shilotri* lands is that in which reclamations were made by associations of rayats on special terms made with Government. This variety of tenure is distinguished from the *shilotri* tenure proper by the term *kularg*. In *kularg khars* the tenants carry out repairs of embankments jointly, each having a share of the land and assessment recorded against his name.

II SOUTHERN KONKAN.

The Khoti Tenures.

58. In the Kolaba (excluding the talukas of Panvel and Karjat which were transferred from Thana to Kolaba in 1883 and 1891 respectively and which nonetheless still belong to what is called the Northern Konkan) and Ratnagiri Collectorates the survey tenure is quite the exception. It prevails generally in the two northern talukas of Kolaba, but in the remainder of that district and in the whole of Ratnagiri it is found only in those villages which happen to be Government property (*khalsa*) and in surveyed *khoti* villages where there are *dhara* lands and *kowli* lands held on new leases. In the northern part of Kolaba there are a few villages held on the *izafat* tenure already described. Otherwise the *khoti* tenure is the prevailing one, though there are a number of proprietary rights in all these villages independent of, and in some cases older than, those of the *khots*.

Its chief characteristics.

59. With regard to *khoti* tenure, its principal features are undisputed, or nearly so. Though most people believe the *khots* to have been at first, and not more than about 350 years ago, simply farmers holding on leases for the improvement of the country, yet it is now generally conceded that they must be considered as limited proprietors. Theoretically their position is very much that of Bengal zamindars without the permanent settlement, for it has never been doubted that they are liable to increase of assessment. But owing to the smallness to their estates and in many cases to the high assessment they have to pay, and to the fact that their villages having descended in most cases by the Hindu law of inheritance are held by a large number of co-sharers, it is much safer to ignore the superficial resemblance which exists between them and the zamindars. The chief undisputed points of this tenure are as follows :—

1st.—The right to hold their villages on payment, in instalments, of the lump assessment fixed on all the village lands by the Settlement Department, provided that, subject to certain rules under the Khoti Settlement Act I of 1880, the members of the *khoti vatan*, authorized so to do, agree on the nomination of a managing *khot* for the year. On failure of payment, or in the event of the members of the *vatan* being unable to agree on a nominee, the village is liable to attachment, but is restored on payment of any loss that may have been caused to Government by the default of the *khots* in addition to the fixed assessment. If such payment be not made within 12 years from the date of attachment the village is ordinarily held to have lapsed to Government.

2nd.—The right to lease land in which there are no rights of permanent occupancy at whatever rents they may arrange with their tenants.

3rd.—The right to collect customary rents from permanent occupants other than *dharekaris*. Under the Khoti Settlement Act I of 1880 rents in kind from such tenants can in certain circumstances be commuted into cash payments of definite multiples of the assessment.

4th.—The right to all lands which may lapse owing to the absence or failure (either temporary or permanent) of permanent occupants.

5th.—It is the duty of the *khots* to collect the assessment from all permanent occupants who are *dharekaris* (and therefore pay only survey assessment) without remuneration, but they receive assistance from Government as superior holders.

And origin.

60. The *khoti* tenure is said to have originated in the Subhedari of Dabhol, which extended from the Vashishti to the Devgad River, and which is nearly coterminous with the district occupied by the Chitpavan Brahmans. Certainly south of the Devgad River, though *khots* are still found, their powers are allowed to be much less than those of the *khots* farther north.

The Dharekari Tenure.

61. The other tenures in the Southern Konkan are, first, the *dharekari,* which differs but little from the *miras* tenure of the Deccan. The *dharekaris* pay only the survey assessment, which is liable to increase only at periodical

revisions of rates ordered by Government, and are now in no respect dependent on the *khots,* though formerly no doubt they paid various cesses to them. They have the same rights of alienation as *mirasdars,* and, wherever the survey settlement has taken place the *dhara* tenure has been merged into the survey tenure.

In the Khed and Dapoli Talukas of the Ratnagiri Collectorate there are a number of proprietors under the names of *dupatkari, pavvini dupatkari,* and *daspatkari,* which are known under Khoti Act as *quasi-dharekaris.* These, however, differ only from the *dharekaris* in that their payments to the *khot,* though fixed, are somewhat higher than the survey assessment, their rights in their land being in all respects similar to those of the *dharekaris.*

Vatandar Kuls.

62. There are also a certain number of occupants generally known as *vatandar kuls,* or under the Khoti Act as occupancy tenants, who, it is acknowledged, cannot be dispossessed by the *khots,* and whose rights are heritable, but not transferable, unless they can prove that such right of transfer has been exercised independently of the consent of the *khot* within the thirty years ending with the revenue year 1861-65. They continue to hold their lands conditionally on the payment of the rent from time to time lawfully due by them to the *khot.* These are supposed to be the descendants of those cultivators who held land in the villages before the *khots* obtained their grants. The remainder of the cultivators where the survey has not been introduced held their lands on payment of a proportion of the crop, the proportion being 1/2, 1/3 or 1/4 according to the customs of the village and the nature of the crop. Under the Khoti Act all these tenants other than occupancy tenants continue to hold their lands subject to such terms and conditions as are agreed upon between the *khot* and themselves, and in the absence of specific agreement they pay rent to the *khot* at the same rates as are paid by occupancy tenants in that village.

Arrangements under Survey Settlement.

63. The survey settlement has substituted for this proportionate payment in kind a fixed cash assessment as the Government share, and under the Khoti Act the rent payable to the *khot* by privileged occupants is as follows :–

1. By a *dharekari* the Survey assessment of his land.

2. By a *quasi-dharekari* the survey assessment of his land, and, in addition thereto, amounts of grain or money respectively set forth in schedule annexed to the Khoti Act.

3. By an occupancy tenant such fixed amount, whether in money or in kind, as may have been agreed upon between the *khot* and the said tenant, or on the expiry of the term for which such agreement shall have been made, or, if no such agreement have been made, such fixed share of the gross annual produce, not exceeding one-half in the case of rice land, nor one-third in the case of *varkas* land, and such share, if any, of the produce of the fruit trees on he said tenants' lands as shall be determined to be the customary amount hitherto paid by the occupancy tenants in that village.

Reclamation leases.

64. Considerable tracts of land on the coast or along the sides of the larger creeks have been granted on reclamation leases. These lands were formerly either salt marsh lands or sandy shore above high-water mark, the former being made into rice fields and the latter into cocoanut gardens. The leases in most cases specify that the land is held on special rates only until the survey shall be introduced. After the introduction of the survey such lands are, therefore, generally held on the ordinary survey tenure.

INAM TENURES.

65. An enquiry into the validity of titles to alienated holdings was tentatively commenced in 1843 in one or two Collectorates of the Southern Maratha Country and, in consequence of the discovery of unauthorized and fraudulent alienations, was in 1851 developed into an organized investigation, which under the title of the Inam Commission or Alienation Department extended to the whole of the Presidency. The Commission at first instituted detailed enquiries into the different titles submitted to it, but after a time this procedure was found inconveniently slow and two Acts were passed (Act II of 1863 for the Deccan, Khandesh and Southern Maratha Country, Act VII of 1863 for Gujarat and the Konkan) giving person who claimed exemption from the payment of full Government

revenue the option of avoiding a scrutiny of their title by the payment of quit-rent. This quickened operations and by 1873 the bulk of the work was finished. (For a fuller account of the proceedings of the Inam Commission see the Narrative of the Bombay Inam Commission, Bombay Government Selection No. CXXXII.)

66. For all practical purposes the tenures on which alienated holdings are now continued may be reduced to the following four principal classes :–

(1) Political. (2) Service. (3) Religious. (4) Personal.

Political.

67. Under the head of "political tenure" are included political pensions and what are known as *jaghirs* and *saranjams*. Grants of this description are to be found almost exclusively in the Collectorates of the Southern Division and in the Nasik and Khandesh districts of the Central Division. *Jaghir* and *saranjam*, though the former is a term of Mahomedan and the latter of Maratha origin, are understood to have similar characteristics, having been originally grants by the State for the performance of civil or military duties, or for the maintenance of the personal dignity of nobles and high officials. Under the British Government, however, no such distinctions are preserved ; and the *jaghirs* and *saranjams* now in existence have with some exceptions, where service is commuted into money payments, no condition of service attached to them, but are continued hereditarily or for one or more generations on political considerations alone.

Service Tenure.

68. The assignments of land or of money, held on what is known as "service tenure" are grants which impose duties on the holders. Such grants were originally made with a view to ensure the performance of certain services in each district and for each village. As no change has been introduced in the constitution of village communities, village service is still rendered in return for the grant of land or of money. But by the introduction of the revenue survey and the organization of a stipendiary police, the former system of district service became obsolete, and the duties of the holders of district service assignments ceased. An arrangement has accordingly been introduced under which the holders of such assignments

become, on repaying a portion of their emoluments, free from all liability to serve.

Religious Endowment.

69. Holdings granted by the former native governments for the support of Hindu and Mahomedan religious or charitable institutions, such as temples, mosques, etc., and continued under British Government, come under the head "religious tenure". Such holdings are tenable in perpetuity, or so long as the institution for maintenance of which they were originally granted or are now held may be in existence. They are entered in the public accounts under the head of *devasthan.*

Personal Tenure.

70. The head of personal tenure comprises that vast body of holdings which, though alienated by the former government under various denominations, have been continued without any distinguishing peculiarity simply as personal *inams* or unconditional grants enjoyed by individuals. Under the operations of the Summary Settlement Acts (Bombay II and VII of 1863) and other subsidiary settlements, personal *inams* are for the most part continuable in perpetuity, and are transferable without any restriction whatsoever. Those, however, which do not come under the summary settlement mentioned above, do not carry with them the right of adoption.

LAND TENURES AND LAND REVENUE ADMINISTRATION IN THE TOWN AND ISLAND OF BOMBAY.

General history.

71. The island of Bombay was ceded to the Crown of England by the Crown of Portugal by virtue of the 11th Article of the Treaty of Marriage between King Charles II of England and the Infanta Catherine of Portugal, dated 25th June 1661. The actual cession, however, did not take place till November 1664, when Humphrey Cooke was practically forced to accede to treaty with the Portuguese on such terms as they would grant. By this convention Cooke renounced on the part of England all pretensions to the dependencies of Bombay and accepted the cession of Bombay itself under

certain conditions. Cooke's convention was, however, subsequently disavowed by the Crown as being contrary to the terms of the treaty and for a time the collection of all Land Revenue on behalf of the Crown appears to have been held in abeyance.

72. In 1668, the Crown of England considering Bombay to be an unprofitable possession transferred it to the East India Company by Letters Patent, dated 27th March 1668. By this Charter the King granted the Port and Island of Bombay to the East India Company in perpetuity, with all the rights, profits and territories thereof, to be held "in free and common socage as of the manor of East Greenwich, on payment of the annual rent of £10." The Company were neither to sell nor to part with the Island.

73. In the next year it was proclaimed that all acquisition of land by individuals prior to 1661 proceeded from imperfect right, but this proclamation appears to have caused so much discontent among the landholders that the Company instructed their President, Mr Aungier, to forego inquiry into title and in consultation with the landholders to fix a lump sum as their rent payment. In accordance with these instructions Mr Aungier drew up an agreement with the representative landholders on the 12th of November 1672. This was confirmed by all parties concerned at a convocation held in 1674.

74. This convention though not signed and ratified by the East India Company has been regarded valid and acted upon. It gave the inhabitants security in their possessions, Government reserving the right to take them for building "cities, towns or fortifications" on reasonable satisfaction to the proprietors. It recognized all land when in occupation as private property subject to Military Service. All uncultivated and waste land, excepting such as by the constitution of the Island was as appendage of the cultivated portion as pasturage ground remained the property of the Company.

75. From 1674 onwards, as the population increased, the Company's lands were proportionately assigned for their accommodation. The Crown Lands were let out for cultivation to the *kunbis,* the produce being equally divided between the Company and the tenants.

76. People were encouraged to stop breaches by the grant of leases of unreclaimed ground for a number of years at a small quit-rent with the

stipulation that they should reclaim the lands within seven years. Marshy lands were similarly drained and rendered fit for cultivation.

77. In 1718, a quit-rent was imposed to reimburse the Company for the charges incurred in building fortifications. This tax may be said to have substituted a money charge for the liability to Military Service reserved under Aungier's convention of 1674. In 1731, this quit-rent was modified. By a resolution of Council, dated 3rd December 1731, the English inhabitants were directed "to pay the same quit-rent for their houses that they had hitherto been assessed in, but for such ground as they might have taken in since the building of their houses or may hereafter take in they shall pay an additional quit-rent of 6 reas[4] for each square yard but be free of ground rent and all natives or black inhabitants to pay for the ground they occupy or should hereafter occupy a quit-rent of 6 reas and a ground rent of 5 reas for each square yard."

78. Since the conclusion of Aungier's convention the lands do not appear to have been allotted on any established system. In 1733 attempts were made to introduce leases for definite terms on the ground that "little regard has been paid by the inhabitants within and without the walls to an order of the 3rd of December 1731", but these attempts proved to be fruitless.

79. Meanwhile efforts were being made to reclaim land from the sea and lands so recovered were assigned to individuals at a nominal rental on condition of their improving them. These lands were known as Salt Batty Grounds. In 1740 a publication was issued giving notice that Government was willing to receive proposals for farming lands in parcels or as a whole. The lands were let at 4 reas a burga and parcels were allotted to different *kunbis*. This rent was raised to 6 reas a burga in 1744 and further to 9 reas a burga in 1748.

80. On the 3rd of January 1758, with a view to reimburse the "prodigious expenses which the Company had incurred in increasing the fortifications and the works on the Island for the security of the inhabitants in general", a tax of 10 per cent was ordered to be levied on the produce of all the landed estates or garden lands belonging to the inhabitants of the Island.

81. The chief events in the land administration in Bombay between

1760 and 1800 were the survey proposals made in the year 1772, the vesting of the Mazagaon estate in the Company by virtue of a decree from the Mayor's Court, dated 10th February 1758, and the subsequent leasing out of the estates in small parcels and the *inam* grant of lands in Parel to the Wedia family in 1783 on the recommendation of Sir Edward Hughes, K.B., Commander-in-Chief of His Majesty's Ships in India, for the very important services rendered by the Parsi Master-builders Manekji Lowji Wadia and Bomanji Lowji Wadia.

82. In 1803 Government directed that the "Engineer's limit" should be declared to the extent of 800 yards from the Fort and issued an order to that effect to the Commanding Officer of the Forces. A general proclamation was also issued on the 13th January 1804 ordering the clearance. The inhabitants displaced from within this 800 yards limit were accommodated in the area subsequently known as New Town or Kamatipura. The allotments of lands made in this New Town appear to have been on the same terms as in the Old Town, viz., on the payment of rent of 11 reas per square yard without any leases for any definite period of time.

83. In the year 1821 another *inam* grant was made to Nowroji Jamshedji Wadia of lands situated in Parel, Naigam and Sion. The Sion lands were, however, exchanged by Mr. Wadia for certain lands in the Island of Salsette in 1854.

84. From 1841 for nearly a decade a great contest was maintained between the Honourable Company and owners of the Salt Batty lands in consequence of Government having resumed certain plots of ground near the Race Course for the purpose of stacking hay, without paying any compensation to the occupants thereof, Government conceiving the ground to be the property of the Company and the occupants to have been merely the tenants-at-will, the occupants themselves setting up a claim of adverse possession against the Company. As a result of this contest the right of the Company over all the Salt Batty lands excepting some reserved for public roads and tanks were extinguished in favour of the individuals who held the same respectively as the immediate rent-payers to the Company subject to the rents then severally payable in respect of them and the Foras Act, No. VI of 1851, was passed embodying the above conditions.

85. In 1861 Government appointed a Committee to consider the subject of the land fortification in the Island of Bombay. This Committee recommended the demolition of the existing ramparts and the distribution of the ground so set free in building allotments. The suggestion was accepted by the Secretary of State in June 1862. After reserving a number of sites required for public buildings most of the rest were sold by public auction on leases for 999 years.

86. In 1885 the third *inam* grant was made to Khan Bahadur Jamshedji Dhunjibhai Wadia for his valuable services in His Majesty's Dockyard, about 300 acres of land situated at Dharavi and Sion being given rent-free in perpetuity.

87. In 1891 Government considering the general inadequacy of the ground rent levied on Government lands in Bombay, appointed a Committee to consider how the assessments could be raised so as to bear a fair proportion to the increased value of land obtaining. On the recommendations of this Committee Government adopted the policy of granting leases of 99 years in the case of lands where for general considerations architectural conditions were considered necessary and for 50 years renewable for a further term of 50 years in the more outlying parts where no conditions in excess of the Municipal Building Rules might be necessary. The basis on which the rent is calculated is a four per cent return on the market value of the land. This policy is the present Land Revenue policy of Government.

88. The Land Revenue Administration in the City of Bombay is administered under Act II of 1876 as amended by Act III of 1900.

Surveys.

89. No records of any authentic survey are available before 1811 although the first mention of survey was made so long ago as 1670-71 and many proposals to this effect were made from time to time since the cession of the Island. The survey which commenced in 1811 and concluded in 1827 was superintended in turn by Lieutenant Hawkins, Captain Dickinson and Lieutenant Tate. The primary object to this survey was for the purpose of ascertaining the number of cocoanut, brab and other trees in each part and the names of the proprietors, but very soon after the

commencement the survey operations were extended so as to define not only the boundaries and extent of the Company's property but of that of the inhabitants in general and to specify the nature of the tenures under which all lands in the Island were held. During this survey southern half of the Island was minutely surveyed and registers showing various details were compiled. The northern half was only topographically surveyed and only the total areas held under the different tenures were denoted in the map. The cost of this survey was Rs. 1,63,000.

90. Between 1844 and 1859 various parts of the Island were surveyed departmentally. These surveys though of considerable use could not be incorporated in the Revenue Survey, as the Traverse points had never been accurately laid down in connection with the trigonometrical stations of the Great Trigonometrical Survey.

91. The next revenue survey of the Island, the record of which for the purpose of the City of Bombay Land Revenue Act is taken to be *prima facie* evidence, was made during the years 1865 to 1872 under the superintendence of Colonel Laughton. Plans principally on a scale of 40 feet to an inch for the southern half and 100 feet to an inch for the northern half of the Island were prepared together with the registers showing the area, the name of he occupant and the tenure of every holding. Boundary marks were fixed to demarcate the outlines of the properties and levels at every 300 feet along the principal roads have been recorded. The area of the Island as determined by this survey was 22 square miles, 105 acres and 4,149 square yards. The cost of this survey was Rs. 3,13,062.

Existing Tenures.

92. The following are the tenures existing in Bombay :–

1. Pension and Tax.
2. Quit and Ground Rent.
3. Toka.
4. Foras.
5. Inam.
6. Leasehold.
7. Sanadi.

8. Newly Assessed, and
9. Tenancy-at-will.

(a) *Pension and Tax.*— The term 'pension' takes its origin from the Portuguese word 'Pencao,' which means a bonus or premium paid for the fee simple on the compromise of a doubtful tenure. The payment of "Pension" dates from Aungier's agreement of 1672 which commuted in consideration of the payment every year of 20,000 xeraphins (Rs. 13,850), whatever rights the Company possessed over the estates which were in a state of cultivation and which were in consequence acknowledged by that instrument to be freehold property. The "Tax", of 10 per cent on the produce of all landed estates, was introduced from the year 1758 to meet "the prodigious expenses" of fortications and works for the security of the inhabitants, but it did not alter the original character. There is no fixed rate per square yard on these lands ; the rents are "lump sums" bearing no uniform proportion to the quantity or value of the land and in many cases give rates as low as a fraction of a pie per square yard. An explanation of the very low rates and the irregularity in the scale is to be found in the fact that 'pension' was originally levied on garden or rice land and the "tax" was levied on the produce calculated at so much per wheel used for irrigation.

The cess on these lands is not subject to revision and is redeemable on payment of the amount of 30 years' rent. Up to 1st April 1912, not less than 2,558 holdings had been redeemed by their proprietors.

Pension and Tax lands are found in the Fort, Girgaum, Malabar Hill, Cumballa Hills and the Mahim Woods. Their area as recorded in Colonel Laughton's survey is 2,551 acres.

(b) *Quit and Ground rent.*—'Quit rent', as its name implies, meant freedom from liability to military service. It was established in 1718 and was money substitute in lieu of the military service reserved by Aungier's convention. The original quit rent does not appear to have been fixed on any uniform system. It was at first imposed on every description of property within the Town Wall but was afterwards extended to properties beyond the walls. By an order of 1731 the quit rent was equalized and fixed at 6 reas per square yard for the English inhabitants, while the Native inhabitants had to pay a "ground" rent of 5 reas per square yard in addition to the "quit rent" of 6 reas per square yard. This distinction accounts for the fact that some properties in the Fort pay quit rent only and others quit and ground rent. The properties in the Town pay quit and ground rent.

Like Pension and Tax lands, the cess on these lands, if less than Rs. 10 per annum, can be redeemed on payment of 30 years' rent. The number of holdings so redeemed by 1st April 1912 was 402.

These lands are situated in Fort, Old and New Towns and in parts of Colaba and Mazagaon. Their area as shown in Laughton's Survey is 973 acres.

(c) *Toka.*—These lands derive their name from the word *toka*, which means a share of the produce. The *toka* lands comprise the greater part of the Company's villages of Parel, Bomnolly, Naigam, Wadalla, Matoonga, Sion and Dharavi. The right of the proprietorship of Government of these lands is founded on the fact that all uncultivated and waste land excepting such as by the constitution of the Island was an appendage of the cultivated portion as pasturage ground was at the date of Aungier's convention. Crown land and was as time went on let out for cultivation. A considerable area under cultivation situated at Sion, Wadalla and Parel, belonging to the Society of Jesuits, was seized and confiscated in 1692 and was similarly let out. The *kunbis* who cultivated the lands paid half the produce to Government *in kind.*

Between 1751 and 1800 the villages were farmed by public auction, one of the condition being that the farmer should not collect from the Kunbis more than the usual *toka*. The farming system was however abolished in consequence of the constant disputes between the farmers and the *kunbis* as well as on account of the alienations made by the latter from the time to time. After its abolition the *kunbis* paid their *toka* directly into the Collector's office, but commuted into money payment the rate of commutation being fixed every year according to the market. Since 1837, however the rate remained fixed at Rs. 20 per moora[5] of rice. In 1879 the rents on these lands were revised and fixed at rates varying from $^1/_3$ pie to 1 pie per square yard per annum. These rates have been guaranteed for 50 years. The next revision will take place in 1929.

The early history of this tenure shows that the lands could be resumed by Government, the *kunbis* or tenants who cultivated the lands being removable at pleasure. But the aspect was changed by the introduction of the revised assessment of 1879.

The total area to *toka* lands ascertained by Laughton's Survey was 1,489 acres.

(d) *Foras* or Salt Batty lands are lands reclaimed from the sea. They derive their name from the Portuguese word "Foro", the meaning of which is rent. The 'old' salt batty lands were recovered from the sea by means of the vellard between Sion and Mahim : the 'new' salt batty grounds by means of the Hornby Vellard. These lands were originally let free of rent in 1703 for 35 years. In 1738 they were again re-let free of rent. In 1740 a low rent of 4 reas a burga was levied. In 1744 it was increased to 6 and in 1748 to 9 reas a burga. The right to alter the rent was challenged by the holders. In 1805 the question of the respective rights of the Company and the holders was put to a legal test before the Recorder, Sir James Mackintosh. Though the verdict was in favour of the Company the rights of the Company still remained an open question and a long series of disputes led to the passing of the Foras Act No. VI of 1851 under which these lands were enfranchised as freehold lands.

Foras lands are situated at Byculla, Parel, Worli, Mahim, Matoonga and Dharavi. Their area as given in Laughton's Survey was 3,408 acres.

Like quit and ground rent lands the cess on these lands, if less than 10 Rs. a year, is redeemable on payment of 30 years' rent. Up to 1st April 1912, 978 holdings have been so redeemed.

(e) *Inam.—Inam* lands are situated at Naigam, Parel, and to the north-west of Sion Fort. Small portions lie near Dadar and Dharavi. The grants were made to the Lowji (Wadia) family in 1783, 1821 and 1885 on account of their excellent services as ship-builders for the Bombay Government Dockyard.

The *inami* lands pay no assessment to Government.

The area is 1,181 acres.

(f) *Leasehold.*—Leasehold lands are held all over the Island under various condition and terms of 21, 50, 99 or 999 years.

The 21 years' leases are generally renewable some at revised rents and some at the same rents but on payment of small fines.

Some of the 50 years' leases are also renewable every 50 years at revised rents but some are renewable for one further period of 50 years only.

A major portion of the 99 years' leases are non-renewable the others being only once renewable. The Mazagaon leases for 99 years are renewable at revised rents.

Some of these 21, 50 and 99 years' leases contain a clause reserving to Government the power to resume the lands on 6 months' notice, if required for a public purpose, on payment to the lessee of the value of the buildings and improvements on the land.

The 999 years' leases are of course non-renewable.

The area at present under lease in Bombay is 462 acres.

(g) *Sanadi.*—The sanads cover a period of 40 years from 1814 to 1854 during which 828 *sanads* were issued. The *sanadi* lands are mostly situated in the New Town. The *sanads* for land in Colaba, which were 188 in number and were all granted in 1815 were cancelled and the lands resumed in the years 1823 and 1866 when the limits of the Colaba Cantonment were extended.

These *sanads* are of two kinds. Under the one the holder is a mere tenant-at-will the land being resumable by Government at pleasure. Under the other the lands can be resumed, if required for public purposes only, on 6 months' previous notice being given and on payment on the value of buildings and improvements to be determined by a committee appointed by Government.

The area held under *sanads* at present is 127 acres.

(h) *Newly Assessed.*—This tenure has its origin in Bombay Act II of 1876. It comprises lands assessed by the Collector of Bombay under Section 8 of the said Act. A general revision of assessment on these lands was made in 1899 and the new rents then fixed were guaranteed for 50 years in some cases and 30 years in others. The assessment is liable to revision at the end of the period of guarantee. These lands are situated mostly in Naigam, Dharavi and Parel. The extent of these lands is 134 acres.

(i) *Tenancy-at-will.*—This term needs little explanation. The lands are granted under agreements which may be terminated by one month's notice on either side. The tenants have no right to build permanent structures on the lands so let to them. These lands are scattered all over the Island. Their present area is 13 acres.

The total area of the Island at present is 22 square miles, 178 acres and 4,736 square yards. The annual revenue is Rs. 2,83,482.

Land Tenures in Sind.

Character of the present tenures.

93. The tenures on which land is now held in the Province of Sind are of a comparatively simple character. Doubtless in the ancient times of Hindu Nationality, as under Brahman dynasties, the same complexity of land tenure prevailed in Sind as in other Provinces of India ; but as successive waves of Mahomedan invasion and conquest passed over the Province, and when finally the bulk of the population had, forcibly or otherwise, been converted to Islamism, the ancient institutions must have gradually decayed, and given way to those brought in by the conquering race. The village system which is supposed, and probably with truth, to have once flourished in Sind, has shared in the common decay. The group of families (Raj) acknowledging generally someone head, the Wadero or headman among Mahomedans, and the Mukhi or chiefman among Hindus, still survive, but all trace of an organization for administrative purposes, all trace of hereditary village officers with assigned duties and remuneration, has long since passed away. Tapedars or Village Accountants and supervising Tapedars have been appointed everywhere, but none are hereditary. The system which was at first introduced into the Thar and Parkar District and a few other localities, of granting *sherees* or small patches of rent-free land, to heads of villages which are continued to the heir, if well-behaved, or resumed if service in the suppression of crime is not properly rendered, has recently been extended to the whole Province and grants are being made on the recommendations of the District Officers. Villages Pagis or trackers are engaged in the pay of the Police Department, but have no hereditary claim to service.

99. In "Revision Settlement" the survey numbers were formed of small size, and full assessment having been placed on each, the zamindar could under certain rules allow his fields to lie fallow and yet retain his lien on them without payment of assessment for the years during which the land was left fallow. If, however, he elected to cultivate when the lands ordinarily should lie fallow he became liable to full assessment upon each survey number which he cultivated.

100. "Irrigational Settlements" have now been applied to all talukas on the lapse of the term of original or revision settlements. One of the defects in original or revision settlements was the attempt, which entirely failed, to classify the land and water-supply, and assess the revenue proportionately. The classification of the land is now abandoned, and the assessment is based entirely on the mode of irrigation adopted, which varies in different talukas and in different groups of villages. This has the merit of leaving it to the farmer to choose the best method of irrigation, season by season, according to the height of the river and the water-supply available. Under this system also the occupants are liable for the full assessment on each survey number when cultivated, but the size of the numbers has been reduced so as to render it possible for each number to be cultivated with one pair of bullocks. The occupants are also permitted to retain their rights over all their lands when lying fallow ; but, to prevent abuse of the privilege, an assessment is charged at least once in five years. Practically, assessment is now levied on cultivation only, to the great benefit of the zamindars and of the revenue. The full rates are high, but in cases calamities such as locusts or floods, remissions are liberally given.

There are 55 talukas at present under "Irrigational settlements." In the Desert of Thar and Parkar (4 talukas), and in the extensive hilly tract adjoining Baluchistan, which is treated as a *mahal,* special arrangements exist for levying a very light assessment, no fixed settlement having been made.

101. There are few tenant rights in existence in Sind. The smaller zamindars cultivate for themselves and the larger through yearly tenants who almost always pay the superior a proportion of the crop, not cash, for the privilege of cultivating, the zamindar being responsible for the assessment. The share paid varies from ¼ to ½, according to the difficulty

and expense of cultivating : the practice of leasing land on cash rent is growing slowly.

Hereditary tenancy.

102. In Upper Sind, in the Rohri Sub-division on the left bank of the river, a species of tenancy exists which requires special notice. This is locally termed, "maurusi haripan," that is "hereditary tenancy or ploughmanship." It is somewhat similar to the *aforamento* prevailing in parts of Portugal and the *beklemreght* in the Province of Groningen, described by M. de Lavaleye, in his article on the Land system of Belgium and Holland in the 1st volume of the Cobden Club Essays. The hereditary tenant pays a quit-rent under the names "lapo," "zamindari," "malkano," "tobro" or "deh kharch" to the proprietor. This quit-rent differs in different villages and even on different crops grown, but seldom exceeds 6 or 8 annas per acre and cannot be enhanced. The settlement of the Government demand is made directly with the tenant and he is, in the land registers, entered as an occupant, the amount of quit-rent payable to the proprietor being also recorded. The right of occupancy is transferable, and in short, is as complete and secure as possible. Up till 1894 the original zamindar was not considered entitled to any assistance under the Land Revenue Code in the recovery of the "lapo" except through the Civil Court, but in November of that year Government announced that they had no objection to such assistance being given in making the recovery from persons whose liability to pay it had been recorded in the Settlement Registers or established by decree or whose title was directly derived from such persons.

103. Besides the "maurusi haris" there exist what are styled "2nd class haris." These are the real tenants of the zamindar, to whom they pay "lapo" and also a proportion in accordance with the custom of the country, of the crop as rent, and as long as they do so they cannot be ousted from their tenancies. In these cases the zamindar pays the assessment to Government.

104. The zamindari system referred to in the last two paragraphs is supposed to have originated in the following manner :—

Under the former Native rule certain individuals were granted the privilege of collecting certain fees on the revenue accruing from the lands of a tract of country, in consideration of their using their influence in bringing it under cultivation and collecting the revenue on the same. They attracted cultivators probably advanced them money on account of the expenses of cultivation, afforded them the protection necessary in the then unsettled state of the country, and aided in the collection of the revenue ; and the "lapo" was the consideration they received in payment of their services ; the "deh kharch" (or village expenses) was probably an extra cess which they levied from their cultivators to meet the cost of entertaining Government officials, guests, etc., etc., and the "malkano" and "zamindari" were other names for the above or similar benevolences. They all, however, now have one common meaning, viz., a charge on cultivation, payable sometimes in kind, sometimes in cash, which the zamindar is, by custom, entitled to receive from the cultivators. The maurusi haris are probably the representatives of the cultivators originally introduced by the zamindars into the deh ; and the 2nd class "haris" the descendants of those who cultivated the zamindars' private lands as yearly tenants, but who, from long enjoyment of their tenancies, have at last obtained from the zamindar the privilege of holding them permanently on payment of the battai (or share-in-kind) rate customary in the district.

105. Till about thirty years ago the zamindars of Rohri claimed the right of lapo on all waste lands brought under cultivation in settled districts, but under a decision of the Judge of Shikarpur, it has been ruled that this right does not exist, and that they are entitled to it only from lands which were under cultivation at the time of introduction of the survey settlement.

106. The very large estates which formerly prevailed in this Province, the property of Muhammadan zamindars, were in danger of gradually being broken up owing to the combination of many untoward circumstances, partly to their not understanding the original settlements and being forced to pay on all the holdings that they claimed as their own, whether cultivated or not, partly to unthriftiness, coupled with the hardness of the law for the recovery of debt and interest. Improved settlements and irrigation, the growth of intelligence and two Encumbered Estates Acts, (1) Act XIV of 1876 as amended by Act XX of 1881 which saved many large holdings and (2) Act XX of 1896 as amended by Act II of 1906 which is in full operation at the present moment, have stayed or retarded the evil. The relief so afforded by the Encumbered Estates Act has been supplemented by the Court of Wards Act which was passed in year 1905

with the object of enabling the executive, without the introduction of chapters III, V, VI, VII and certain sections of other chapters of the Deccan Agriculturists' Relief Act has also resulted in great benefit to such of the landed proprietors as have not received or cannot receive protection under the Encumbered Estates Acts. In former years Hindu zamindars were rare in Sind ; now they are to be found in thousands, partly owing to their having foreclosed mortgaged estates and partly because they find it a profitable investment of capital. Fresh grants of land to the improvident classes are, however (since the passing of the Bombay Land Revenue Code Amendment Act), now for the most part made on the condition that they shall not in any way transfer the land except with the permission of the Collector.

Rent-free tenures.

107. The rent-free or partially rent-free tenures comprise Jagirs, charitable grants (*khairats*) and garden grants. Jagirs are ranged under four classes, determined by the period at which the original alienation was made. Thus, the first class comprises alienation granted prior to the accession of the Talpur Dynasty, A.D. 1783 ; the second comprises alienations granted in the earlier years, and the third and fourth those granted in the middle and concluding period respectively of that dynasty. Jagirs of the 1st class are permanently alienated, those of the 2nd class are alienated subject to partial resumption and in certain cases to a payment in lieu thereof on succession, and those of the 3rd and 4th classes eventually lapse wholly to Government. Besides these there are lands permanently alienated to what are known as the four Great Talpur Families. In these, succession has been regulated on principles similar to those laid down for second class Jagirs, but in settling the claims of the four families, fixed rules were departed from in individual cases with a view to a more equitable and liberal treatment of chiefs whose claims called for special consideration.

Patadari grants.

108. A distinct class of permanent alienation is found in the neighbourhood of Shikarpur, namely, what are termed "Patadari grants." These are said to have been originally grants under leases (*pata*) of reduced assessment, made by the Afghan Government to Pathan settlers in North Sind. However this may be, they since acquired the form of assignment of

a fixed proportion of revenue on certain lands, and as such they have been recognised and confirmed by our Government. The revenue alienated under this head amounts to Rs. 28,317 (1911-1912).

Charitable grants.

109. The *khairats* or charitable grants principally to Sayads, involve the alienation of a revenue of Rs. 2,81,249 (1911-1912). These also are permanent alienations, having been so recognised by the British on the ground of length of enjoyment.

Frontier grants.

110. Besides these ordinary alienations there are large tracts of land in the Upper Sind Frontier District, granted rent-free to Baluch chiefs and their tribesmen. Some of these grants are in perpetuity, others for life but all subject to good behaviour and loyalty, also to the payment of *hakabo* (water-rate) or any other local cess legally imposed on them. The area thus granted amounts to 33,514 acres in round figures.

111. The minor alienations are of three kinds—

(1) Garden grants.

(2) Huri grants.

(3) Seri or village service grants.

Garden grants.

112. Under both Afghan and Baluch rule in Sind much liberality was shown in remission of revenue on land brought under garden cultivation. Garden grants are found scattered all over the province.

They are divided into two classes—

(1) Wholly rent-free.

(2) Paying reduced assessment subject to certain stipulations. These lands are transferable, and being valuable property, are frequently sold and mortgaged. The extent of land thus alienated is 2,236 acres.

Huri grants

113. Owing to the tree-less character of he country throughout the greater part of Sind, Mr. Frere, Commissioner in Sind, in 1858, in exercise

of the authority then vested in the Commissioner, sanctioned the grant of lands free of rent for the purpose of growing trees. This concession, which has since been continued, is not really of the nature of a land alienation ; only the rent due on the land is foregone so long as they are used for the purpose for which they are granted. If any land so granted is cultivated with crops, full assessment is levied. These grants are transferable, the transferee being bound by the conditions of the grant. The area thus granted in only about 16,015 acres.

Seri grants.

114. The Seri grant is generally made for the promotion of cultivation and for service in the prevention and detection of crime, in the collection of Government demands, etc. These grants are personal and for one life only, though continuable to successors. The area granted rent-free is 11,291 acres.

APPENDIX I.

Revenue Survey and Assessment : Exposition of the policy of Government in regard to — Protection from Assessment of the increased value of land due to improvement made by the occupant.

No. 2619.

REVENUE DEPARTMENT

Bombay Castle, 26th March 1884.

RESOLUTION of GOVERNMENT.

His Excellency in Council desires in this Resolution to state the principles by which Government regulates its action in regard to that portion of the produce of land which by custom belongs to the State, that is to the public, and forms part of the public revenues devoted to the cost of governing the country.

2. The law is contained in the Bombay Land Revenue Code (Act V of 1879) which repealed and took the place of the Bombay Survey and Settlement Act I of 1865. Under Section 214 of Act V of 1879 arc framcd rules for carrying out the purposes of the Act which after publication have the force of law.

3. By Section 69 of Act V the right of Government to mines and mineral products in all unalienated land is expressly reserved wherever it has not become vested in the occupant of such land.

4. Section 37 enacts that "the bed of rivers, streams, nalas, lakes and tanks, and all canals and water-courses and all standing and flowing water . . . which are not the property of individuals, or of aggregates of persons legally capable of holding property, and except in so far as any right of such persons may be established in or over the same, and except as may be otherwise provided in any law for the time being in force, are, and are hereby declared to be, with all right in or over the same, or appertaining thereto, the property of Government."

5. Section 55 of Act V gives power to fix rates for the use of water the right to which vests in Government. The Bombay Irrigation Act VII of 1879 gives power to charge rates for the use of canal water. But in these cases the rates are not part of the assessment of land to the ordinary land revenue, the water being such as is capable of treatment as a distinct marketable commodity the property of Government and purchasable for agricultural uses.

6. These rates being left aside, there remains the assessment of the ordinary land revenue according to the productive quality and inherent advantages of each plot of ground known as a survey number.

7. By Section 73 of Act V the right of occupancy of land is declared an heritable and transferable property and by Section 68 an occupant under a survey settlement is entitled to the use and occupancy of his land in perpetuity, conditionally on the payment of the amounts due on accounts of the land revenue for the same. It is manifest then that the security of the tenure depends on the manner in which the assessment of the land revenue is regulated.

8. Section 95 of Act V gives power to the Governor in Council to direct the survey of any land with a view to the settlement of the ordinary land revenue and to declare the assessment fixed for a term of years (Section 102). The Governor in Council may (Section 106) at any time direct a fresh revenue survey or any operation subsidiary thereto, but the assessments cannot be enhanced until the original term of settlement has expired.

9. At the second or "revision" survey settlement, the assessment fixed at the first or "original" survey settlement may be altered partly by correction of the survey record or measurement and classification, and partly with regard to the increased value of the land from a rise in agricultural profits.

10. When the survey record has been made correct, it remains an authoritative and sufficient standard of the relative value of survey numbers or fields, and the first reason for a revision survey ceases to exist. The second reason is permanent, because agricultural profits are always subject to increase and decrease. But this part of the revision of assessment may be carried out without the employment of a Department of Survey when the survey record is once complete.

11. The completion of the survey record therefore by revision where it is now imperfect is one operation which will improve the position of the survey occupant, by putting an end to such disturbance and uncertainty as are inseparable from the remeasurement and reclassification of soils.

12. Revision has hitherto been undertaken only when an original settlement period expires. If this practice were maintained the operation would be greatly protected and the highly skilled Survey establishments would be dissipated for want of full-time employment. It has therefore been resolved that the completion of the survey record should be carried out at once with the full strength of present establishments, and it is estimated that in this way field operations of the survey in this Presidency may be completed within a period of eight years. Current settlements will remain unaffected until their term expires, as is stipulated by Section 106, Act V : "no enhancement of assessment shall take effect till the expiration of the period previously fixed" for the currency of a settlement by the Governor in council under Section 102.

13. Thus far the duration of revision operations. Next as to their scope. The policy of this Government has always been opposed to the remeasurement and reclassification of land in revision survey beyond what is absolutely necessary to obtain a correct survey record. The Governor in Council has therefore insisted that before any reclassification of soil is permitted, the reasons should be fully explained by the Survey Department and that no such operation should be commenced without the express

sanction of Government. It has been found, however, that in some districts a partial or even a complete resurvey and revaluation was inevitable. The reason of this is that in the first years of the Revenue Survey the work was too imperfect to be accepted as a standard. The classification of soils adjudged to be culturable was faulty. The value of the richer soils was under-estimated and that of the poorer soils over-estimated, and the extremes of the scale were not adjusted to the difference in productive capacity. It was found on revision that to obtain a just standard of relative value it was necessary to raise the better soils and to lower the poorer soils about one class, or 2 annas in the rupee scale. Again, the appreciation of the vast area then lying out of cultivation was rough and indiscriminating, so that large plots of easily cultivable land were thrown into survey numbers and left unassessed under the name of *pot-kharab.*

14. Therefore since the commencement of operations of revision in the Poona District in 1867-68 it has been incumbent on the Government, in the interest of the public revenues, to sanction for each tract brought under revision such extent of revaluation as was proved to be necessary, amounting in some tracts to a partial remeasurement and reclassification and in others to measurement and classification *de novo.* As the early settlements have nearly all expired, the revision is almost complete in those areas in which a virtually new survey was necessary. The work will be in future confined to partial remeasurement and revaluation, and when this is completed remesurement and reclassification will cease altogether to be operations attendant on a revision of assessment.

15. Moreover, as the revised survey record is sufficiently correct for the purpose of a standard, His Excellency the Governor in Council has resolved that it shall be accepted as final and not subject to any future general revision. This resolution secures from any further general alteration of the valuation of land for revenue purposes the whole of the Southern Maratha Districts except a few talukas, and the greater portion of the Deccan. In the districts of Ratangiri and Kanara, in which original settlements are still in progress, the work of the survey is sufficiently accurate to admit of the extension of the same guarantee to them. The power of Government to direct a revaluation of soils will therefore be exercised almost solely in the province of Gujarat, the districts of Thana and Kolaba, and in Khandesh and Satara ; and in these it is believed that a partial resurvey will suffice.

16. Before leaving this part of the subject it is necessary to speak of the arable land which under the name of *pot-kharab* was included unassessed in survey numbers at the early settlements. The Government has been inclined ever since 1874 to leave the profit of bringing such land into cultivation to the occupant. But it was found that the area thus treated in the early settlements was so large that to forego assessment of it would occasion an unjustifiable sacrifice of the claims of the public revenue. Action in the matter was therefore postponed. But the settlements marked by lavish indifference to *pot-kharab* have now come under revision. About the year 1854 a more careful system was introduced under the rules of the Joint Report. His Excellency the Governor in Council has therefore resolved that the Settlement officers shall, in the operation for revision settlement of land originally settled after 1854, as a general principle accept and confirm as exempt from assessment whatever area was entered as a *pot-kharab* in the classification of land at the original settlement. In other words, as a general rule, land which, though arable, was at the first survey included in a survey number as unarable and was left unassessed, shall also be left unassessed at the revision settlement for the benefit of the occupant.

17. This concludes the review of the operations proposed for the completion of the survey record. It remains to examine the law and principles by which the periodic increase of land revenue assessment is regulated, and particularly those which protect from assessment the increased value of land due to improvements made by the occupant.

18. First with regard to the law, Bombay Act I of 1865 contained the following provision :–

Section 30.—It shall be lawful for the Governor in Council to direct at any time a fresh survey or classification of soils or revision of assessment, or all or any of these combined, but the assessment so revised shall not take effect till the expiration of the period of previous guarantee given as provided in Section XXVIII. Such revised assessment shall be fixed, not with reference to improvements made by the owners or occupants from private capital and resources, during the currency of any settlement under this Act, but with reference to general considerations of the value of land, whether as to soil or situation, prices of produce, or facilities of communication.

This section is re-enacted as Section 106 of Bombay Act V of 1879, but the following section adds a proviso :–

107. Nothing in the last preceding section shall be held to prevent a revised assessment being fixed :

(a) with reference to any improvement effected at the cost of Government, or

(b) with reference to the value of any natural advantage, when the improvement effected from private capital and resources consists only in having created the means of utilizing such advantage, or

(c) with reference to any improvement which is the result only of the ordinary operations of husbandry.

19. Attention will now be directed to Section 107.

The principles which Governor in Council desires to maintain are :—

(1) That enhancements of assessment shall be based on "general considerations" and not on the increase of value in particular fields.

(2) That the occupant shall enjoy the entire profit of improvements made at his own cost.

20. These principles being applied to the interpretation of Section 107 it is observed that "reference to general consideration of the value of land" means reference to increased value due to extraneous causes distinct from the result of expenditures of money or labour by the occupant. For instance, a railway which affords a better access to markets is such a cause. Its value may be judged by examining the scale of prices over a long period and noting the proportion of increase which appears to be permanent. Again, by obtaining returns of the selling and letting value of land.

21. The rise in value may be due to improvements made by the landlord—in this case to State. Clause *(a)* enacts that such improvements effected at the cost of Government may be considered in fixing a revised assessment.

22. The interpretation of Clause (*b*) is more doubtful and will be further considered below.

23. Clause (*c*) was intended to meet the case of *pot-kharab* and also would apply to cases where waste land has been assessed at very low

rates in order to encourage its cultivation. This latter case however does not occur in Bombay and the clause is of no practical use (to meet it). Another course is taken under rules subsidiary to Act V with

(1) land the bringing of which under the plough "will be attended with large expense";

(2) the reclamation of salt land.

Such lands are given by contract free for a certain term and at the end of it on a rent gradually rising up to the full assessment.

24. So far then in this Presidency the condition on which assessments are enhanced on revision do not affect the value of improvements made by the occupant. The case of these has now to be considered. In other words, what is the effect of Clause (*b*) of Section 107 on the assurance given in Section 106.

25. His Excellency in Council desires to regulate the action of Government in this matter by the broad principle that occupant of land pays for the use of all advantages inherent in the soil when he pays the assessment on the land. Among inherent advantages he would include subsoil water and rain water impounded on the land, and he would secure to the occupant altogether free of taxation any increased profit of agriculture obtained by utilizing these advantages through expenditure of labour or capital.

26. His Excellency in Council has no desire to claim any part of such profit for the State either immediately or after a certain term of exemption. There may be provinces where some reservation is necessary, but in the circumstances of Bombay His Excellency in Council is convinced that the material interest of the country will be more truly advanced by laying down a broad principle that the occupant may apply labour and capital to the utilization of all inherent advantages in perfect security that the profits acquired by this labour and capital will never be taxed by the State, than they would by reserving a discretion to tax these profit attended by a feeling of uncertainty when and how they may be taxed. The encouragement of higher cultivation in a fully cultivated province is of infinitely greater public importance than the small prospective increase of the land revenue which may be sacrificed by guaranteeing to the occupant the whole profits of his improvements.

27. This Government has already acted on the broad principle stated above. Wells are the universal and most important means of utilizing inherent advantages. The Government in 1881 issued (Government Resolution No. 6682, dated 10th November 1881) a general assurance that Section 107 (*b*) of Act V of 1879 is not held applicable to wells constructed at the expense of the owner or occupier of the soil in which they are dug. This rule was in fact partially in force (as a rule for guidance in revising assessments) as early as 1871 : it was extended to the whole of the Deccan and Southern Maratha Country in 1874 : and was made a rule of general application in 1881.

28. It is clear therefore that as regards the commonest form of agricultural improvement the Government has given complete assurance to any occupant who proposes to construct a well, that the increase of profits resulting from it will not be considered as a ground for increasing the assessment on revision. If it is argued that this assurance is not in the terms of the law but in an executive order, on the other hand it is to be remembered that the revision settlements made in subjection to it are unalterable for 30 years. It was also notified in 1881 that if any other kind of improvement is contemplated, Government will decide at the request of an application for an improvement loan, whether Section 107, Clause (*b*), applies to his project or not. The same assurance can of course be obtained if the improvement is made by means of private capital.

29. These executive orders were promulgated at a time when, according to the custom of preceding rulers, old wells existing at the time of the original survey settlements, and in many cases known to be the property of Government, had been subjected to special water assessment. With regard to these it was in 1874 made a rule applicable to the whole of the Deccan and Southern Maratha Country, that in case of old wells constructed before the first settlement, all special water assessment should be abandoned, and only the maximum dry-crop rate should be levied. This rule was made of general application in 1881.

30. These rules are important at the present time in connection with operations for revision of the original settlements in the province of Gujarat which are about to be commenced.

31. His Excellency in Council entirely concurs in the soundness of the principle approved by the Government of Bombay in 1866 and 1868 (Resolution, Revenue Department, No. 2110, June 8, 1886) that the assessment by a light rate of the water-producing qualities of the soil is preferable to the system of assessing highly only such lands as are found to be already supplied with wells. In a Resolution, Revenue Department, of March 27, 1868, the views of the Government were thus expressed :—

"In regard to special taxation of wells, it is said with truth that water is, like mineral wealth, fairly taxable by the landlord when used by the tenant. His Excellency in Council, however, considers that the first principle of its taxation should be that which governs our taxation of the land itself, that is the capability of being used rather than the use itself. If water of good quality be easily available near the surface, it is more reasonable to tax such land by light additional rate, whether the water be used or not, than to lay an oppressively heavy tax on those who expend capital and labour in bringing the water into use".

32. Difficulties were experienced in carrying these views into effect, but the hope was expressed that when the time for a revision settlement should come, means might be found for abandoning the special rates imposed on existing wells. The subject has again been under the consideration of Government and sanction has been given to the adoption in the survey settlement of parts of the Panch Mahals of the plan of taxing subsoil water advantages by a scarcely noticeable increase of the soil rates on the land possessing such advantages, all special water rates being abandoned. The result of this experiment will form a guide for the introduction of a similar reform in the revised settlements of Gujarat.

33. In the Land Improvement Loans Act of 1883, Section 11; it is enacted—

11. When land is improved with the aid of a loan granted under this Act, the increase in value derived from the improvement shall not be taken into account in revising the assessment of land revenue on the land.

Provided as follows :—

(1) Where the improvement consists of the reclamation of waste land, or of the irrigation of land assessed at unirrigated rates, the increase

may be so taken into account after the expiration of such period as may be fixed by rules to be framed by the Local Government with the approval of the Governor General in Council.

In the debate in Council on this section it was explained that the proviso has regard to such circumstances as those of large tracts in the Punjab, where there is a very large amount of waste land unoccupied and a very sparse population. The land in its unirrigated state is of very little value and is assessed at about one anna per acre, but as soon as water is brought in, it can be assessed at 14 annas or one rupee per acre. But in districts where the land is fully cultivated and where there is a very small margin of waste and a very full population it was held that section was properly applicable without the proviso. In Bombay, provision is made for bringing land into cultivation under special difficulties and for the reclamation of salt lands by agreements or leases under which the land is given for a certain term rent-free, for a further term at a low rate per acre, and is then assessed like other land adjoining. The land when brought up to the level of ordinary cultivation is thus assessed at the ordinary and not at a special rate in pursuance of a contract with the reclaimer. Except in these special circumstances, land is not in this Presidency assessed below the value of its natural advantages because it is waste, and having regard to the policy stated as to wells, His Excellency in Council sees no probability that improvements consisting of "the irrigation of land assessed at unirrigated rates" will at any period be taken into account in estimating the agricultural profits on which an increase of assessment will be based.

34. His Excellency in Council is led by these remarks to consider whether the three clauses of Section 107 of the Land Revenue Code are necessary for the security of the land revenue. Having regard to the power reserved under Section 55 to fix rates for the use of the water of streams and tanks which are vested in the Government, and under the Irrigation Act to charge rates for canal water and percolation and leakage rates, to the policy declared with reference to subsoil water drawn from wells, and to the system of reclamation leases described above, His Excellency in Council considers that Section 107 or at any rate Clauses (*b*) and (*c*) are unprofitable to the land revenue. If in some case, not at once perceptible, an increase of land revenue might be claimed under these clauses without violating any of the pledges given by Government from time to time, and

this is very doubtful, His Excellency in Council is satisfied that no such advantage is comparable to the disadvantage of retaining on the Statute-book a proviso which is of such doubtful significance as to be capable of discouraging the investment of capital in agriculture. The repeal of Section 107 in whole or in part will therefore be taken into consideration.

35. The next point to notice is the limit which Government imposes on the percentage by which the land revenue assessments may be enhanced by the Survey Department on revision.

36. By Resolution, Revenue Department, No. 5739 of October 29, 1874, the following Regulations were laid down for certain districts in the Deccan :—

"1st.—The increase of revenue in the case of a taluka or group of villages brought under the same maximum dry-crop rate shall not exceed 33 per cent.

"2nd.—No increase exceeding 66 per cent should be imposed on a single village without the circumstances of the case being specially reported for the order of Government.

"3rd.—No increase exceeding 100 per cent, shall in the like manner be imposed on an individual holding.

"It is desirable here to state the principles which should be adopted in dealing with the last description of increases. Putting fraud or obvious error in the calculation of the original assessments out of the question these excessive increases in individual cases will be found to be due to one of three causes :—

"1st.—To the assessment of land which was deducted by the original survey as unarable and unassessed, but nevertheless included within the limits of the original assessed number.

"2nd.—To enlargement of the original assessed number by portions of neighbouring lands unassessed at the original settlement having been with or without permission encroached upon by the rayats and cultivated together with the original assessed numbers.

"3rd.—To the alterations that have been made (1) by the adoption of a different valuation scale and (2) by putting a higher value on the soils themselves.

"As regard the second cause, His Excellency in Council is of opinion that lands so appropriated must be regularly valued and assessed, no matter what increase in assessment may thereby result.

"As regards the last cause, it must be borne in mind that the officers employed in the infancy of the survey worked on varying scales of valuation, and that the system they severally adopted were consequently more or less tentative or experimental. It was not till after the lapse of a few years that the then superintendents of survey were able to fix upon a uniform system of valuation which was subsequently embodied in the Joint Report. However much therefore His Excellency in Council would wish to avoid extreme increases in the assessment on individual holdings, there can be no doubt about the superiority of the Joint Report system, and of the absolute necessity for determining and upholding a classification of soils based as far as possible on correct and uniform data.

"It is understood that the Joint Report system was generally adopted a very few years after the introduction of the early assessments, and that consequently no alteration will be required to be made at future revisions. Explanation on this point should, however, be clearly given in future, and also for each future revision in respect to the extent to which it has been found necessary to alter and depart form the classification value originally fixed on the different descriptions of soils. The smallest extent of variation from the old valuation consistent with the principle laid down in the last paragraph should be permitted, and the greatest care should be taken to keep the valuation of the poorest and lighter soils low.

"If the above rules are adhered to, cases in which the enhancement of the assessment in individual holdings will be found to be in excess of the prescribed limit will probably be very few. In order to prevent excessive individual increases, the fixed standard of valuation must not be abandoned. It will always be optional with Government to remit wholly or in part, or for a particular period, such proportion of the increase in excess of 100 per cent as may seem necessary ; but the correct value of the land must be carefully ascertained on a uniform basis, and the proper assessment thereon duly calculated and recorded."

37. These rules have not been formally extended beyond the districts for which they were framed. The reason of this is to be found in the

imperfection of the measurement and classification done in the earliest years of the survey. The revision of the earliest original settlements has, however, been effected, and the limits above set forth can now be adopted, as in fact they have been in the revision settlements of the past two years, without injustice to the public interests. His Excellency in Council is therefore now able to direct that these limitations of enhancement shall be observed in the revision of all original settlements of which the term expires after the revenue year 1883-84.

38. His Excellency in Council will state in conclusion the views of Government as to the collection of the land revenue. It is often asserted that the rigid exaction of the land revenue in good and bad seasons is incompatible with the sustained solvency of the rayat. It is, however, to be noted in the first place that in a revenue settlement everything affecting the security or insecurity of agriculture in the tract under settlement is weighed and the maximum rate of each group of villages is graduated accordingly. No consideration is more potent in the adjustment of rates than the security or insecurity of the crops in the area under settlement. A taluka is often divided into five or six groups for no other reason than the comparative certainty of the rainfall. Thus allowance is made in assessments for the fluctuations in agricultural returns caused by variations of season by what may be called a standing remission co-extensive with the settlement in favour of the less fortunate tracts. The principle certainly is that the assessment thus carefully adjusted to the average production should be punctually paid. But even in ordinary years the practice stated in the passage from the Report of the Famine Commission has been pointed out to the Collector as a guide.[6] And when any agricultural disaster which can be called abnormal occurs, the principle of rigid exaction is unhesitatingly set aside. In the recent years, land revenue instalments have in fact been frequently suspended. If it is found possible to collect these instalments in subsequent prosperous years, the advantage attributed to rents in kind is secured, viz., that the rayat pays when he has wherewith to pay and is excused payment when he has not. If not, the arrears are remitted. If the disaster is serious, remission is sanctioned rather than suspension, and always a careful enquiry into individual cases is held before it is decided whether the suspended land revenue should be collected or remitted. The reason why the subject of remission is not treated in the Land Revenue Code is that each case is considered by the Government to

whom every agricultural disaster is promptly and fully reported. But in order that the policy of Government may be understood and that the action of the Collectors on such occasions may be uniform, the following rules have been added to the Provincial Famine Code :—

"A.—SUSPENSIONS AND REMISSIONS OF LAND REVENUE."

"138. When a Collector has clearly ascertained that an abnormal failure of the harvest, causing total or almost total destruction of the crops over a considerable area, is certain, he is authorized to suspend the collection of the next ensuing instalment of land revenue in such area and any subsequent instalment or instalments falling due while the failure continues. The Collector shall forthwith report his proceedings, stating fully the reasons for his order and the extent of its application, with all other particulars, to the Commissioner for the information of Government.

"139. The Collector will cause the occupants whose land revenue is suspended distinctly to understand that such suspension is provisional only, and that it will be decided after subsequent investigation whether the land revenue suspended will be ultimately remitted or collected.

"140. As soon as possible after the failure of the harvest has ceased, the Collector will conduct a careful investigation into the loss of crops sustained by each occupant whose land revenue payment has been suspended, and its effect on his ability to pay the suspended instalments, and will submit to Government through the Commissioner his recommendations for the remission or collection, or partial remission and collection, of the suspended land revenue.

"141. In framing his recommendations the Collector will consider whether the loss of harvest in each case has been total or partial, whether the occupant has been left without means or possesses a reserve of means or capital, whether he has lost or preserved his plough cattle and agricultural stock. If the occupant has sub-tenants the Collector should ascertain whether he has recovered his rents from them or remitted them. On these and similar considerations the Collector will decide whether total, partial or no remission should be recommended.

"142. In no case should the Collector apply such pressure to obtain payment as will cause an occupant to sell his plough cattle or agricultural implements, or prevent or retard the resumption of agriculture. The recovery of arrears, if any, should be from a surplus of means after sufficient is allowed for the subsistence of the occupant and his family and the restoration of his position as a revenue payer, and occupants should not be driven to borrow from savkars in order to pay arrears.

"143. For the payment of arrears of suspended revenue, if ordered, the Collector may fix such instalments, extending over such period, as the circumstances of the occupant may require".

39. The principles stated in this Resolution as to the non-assessment of the value of improvements made by the occupant are as applicable to Sind as to the districts of the Presidency proper. But the course of survey and settlement in Sind has not been parallel with that in the latter districts. The date from which the survey record may be accepted as complete must therefore be placed much later in Sind, or about 1875-76. Again, while the soil assessment can be fixed so as not to require further revision, the water assessment cannot so be fixed. The productive value of land in Sind depends far more on the water-supply than on the quality of the soil, and the water-supply is a factor in the calculation of assessment to which permanency does not yet attach. The water is not an inherent advantage, but one obtained with some uncertainty and variation form without. A large proportion of the assessment is therefore a charge for water made available by external agencies other than the capital or labour of the occupant. A charge for its use might be made at any time, and if the charge is deferred until a revision takes place, the revised rates which include both soil and water assessment, cannot be restricted by a maximum limit of enhancement applicable to quite different conditions. The comparatively large enhancement in some of the recent revision settlements in Sind is chiefly due to an added charge for the use of increased water-supply of which advantage was taken by occupants during the currency of the previous settlement, but for which nothing extra was paid until the revision took place.

40. His Excellency the Governor in Council has now reviewed the whole of the subject proposed in the first paragraph of his Resolution. The land revenue assessment are based on most careful inductions of all relevant facts. There certainly are difficulties in reaching assurance as to the exact incidence of assessment rates. The attachment of the people to

their land qualifies the precision of the test supplied elsewhere by land passing out of cultivation when the rent is high in proportion to that on other land of similar quality. Data of the rents at which land is leased by private persons are not largely available. But as far as they are known they go to prove that the assessments are moderate. The incidence of the land revenue on the gross produce in Bombay was estimated in the Report of the Famine Commission at 7.6 per cent. The crop experiments made in recent years show that it is not in excess of that proportion. The object of this Resolution is to make publicly known the grounds of assurance that the land revenue will not be capriciously or excessively enhanced and that no part of the profits of occupants' improvements will be taken from them in that name. His Excellency in Council believes that this assurance is as complete and that the system as now explained approaches as nearly to a permanent settlement of the State rights as is possible with justice to public interests in a country of which the resources are still far from fully developed.

J. NUGENT,
Secretary to Government.

Communicated to the Commissioners of Divisions, all Collectors, etc., etc.,

with copies of Government Resolutions :—

A.—No. 1028, dated 25th February 1874.

B.—No. 6682, dated 10th November 1881.

C.—No. 8989, dated 7th December 1883.

Accompaniment A.

Revenue Survey and Assessment.

No. 1028.

REVENUE DEPARTMENT

Bombay Castle, 25th February 1874.

Read again the following papers :—

Letter from the Survey and Settlement Commissioner, S.D., No. 1900, dated 17th November 1873—Soliciting, with reference to the revision of settlements in the Southern Maratha Country now about to be commenced, a reconsideration of the order contained in Government Resolution No. 4050, dated 22nd August 1871, regarding the assessment of well lands.

Memorandum from the Survey and Settlement Commissioner, N.D., 2247, dated 5th December 1873—Submitting remarks on the above.

Memorandum from the Revenue Commissioner, S.D., No. 160, dated 15th January 1874—Forwarding the above, and stating that he hopes to submit his views in a few days.

Memorandum by the Survey and Settlement Commissioner, S.D., No. 124, dated 26th January 1874—Stating in reply to a reference made, that no inconvenience will result from the postponement of a decision on the above question which has no practical bearing on the revision settlements of this year.

Resolution of Government on the above, No. 520, dated 30th January 1874.

Read also a memorandum from the Revenue Commissioner, S.D., No. 304, dated 27th January 1874—Submitting, as promised in his memorandum of the 15th idem No. 160, his views on the letter from the Survey and Settlement Commissioner, S.D., No. 1900, dated 17th November 1873.

RESOLUTION.—Colonel Anderson requests that the orders of Government in respect to the revision of the assessment on lands irrigated form wells may be reconsidered. He objects to them as involving a needless sacrifice of public revenue.

2. Those order are—

(1) That in the case of old wells constructed before the first settlement in dry and arid districts, all special water assessment should be abandoned, and the maximum jirait rate alone levied.

(2) That in the case of new wells constructed subsequent to the first settlement the ordinary dry-crop rate should be imposed without any addition whatever on account of the new wells.

3. The question has now been very fully discussed. His Excellency Governor in Council has no hesitation in reaffirming the second order which has been approved of by the Secretary of State, which has already been productive of good results in encouraging the construction of new wells and which is based on the broad and liberal principle laid down in Section XXX of the Survey Act, namely, that improvements made during the currency of a settlement are not to be taxed.

4. The opinions that have been elicited during the course of the present correspondence convince Government as to the policy and expediency of the first rule. It was intended in the first instance to be applicable to the drier talukas of the Deccan Collectorates, where the rainfall is, as a rule, light and uncertain. His Excellency the Governor in Council is now pleased to decide that it should be generally adopted in the Deccan and Southern Maratha Country, but that the Survey Commissioners should at their discretion be empowered, in the case of districts where well irrigation has been carried on on an extensive scale, to impose an assessment which should in no case exceed a well assessment previously levied.

5. Budkis of permanent construction are to be treated as wells. There is no objection to the plan which Colonel Anderson states he has adopted of classing at a higher rate land within a certain distance from a stream from which water can be obtained by means of budki. The same principle may be adopted in the case of land which is found to derive benefit from its proximity to a tank. This should form part of the regular process of classification, in order that it may be tested by the Classing Assistants in the same manner as other classification returns.

E. JAMES,
for Chief Secretary to Government.

Accompaniment B.

Advances—

No. 6682.

REVENUE DEPARTMENT

Bombay Castle, 10th November 1881.

Submitting the report called for by Government Resolution No. 1389 of 8th March 1881 on extract Section 3, Chapter IV of the Report of the Indian Famine Commission, Part II, regarding Government loans to facilitate land improvement.[7]

RESOLUTION.—Government are unable to see that any discouragement to improvements made by private capital need be caused by Section 107, Clause (*b*) of the Land Revenue Code. Government are competent at any time to declare how they interpret that clause and to notify that it will not be held to apply to any particular class of improvements. Government are now prepared to give a general assurance that Clause (*b*) will not be applied to wells dug at the expense of the owner or occupier of the soil. In the same way in any other specific case, Government will decide at the request of an applicant for an improvement loan, whether the clause applies to the project or not. Government are also willing to give general application to the two rules as to wells in force in the Deccan and Southern Maratha Country (Nairne's Handbook, page 158-9). The Survey Commissioner may prepare a notification in accordance with the above views and report whether any modification in the way of greater liberality or security is called for.

J. MONTEATH,

Acting Under Secretary to Government.

Accompaniment C.

No. 8989.

REVENUE DEPARTMENT

Bombay Castle 7th December 1883.

Read again the following correspondence :—

Letter from the Government of India, Revenue and Agriculture Department, No. 539-R., dated 15th May 1883, and enclosures.

The Government of India have recently been in communication with the Secretary of State regarding the principles on which future revisions of land revenue assessment should be made in Northern India, and the Secretary of State has suggested, in giving his assent to the general principles which the Viceroy in Council advocated, that the Government of Bombay should be addressed with a view to ascertaining whether similar principles *mutatis mutandis* might not be applied in the rayatwari districts of Southern India. I am accordingly instructed to forward copy of a letter recently addressed to the Government of the North-Western Provinces in which these principles are formulated. There is much in that letter which is wholly inapplicable to the state of things in Bombay, but on the other hand one at least of the leading principles therein inculcated has for years past been an accepted feature of the Bombay system ; in other respects the Government of India thinks that that explanation of the principles which underlie the relations of the revenue payers to the State will be found not to be fundamentally at variance with the Bombay system. I am to enquire if, in the opinion of His Excellency the Governor in Council, the more extended application of them to the Bombay revenue system is considered practicable or expedient. The objects which the Government of India has in view are to avoid as far as possible the harassment and expense inseparable from re-survey and re-classification of soil, at every recurring resettlement, to give the revenue payer a means of estimating beforehand with tolerable accuracy what his enhanced revenue should be, and with this object limiting enhancements to the three grounds of rise in prices, additional cultivation, and improvements made at Government expense. It is not supposed that the detailed method of applying these principles, which is suggested in paragraphs 16 to 30 of the letter to the North-Western Provinces Government, will be found applicable to Bombay, but a consideration of these paragraphs may suggest other methods more applicable to that Province, and will at all events render portions of this letter more easily intelligible.

2. There has been much in the correspondence which of late years has passed between the Government of Bombay Her Majesty's Secretary of State and the Government of India, which has led the Government of India to think that the Bombay Government will, on some of the questions which come under discussion in the letter to the North-Western Provinces hold similar views to those of the Government of India. His Excellency in Council is constrained to admit that proposals made by Sir Phillip Wodehouse, of which the main object was to remove the annoyance of the re-measurement and re-classification of land, received some check in consequence of the objections raised by the Government of India itself to an important part of his recommendations. But since the date of the correspondence on the subject, which ended with letter No. 7046, dated 15th December 1875, from the Bombay Government, so much light has been thrown upon the circumstances of the Bombay assessments by the full and clear reports of Colonel Anderson, Mr. Stewart, and other officers engaged in the settlement of the land revenue in the Presidency, that the Government of India is able to revert to the proposals of 1874 with some confidence that the principles therein contained will be found in many respects to agree with those now put forward by the Government of India. On the main point indeed, as has been already implied, the Bombay scheme of 1874 and that included in the present letter to the North Western Provinces agree entirely ; viz., in the desire to do away with the troubles, difficulties, and expense of re-measuring and re-classifying land.

Sir P. Wodehouse appears to have desired to concede to the proprietors of land the whole of the assets realized from the part of the cultivated area of each survey number which at the time of assessment had not been recorded as under cultivation. This at least seems to have been the proposal for districts assessed after 1848. The Government of India would now ask whether the Government of Bombay would be inclined to renew this suggestion with such modifications as may now seem desirable.

3. A good deal of correspondence has arisen in regard to the burthen of enhancement imposed at the time of re-settlement in some of the Bombay districts. The Government of India does not, in referring to it, now wish to enter into any discussion on this part of the subject, but desires merely to ask whether in the case of those districts in which it is impossible to resign the enhanced revenue due to the extensive cultivation of land (known it is believed as *pot-kharab*) which was not included in settlements before 1848 in the assessable area, it would not in the opinion of the Bombay Government be desirable to make the enhancement progressive in all cases in which the increment of revenue bears a high proportion to the former assessment.

4. The most important question connected with the proposals of the enclosed letter is that of eliminating the process of re-valuing the land. The Government of India would ask, first whether it may be understood that in those districts, if any in which the increment due to the cultivation of *pot-kharab* can be resigned, no new valuation of the soil will be necessary, and that the existing revenues can be accepted as the initial revenues ; and secondly, whether any date can be selected in regard to which it must be accepted that all assessment made previous to it were of such a nature as to require a new valuation in their case, but not in the case of districts assessed after that date ? The anxiety of the Government of India to avoid the re-classification of soils under all circumstances where it is possible to do so will not escape the attention of the Government of Bombay, and its views on this question will, it is hoped, receive earnest consideration at its hands. The Viceroy in Council trusts, indeed, that some definite programme may be found possible under which the revenues of a certain number of districts may at once be accepted as initial revenues which can in future only be enhanced on certain will-defined grounds such as those given in paragraph 13 of the enclosed letter.

5. Finally, the Government of India wishes to make some allusion to the position of those tracts of which the produce is so precarious as to prevent the offer of a fixed and uniform assessment from possessing the

advantages which in normal tracts it possesses. In connection with this matter it invites attention to the Resolution No. 58-R., dated 12th October 1882, on suspensions and remissions in Northern India. It might perhaps be found desirable to adopt a system of collecting revenue in such tracts which may include an acknowledged and definite system of suspensions and remissions. The great object in laying down rules, however elastic they may be, for suspensions and remissions, is to establish the principle as a definite and integral portion of the Revenue Code, which will not be dependent on the varying views on individual revenue officers or even of successive Governments. It is understood that in practice suspensions and remissions are now freely resorted to, especially since 1877, but it seems desirable that an element, on which in certain tracts the security of the Bombay revenue system depends so largely, should, so far as the conditions permit, be reduced to a system, and take an acknowledged and prominent place in the rules by which the revenue officers of the Province are guided.

6. The Government of India, without asking at the present moment for anything like a detailed reply as to the method by which the principles above referred to can be applied to Bombay, would be glad to receive an early expression of the opinion of the Bombay Government as to their general applicability in whole or in part to the revenue system of the Presidency.

Letter from the Government of Bombay, Revenue Department, to the Government of India, No. 6340, dated 27th August 1883, and accompaniment.

I am instructed to reply to your letter No. 539-R. of the 15th May.

2. I am to say that His Excellency the Governor in Council is in entire accord with the Government of India on the general principles enunciated in your letter and its enclosures ; he considers that those principles are generally applicable to the revenue system in this Presidency, and he has directed me in this letter to explain how and with what modifications of existing arrangements they may be adopted.

3. Before addressing the Government of India on this important subject, His Excellency in Council desired to avail himself of the knowledge and experience of the Commissioner of Survey. Mr. Stewart has furnished an able review of the present position of settlement operations in Bombay with suggestions for a modification of plan to meet the views of the Government of India. A copy of his letter is enclosed and I am to say that His Excellency the Governor in Council concurs in almost every point in the opinions and proposals which it contains.

4. The object of the Government of India is to reduce and abridge as far as is practicable the annoyance, expense, and uncertainty inseparable from the re-survey and re-classification of soil, and to enable the revenue payer to forecast with tolerable accuracy what a future enhancement of revenue will be by clearly defining and limiting the grounds on which such enhancement will be based.

5. There is, as you remark in your letter, a great difference in the method of revenue settlement pursued in the North-Western Provinces and this Presidency respectively. In the former a revenue settlement is made on mixed considerations of what the landholder's assets are and what they might be, and object is to assess for a fixed term a lump revenue payment on the estate or village. In Bombay the work of the Survey Department proper is to prepare a complete record of the correct areas of fields, and the relative value of each as measured by the return obtained from its cultivation. This survey record does not itself settle the Government land revenue due on the field, but supplies a scale for adjusting it equitably according to the quality and advantages of the land. The object of our measurement and classification of soils is thus distinct from the assessment and variations of revenue rates, and is attained when the survey record is accurate and complete enough to be finally accepted as guaranteeing the relative fairness of any rates which it is decided to impose. At the same time, as the relative value of every field has to be distinctly estimated, it is clear that the operation must be as scientific as possible and the necessity of revising the rough and uneven work of the early years of the survey is explained.

6. Mr. Stewart has given (paras 16 to 21) an estimate of the field operations still necessary before the Survey record can be accepted as

complete according to these views. When these operations are finished the record will remain as an authoritative and sufficient standard of relative values by which assessment may be adjusted to each field through calculations made in the Collector's office. The work remaining to be done is not much ; but if the correction of the survey record in each taluka or group is, as at present, deferred until the current settlement expires, it will be protracted into the next century, while the existing highly skilled establishment will be dissipated for want of full-time employment. Mr. Stewart therefore proposes that the completion of the survey record should be carried out at once with the full strength of present establishments and expects that in this case all field operations in the Presidency may be completed within a period of eight years. Current settlements will not of course be altered until their term expires and it will be necessary to explain carefully to the landholders under unexpired guarantees what the object of the operations is. I am to say that His Excellency in Council entirely concurs in this proposal and believes that it will commend itself to His Excellency the Viceroy in Council as in complete concordance with the policy approved by the Government of India.

7. I am next to advert to the question asked by the Government of India, whether the Government of Bombay is now inclined to renew with such modifications as may seem desirable, the concession proposed by the Government of Sir P. Wodehouse in 1874, that land which, though arable, was included in a survey number as unarable and unassessed at the original settlement, should at the revision settlement be again left unassessed for the benefit of the occupant. I am to say that His Excellency in Council considers that this concession, if granted absolutely as proposed in 1874, would have resulted in unnecessary loss of revenue, regard being had to the quality of the survey record as then unrevised in some of the districts first surveyed. But the position is now different, and this Government is prepared to sanction the concession as a general principle in talukas and groups the soils of which were classified subsequent to the year A.D. 1854. This subject is discussed in paragraphs 13-15 of Mr. Stewart's letter. As Mr. Stewart observes, this decision of Government on the future treatment of *pot-kharab* removes the necessity for the progressive increments of revenue suggested in the 3rd paragraphs of your letter.

harvests and by the inflation and contraction of trade in some exportable product, and these cannot been foreseen. It may be hoped that when the country is better protected from famine, railways and roads are more generally distributed, and the export trade has obtained a stronger hold on foreign markets, the oscillations in agricultural profits will be less marked. In the meantime it is not easy to formulate a rule of proportions between revenue enhancements and prices.

15. Mr. Stewart has suggested (para. 27) that it may not be expedient in the interest of the existing peasant occupants of Bombay to reduce to very precise and narrow limits the declared grounds on which alone the Government will increase its land revenue demand. The Government of India will probably not concur that uncertainty should be retained in the definition of these grounds after it has ceased to be necessary, because it acts as a deterrent on the moneylending class, who might be inspired by certainty of assessment to supplant the present holders of the land. Anything which may operate to hold back capital from agriculture is an evil. But while the reasons for enhancement tend to merge into the one general ground of a substantial increase in agricultural profits, I am to say that His Excellency in Council would not recommend until the survey record is complete any change in the principles of revision laid down in the Land Revenue Code.

16. I am finally to refer to your remarks on the subject of suspensions and remissions Mr. Stewart (paras. 28-30) has pointed out and illustrated the fact that it is an important part of the survey valuation of land to make full allowance in the assessment rates for the uncertainty of the harvest in tracts where the rainfall is irregular. The system provides relief for ordinary or partial failures of harvest by what is in fact a standing remission. This relief is embodied in the survey record and operates mechanically and independently of "the varying views of individual revenue officers or even of successive Governments." Remissions on a large scale are, therefore, properly limited to exceptional calamities, such as a visitation of locusts, famine, or agricultural depression caused by bad seasons following famine. The reason why rules have not been formulated for such remissions in this Presidency is that, the occasions being exceptional, the facts are always reported at once for the special orders of the Government and I am to say that His Excellency in Council believes that

it may be claimed for the Bombay revenue system that no failure is probable in the conveyance of timely information to the Government. In these circumstances formulas are not needed for the guidance of Government. But His Excellency in Council is willing to believe that it may be an advantage to the district officer to be in possession of a clear and simple statement of the policy of the Government on the whole subject of suspensions and remissions. In regard to ordinary years there is some reason to think that the Collectors in following the processes of the Land Revenue Code for the recovery of revenue may lose sight of the sound views stated in the passage of the report of the Famine Commission quoted earlier. And in seasons of exceptional distress some rules of action may be a useful guide to uniformity in the Collector's recommendations of suspension and remission. I am to say that His Excellency in Council therefore proposes to refer this subject for the consideration of the Committee which has lately been appointed for the preparation of a Provincial Famine Code, and to decide on their report what instructions it is advisable to issue.[7]

17. I am to say in conclusion that as Mr. Ozanne has now taken up the appointment of Provincial Director of Agriculture steps will at once be taken to organize under his direction, in cooperation with the Survey Commissioner, (Mr. Stewart's para.17) "a competent staff whose duties will be to keep the village maps up to date, to correct from time to time the field registers, and to record from year to year the statistical information which has to be considered at the time of revising the rates."

18. His Excellency in Council desires me to say that he will be glad to receive an expression of the opinion His Excellency the Viceroy in Council on the views stated in this letter before action is taken to carry them into effect.

Letter from the Survey and Settlement Commissioner, No. 1360, dated 27th June 1883, referred to in the foregoing letter form the Government of Bombay.

I have the honour to acknowledge the receipt of your memorandum No. 4414, dated 11th instant, forwarding for my opinion a letter from the Secretary to the Government of India, Revenue and Agricultural

Department, dated 15th May 1883, in which the Government of Bombay is asked to consider and report as to the extent to which certain principles laid down for the guidance of the Government of the North-West Provinces in future revisions of assessment can be made applicable to this Presidency.

2. The two main principles which the Government of India's letter is intended to inculcate may be briefly stated as follows :—

1st.—That to avoid the trouble, annoyance and expense under the present system of revision of assessments, the process of re-valuation of land should be eliminated in future from the scheme of land assessment. Or in other words, that the agricultural value of the land having been once ascertained with tolerable accuracy, that value should be taken as the basis for future adjustment.

2nd.—That the future assessments of land revenue should be arranged under such rules and in such a manner as will enable the proprietors of land to forecast with tolerable precision and without official aid the enhancement of revenue to which they will in future be subject, so that an element of certainty of assessment may be to some extent introduced into the settlement.

3. With regard to these two principles I think I may safely say that the first is one which is thoroughly accepted in the Bombay system of settlement and has been fully recognized and expressed in the orders of Government for several years past, and that although the second principle has not yet been fully developed as part of the settlement system in this Presidency, a considerable step towards its realization has been made by the legal restrictions on enhancement of assessment in revision provided in the Land Revenue Code and by the limits which have been placed on revenue enhancement by the orders of Government in 1874. Although it may be open to doubt whether under the rayatwari system of Bombay a certainty of the future range of assessment will be altogether favourable to the interests to the rayats themselves, as distinguished from the capitalists who are rapidly acquiring their lands, there is nothing in the Bombay system itself which will stand in the way of the carrying out of the wishes of the Government of India, if it be decided that the time is ripe for the introduction of this principle in its entirety.

4. The subject of the re-measurement of land in this Presidency is so closely connected with that of re-classification as an operation of revision that the absence of reference to it in the letter to the Government of the North-West Provinces may excite some surprise. The reason, however, is that in the North-West Provinces the whole area surveyed for the original settlements between 1833 and 1844 has been already brought under one revision of rates and the original measurements and maps have been altered and corrected up to a comparatively late date ; whereas in this Presidency we have been and are still engaged in reviewing, and in many instances re-doing, the old work which cannot be fully accepted as accurate. And not only have the whole of the original measurements in the North-West Provinces been once revised in the ordinary course, but the later surveys have been carried out by the costly Imperial cadastral agency, which must supply all the data for a settlement on the broad basis of that of the North-West Provinces in a form which could scarcely be improved upon. It must be clearly kept in view, therefore, that the Government of India, in laying down principles for the observance of the Government of the North-West Provinces, is alluding to an approaching revision of an already revised valuation, while the operations in progress in this Presidency are directed to the carrying out of a first revision only.

5. Between the valuation and appraisement of land which forms an integral part of the North-West system in its latest development and the minute classification of soils in the Bombay Presidency, there is a very great difference both in the method of procedure and in the objects aimed at. In the North-West the valuation of the soils is performed by the settlement officer on a simple inspection of the fields of each village, his object being to group the lands into homogeneous areas according to their distance from the village and the natural and artificial qualities of their soil. To the areas so classified average rent rates calculated on very minute local inquiries and local examination of accounts and records are applied, and on a percentage of the total rental so arrived at, the Government revenue of the estate is fixed. The classes of soils employed for this operation are so few and simple, that it is impossible to think that this part of land valuation is that which causes trouble and annoyance to the people. It is much more likely that the elaborate local inquiries and researches of the settlement officer to ascertain actual

rent rates, or to estimate average rent rates when actual rents cannot be ascertained, are the real cause of harassment and vexation. Under the Bombay system no inquiries of the latter kind are required to be made in the village, and if re-valuation is soils is alleged to cause harassment and annoyance to the people, it must be shown to be caused by the single technical operation of re-classification in the field, which is the only one of which the individual rayat has any cognizance. I am inclined to believe that much of the odium which has attached itself to revision operations in Upper India on account of the inquisitorial nature of the local inquiries into rents and the scrutiny of accounts and records involved in the appraisement of the land has been saddled on the Bombay system from an idea that the process of the valuation of the soil must be somewhat similar. In paras. 22 to 30 of my report on future operations in Khandesh, No. 1714, dated 3rd September 1882, I have taken occasion to combat the main charges levelled against us under this head. But my object in bringing to notice the vast difference in the two processes is not to continue a discussion on this question nor to gainsay the fact that the re-classification of lands is a thing to be avoided as far as possible, but to show that although the Government of the North-West Provinces, in settling for the revenue with holders of villages and large estates, may be able to accept a land valuation of "tolerable accuracy" as the basis of their assessments, the Government of Bombay in settling for the payment of revenue with individual rayats, many of whom are small holders, cannot afford to stay its hand in the matter of re-classification of the soils until it is assured that the standard of classification is thoroughly fair and equal and that each holding or recognized parcel of a holding has been subjected to an intelligent estimate of its relative productiveness.

6. The classification of soils in the Bombay Presidency differs in the first instance from that of the North-West Provinces in being an operation wholly apart from the duties of the settlement officer. It is a duty preceding settlement performed by a special agency and is as detailed and technical as the soil-classification of the North-West is broad and general in its aims. Each survey field or subordinate survey field (pot number) is classed separately on its own merits by digging to ascertain depth and careful analysis of soil, and the average

classification arrived at is expressed in fractions of a rupee according to a prescribed valuation scale. Beyond recording the distance of the field from the village, which is an important point as affecting the facility of obtaining manure and such facts as may be necessary regarding irrigation and tree-growth, the functions of the Bombay soil-classifier end here. I may mention that it has been the practice hitherto for the classer during his stay in the village to record facts regarding population and livestock ; but I have recommended that even this duty should be discontinued.

7. Although the classification valuation of the field itself is no guide in deciding the pitch of the rates of assessment, it is however the great factor by which the incidence of the assessment on each field is graduated. When the maximum rate, i.e., the rent charge considered applicable to the best, or what is technically termed 16 anna soil, is decided for a village or group of villages, the assessment per acre of the lower classed fields is decided at once by the proportion their valuation in annas bears to 16 annas. The necessity of a careful and accurate field classification cannot therefore be too highly estimated. If the classification is relatively fair and equal, periodical enhancements of the maximum rates may be made upon its basis only without any hesitation ; if on the other hand it is unequal and ill-balanced, every successive application of an enhancement will add to excessive rating on the one hand or undue leniency on the other. A good classification in itself will not prevent the imposition of too high or too low an assessment, but it is complete safeguard against relative inequality in assessment. Moreover, if over-assessment is caused by a too high pitch of the maximum rates, the mistake can be remedied with no appreciable expense by a lowering of the rate and the application of the classification thereto ; but when relative over-assessment is caused by an unequal classification, there is no remedy for it but an expensive course of field operations.

8. The above remarks will, I think, tend to show what a much greater stake is involved in the field-to-field classification of Bombay than in that portion of the land valuation in the North-West Provinces which is connected with the distinguishing of soils. In fixing the lump revenue to be paid by a village community or a zamindar, some little roughness in the classification of the lands under the main heads of soil will not ordinarily

be perceptible ; and if the valuation of one portion of the estate is somewhat low, a high valuation of another portion may counterbalance the effect. But this is not possible in the case of the small parcels of land on which the settlement is made in Bombay, where no "tolerably accurate" classification will suffice. It is essential to obtain as accurate a classification once for all as is possible with the experienced agency supervising staff which we now possess.

9. From the earliest period of the present Bombay system of settlement, it has been a fundamental principle that no form of assessment can be suitable to the rayatwari tenure, unless founded upon a close examination of soils. The conclusion arrived at by the Government of India, after reviewing the progress of settlements in the North-West Provinces in para 7 of their letter, are substantially those which have been formulated and accepted by the exponents of the system in this Presidency for upwards of forty years past. It is possible that, as a corollary of the views now expressed by the Government of India, the system of land classification in this Presidency would be considered too minute an attempt to obtain an exact valuation of agricultural land ; but the time has apparently passed for a modification of the system when, with the exception of four talukas, the entire area of the Presidency has been so treated, and when fair progress has been made to revise the oldest portion of the work.

10. It may be asked why, if such a detailed examination of the soils has once been made, it should be necessary to do all or any of the work over again. The answer to this is that when the first districts were settled, the processes and standards of classification varied in all parts of the Presidency, and the scales adopted for valuation were for many years purely tentative and experimental. Native classers had to be slowly and painfully trained to a proper discrimination of the qualities and defects of the various kinds of soil. Owing to the almost certain sacrifice of revenue which at first attended the operations of the settlement officers, funds were scantily allotted, and the controlling staff was insufficient for proper and systematical test. It has been found hitherto in revising the old work that when compared with the standard which has been adopted in recent settlement and which has remained fairly constant, there is a serious under-estimation of the value of the richer soils and a corresponding over-

estimation of the poor soils. In most districts hitherto entirely re-classed or partly re-classed with a view to adjustment, it has been found that to obtain a true relative valuation the better soils have had to be put up and poorer soils lowered about one class, or 2 annas in the rupee scale. An undue lowering by one class of the value of a 16 anna field is equivalent to a loss ot the revenue of 12½ per cent on that field, but it is a much more serious consideration that the over-valuation of a 4-anna field to even half that extent will produce a relative over-assessment of 25 per cent.

11. Various reasons have been given for the faulty standard of the old classers. It has been suggested that as the country at the time of the early settlement was in a very impoverished condition and the best lands were lying waste on account of the weight of the previous assessment, there was a special object in keeping the valuation of such soils low, in order to tempt their recultivation. It is certain that the poorer soils were those which were at that time under the most constant cultivation, and their well-tilled appearance, in contrast with the good soils which were untilled and overgrown with weeds, may have had much to do with the relative error which is found in all the old classifications. However this may be, the fault is gradually found to decrease as districts were reached in which cultivation had become more general, while after the great rise in value of land in 1862 to 1865 there appears to have been a re-action towards a rather over-valuation of the better classes of soil. For about the last ten years only has the standard which now prevails been consistently followed. It has been adopted by a general consensus of opinion among the most experienced classing officers, many of whom had witnessed every stage in the development of the system, and is believed to give as true a relative valuation of all classes of soils as can be reasonably expected. To such perfection have our experienced classers been trained in its use, that the average difference between the original classification and test is usually less than 6 pies.

12. It is not only on account of the faulty standard of classification of culturable soils that the necessity has arisen for revising the old classifications, but on account of the lax system which obtained in distinguishing the culturable from the unculturable portion of a survey field. I have on several former occasions explained how large parcels of

really culturable land came to be thrown into survey numbers under the head of *pot kharab*. The practice was chiefly prevalent in those surveys conducted before 1850—the year in which the Joint Report Rules were finally published—but it was not for some time after that a close examination was made of those portions of a survey number which were out of tilth to ascertain their productive capabilities. The facilities for this lax system were, however, much narrowed when the sub-division of the land into fields according to the principles of the Joint Report became general. In the large survey fields which existed before that time, often from 60 to 200 acres in area, there was a temptation to laxity which could not exist when the maximum size of survey field came to be fixed at about 30 acres only.

13. In paragraphs 2, 3 and 4 of the Government of India's letter three important questions are asked :—

1st.—Whether the Government of Bombay is prepared to renew the suggestion made in paragraph 7 of Government Resolution No. 5739, dated 29th October 1874, that the same area of land shall upon revision be deducted from each number as unassessed (*pot kharab*) as was allowed at the original settlement ?

2nd.—Whether, if the Government of Bombay considers it impossible to resign the enhanced revenue due to the cultivation of *pot kharab,* it would not appear desirable to make the enhancement progressive in all cases in which the increment of revenue bears a high proportion to the former assessment ?

3rd.—Whether any date can be selected in regard to which it may be accepted that all assessments made subsequent to it are of such a nature as to require no new valuation of soils ?

14. As regards the first question, I consider that the time has now arrived when steps may be safely and equitably taken to meet the wishes of the Government of India. Owing to the great reduction in the area of the survey field and the close and detailed inspection of each field which the Joint Report inculcated, the opportunity for the classers to slur over the examination of the fields became much diminished, while the development of the survey system and the increase of the controlling staff rendered the test and general supervision of the

work year by year more efficient. There are very strong indications now that we are approaching the revision of valuations made at a time when land was only entered as *pot kharab* because it was really unfit for cultivation, and if we go on assessing such land much longer, we shall be running a risk of taxing improvements of a nature over and beyond the ordinary operations of husbandry. A step, therefore, which in 1874 would have resulted in giving large areas of land to persons wholly unentitled to them at a mere quit-rent seems now to be very advisable on broad principles of justice, and the cancelled orders of 1874 may, I think, with great advantage and without any appreciable sacrifice of revenue be repeated in 1884. I only refer of course to the general principle involved, as some modification of the rule may be necessary in practice to meet cases where land was entered as *pot kharab* for reasons other than because it was believed to be uncultivable, as in cases where land was formerly covered with buildings now removed, or was used as burialground now abandoned, or formed the bed of a nala which has now silted up, and so on.

15. If the above concession is made regarding *pot kharab*, I do not consider that it will be necessary or advisable to confuse the simple system of collection now in force by treating enhancements arising from its assessment in an exceptional way. The time when increases of revenue on account of assessment of *pot kharab* were really appreciable has all put past, and in the early settled districts, such as Nasik and Ahmednagar, where the system was most lax, the enhancements on this account have already been levied for several years in full. Some of the profits which have been proved to have accrued to holders of survey fields owing to the wholesale inclusion of *pot kharab* in their occupancies, which they could deal with as they chose for the period of settlement, are so vast that but little sympathy can be felt for them if all their cultivable land is now assessed at a fair and moderate share of its estimated rental.

16. The third question of the Government of India must be treated in connection with the subject of re-measurement, as that operation is usually followed by a certain amount of re-valuation of land. I will endeavour, as far as a very careful study of the question will permit me, to forecast the amount of re-measurement and re-classification

which must be performed by this Department before we have a sound basis upon which the revenues to be accepted as initial revenues can be confidently founded.

17. In discussing this question I will take it for granted that with the formation in this Presidency of an Agricultural Department early attention will be directed to the organization of a competent staff, whose duties will be to keep the village maps up to date, to correct from time to time the field registers, to divide occupancies, when necessary, and to record from year to year the statistical information which has to be considered at the time of revising the rates. The absence of such a staff at present is one of the weakest point of our system and the earlier it is provided and set to work in all settled districts the less will be the review of the measurements and valuations which will have to be made when the time for each revision comes round.

18. The districts of this Presidency may be considered in three distinct classes :—

1st.—Those in which a revision of rates has been carried out or is now being carried out.

2nd.—Those in which the original settlement has not yet expired.

3rd.—Those which are now being settled for the first time.

In the first category come the Deccan districts of Poona, Sholapur, Nasik and Ahmednagar, and the Southern Maratha Collectorates of Dharwar, Kaladgi and Belgaum. In the Dharwar Collectorate the revised rates have been completely introduced ; in all the other Collectorates there is some little work remaining to make the revision complete, but in the course of two more seasons the whole area of these districts will have been brought under the field operations sanctioned by Government as necessary previous to revision of rates. In the second category come the five districts of the province of Gujarat, the Konkan districts of Thana and Kolaba and the districts of Khandesh and Satara. The third class comprises the districts of Ratnagiri and Kanara, of which small portions still remain to be surveyed for the purpose of original settlement.

19. In the districts comprised in the first class the operations of re-measurement and re-classification have been in some cases total, and in

other cases partial, but the work on the whole has been and is being, so completely and carefully carried out, that there can be no objection for Government to declare that the valuation of soil should be accepted without any future re-doing for the purpose of revenue settlement. But much of course depends on whether a competent staff of trained hands is at once employed to ascertain and make up to date all corrections and alterations necessary in the village maps and records.

20. Regarding the districts of the second class I find myself unable to give the same general guarantee although much trouble in field operations may be saved by the early organization of the staff alluded to above. In Khandesh the old survey and soil valuation was admittedly partial and imperfect, the early reports clearly contemplating that deficiencies should be made good at the conclusion of the first period of settlement. In the earlier settled portion of Thana and Kolaba the only attempts at accuracy made were with regard to the lands cultivated with the rice and rabi crops, the *warkas* and hill lands being very roughly measured, and their area computed in a manner which would not now be tolerated. In the Collectorates of Gujarat the measurements were from the beginning conducted with greater care, the level character of the country being favourable to accuracy; but the early measurement and the classification of rice and garden lands in Ahmedabad and Kaira will require partial re-doing, and some operations will be necessary throughout the province to divide clubbed occupancies, so as to comply with the law as contained in Rule 55 of rules under section 214 of the Land Revenue Code. In the district of Satara both measurement and soil valuation have been comparatively carefully conducted throughout and although it may be advisable to make partial test of the work to be sure that it is up to the standard of excellence now aimed at, the operations will, it is hoped, be comparatively insignificant and inexpensive. Finally, I have every hope that the field operations for original settlements which have been or which are now being carried out in the Ratnagiri and Kanara Collectorates, will be found to be so detailed in their nature and so generally accurate in all material points, that revised rates may be introduced upon their basis with ease and confidence.

21. I will endeavour to show in a tabular form the forecast which I venture to make regarding the extent of field operations which will be requisite in future revision settlements :—

No.	District.	Under what Description of Settlement	Duration of operations for existing settlement.		Operations necessary at future revision of rates.	Remarks.
			From	To		
1.	Ahmedabad	Original	1851	1862	Partial re-measurement Re-classification of rice and all irrigable lands.	
2.	Kaira	Do. ..	1857	1868	Do ..	
3.	Surat	Do. ..	1859	1873	Do. ..	
4.	Broach	Do. ..	1863	1877	Do. ..	
5.	Panch Mahals.. ..	Do. ..	1865	1882	Do. in first settled talukas only.	
6.	Khandesh	Original	1854	1870	Partial re-measurement and re-classfication throughout	Original survey only partial. Revision operations commenced in one taluka as sanctioned by Government Resolution No. 6592, dated 23rd September 1882.
7.	Nasik	Partly revised	1871	Unfinshed	None	One taluka only remains unrevised operations in progress.
8.	Ahmednagar	Do. ..	1876	Do.	None	Field operations towards revision completed in three-fourths of the district.
9.	Poona	Do. ..	1867	Do.	None	Revision field operation in two remaining talukas sanctioned and in progress.
10.	Sholapur	Do. ..	1872	Do.	None	Two talukas remaining of which original rates not yet expired.
11.	Satara	Original	1855	1864	Partial re-measurement and re-classification throughout	
12.	Belgaum	Partly revised ..	1879	Unfinished	None	Field operation towards revision completed in three-fourths of the district.
13.	Dhawar	Revised	1874	1850	None	
14.	Kaladgi	Partly revised ..	1874	Unfinished.	None	Revised field operation completed.
15.	Thana	Original	1854	1867	Partial re-measurement and re-classification.	Revision operation just commenced in one taluka as sanctioned by Government Resolution No. 8263, dated 25th November 1882.
16.	Kolaba	Do.	1854	1867	Do.	
17.	Ratnagiri	Partly settled	1866	Unfinished.	None	Field operation nearly complete.
18.	Kanara	Do. ..	1863	Do.	None	Field operations complete, except in one taluka.

22. It will be seen from the above table that in all districts in which revision operations will take place after this date it is expected that there will be no general re-measurement and re-classification at all. The operations will be confined to partial re-measurement and re-classification, no step towards which is under existing orders taken without the express concurrence of Government. After the partial measures necessary to place the work on a satisfactory footing, re-measurement and re-classification will cease altogether to be operations attendant on a revision of rates.

23. In paragraphs 16 to 19 of the letter to the Government of North-West Provinces I observe that independently of the fact whether the period of existing settlement has expired or not, it is urged upon that Government that in all adequately assessed districts the existing revenue should be taken as the initial revenue upon which future adjustments on revision shall be directly based. Also that in districts in which the existing revenues are not considered to be adequate fair revenues should be fixed without delay for adoption as the initial revenues, and that in districts where the necessary data are not available initial revenues should be ascertained as soon as possible after the required survey and valuation. It seems to me that we may to some extent adopt the principle here advocated as a part of our programme. It is not necessary that in Bombay we should at once fix certain revenue to be adopted at future revisions as the initial revenues of the tract : all that we require is an accurate initial valuation of the land field by field which may be accepted as the basis of our revenues in future revisions. If we once have a good valuation of each field, the assessment can be fixed at any time on whatever maximum rate may be considered suitable. I would propose that, instead of waiting until the period of original settlement expires in each taluka of a district, we should proceed at once to review the work over the whole remaining area of the Presidency, so as once for all to secure a correct initial field valuation. The great advantages of so doing will be performed by the present staff which has attained a pitch of excellence in surveying and soil-valuing which no new staff could ever hope to attain, and instead of the remaining work being done at straggling periods and with reduced establishments until well into the next century, as will be the case if we are to await the expiration of each settlement, everything that is necessary for future

prices is of course the most important of all the considerations which sway the settlement officer in proposing a Bombay revised settlement, and it may be said that the general considerations which are enumerated in the Code are simply collateral ones upon which hinges the main question, viz., what proportion of the rise in values to which they have contributed should be added to the Government revenue. The third point is fully provided for in section 107 of the Land Revenue Code, and is of course an indispensable consideration in the revision of rates.

27. If it be conceded that certainty of assessment to some extent will be an improvement in our present system, that the fixing of these three considerations as the only grounds for enhancement of assessment will conduce to the attainment of that object, and that a certain sacrifice of prospective revenue may be made to ensure it, I see no real difficulties in the way of adopting the proposal. But it would be well before taking this step to consider whether this plan, which has approved itself to the Government of India with a special view to the zamindari system of the North-West, is a desirable element in a system which deals with individual rayats holding small parcels of land, and the majority of whom are totally uneducated and unintelligent. It appears to me that the sacrifice we would make by tying our hands to attain this end might prove to be fruitless of advantage to those whose interests are really sought to be promoted. The business-like zamindar of the North-West or the intelligent heads of a village community with whom the revenue is settled may be enabled to peep into the future and to obtain an insight into their future liabilities, but there is little likelihood that the average Bombay rayat will be able to avail himself of the facility for another generation at least. There is great reason to fear, moreover, that by binding ourselves down to re-assess upon grounds which may be readily discounted we shall be putting into the hands of the capitalist or moneylender one more weapon against the ignorant rayat and will be supplying him with an advantage for which his keen intellect will very soon find a use. I have already alluded to this subject in much the same terms in paragraph 29 of my report to the Secretary to Government, Revenue Department, No. 1714, dated 3rd September 1882. For my own part I would prefer to see the present general considerations retained in our rules for fixing revised assessments until the standard of intelligence among the rayats is very considerably higher.

28. I have only to notice one more point, and that is the desire of the Government of India that the question of remissions and suspensions of revenue in years of failure of crops should be introduced into our Land Revenue Code as an integral part of our system of revenue collection. I have very carefully perused the Circular of the Government of India, No. 58R., dated 12th October 1882, and have given its contents much thought and attention. It is admitted therein (paragraph 5) that in Bombay "the principles underlying the proposals which it contains already to a greater or less extent form part of the settlement system," but I would go further than this and say that there is not a single point raised by the Government of India with a view to the carrying out of these principles in the collection of revenue in the province under its direct control, which is not more fully and even more carefully considered and worked out in the preliminary operation of settling the revenue in this Presidency. In the process every subject affecting the security or insecurity of the tract as regards rainfall and crops is weighed, and the maximum rate of every group of villages is graduated accordingly. The whole efforts of the Survey and Settlement Department, from the first operations of measurement to the final duty of proposing revenue rates, are directed to collecting information regarding the climate and its effect on the produce of the soil. The Assistant Superintendent who measures the land, the officer who follows him to classify it, and the Superintendent and Survey Commissioner who supervise the operations, have the most ample opportunities for recording every peculiarity of climate, and when proposals for rating are made it will be found that there is no greater reason for differentiation of the rates than the security or insecurity of the crops in the area under settlement. It is a common thing to find a single taluka divided into five or six groups for no other reason except certainty or uncertainty of rainfall, and of all the considerations upon which rates are fixed this is unquestionably the most fully discussed and the most important. If the point were to be in any way neglected, the whole system of settlement in the Bombay Presidency would be at once shaken to its very depths. It is probable that the great variations of climate in the Bombay Presidency, especially in the belts of country between the Western Ghats and the plains of Central India, have tended to attract more attention to this subject in the process of settlement than in any other part of India.

29. Instances to show the extent to which climatic differences affect the maximum rates are not difficult to find. Let us take the district of Satara which stretches from the Ghats inland for a distance of about 75 miles. In the western villages where the rainfall is heavy and seasonable, the maximum dry-crop rate is as high as Rs. 3-0-0, while in the most eastern villages the prevailing maximum rate is only Re. 0-15-0. For this great distinction there is no reason but that in the one case good seasons are fairly frequent, while in the other they cannot be depended upon. Take again the instances of Indapur, the most easterly taluka of the Poona District, and Savda which holds the same position in the Khandesh Collectorate. The situation of these talukas with regard to the sea coast and the Ghats is fairly similar. They differ but little in the matter of soils, both containing a considerable area of the best soil of the 1st order, classed at 16 annas. This soil in Indapur is rated on revision principles at Re. 1 per acre only, while in Khandesh it bears an original settlement rate of Rs. 2-6-0. As both talukas are intersected by the railway and have excellent roads and markets for the disposal of produce, there is not a pin to choose between them in these respects. But the great difference in the maximum rate which regulates the assessment of all classes of land is caused by the fact that whereas Indapur is a district which possesses a capricious climate, Savda is situated in a part of the country which for some hidden reasons has a particularly steady rainfall. The revenue rates fixed for Indapur admittedly contemplate only one good year in three, and allow for a bad one in the same period while the rates in Savda are pitched on a tolerable certainly of a fair annual crop. If our system were such as to rate lands in Indapur and in Savda upon their possibilities of production, instead of as now on their probabilities then the necessity of allowing for remissions and suspensions in the former would be paramount. The effect of a rule which would bind a revenue officer to allow remissions in a district like Indapur every time there was a crop below a certain average, would simply be to file concession upon concession on exactly the same grounds and to diminish still further an already very attenuated rent-charge.

30. While I am respectfully of opinion that any addition in this direction to our methods of revenue collection would be a work of supererogation and would be nothing less than admitting that a fundamental principle of our system had not been sufficiently observed in fixing the

assessments, there remains the question of how to deal with abnormal or "catastrophic failures" which are apart from the constantly recurring agricultural ills of the district and beyond the ken of the Settlement Officer. Although in districts of capricious rainfall normal failures are recognized and discounted, it is impossible to take into consideration great calamities or a succession of calamitous circumstances of the nature which has been experienced in some districts of this Presidency within the last 8 years. There could be no serious objection to make some provision in the rules to regulate the extent of failure which should be considered as abnormal, and in which case the ordinary machinery of collection must be set aside. Any regulation of this kind, however, would be very difficult to frame, and I am of opinion that there is a distinct advantage in leaving the treatment of such cases to the Local Government. When an abnormal failure does occur owing to scarcity of rain, the ravages of locusts or other such causes, it cannot remain unnoticed, and recent experience has shown how much more strongly and more efficiently than if guided by hard-and-fast rules the Government of this Presidency has been able through its local officers to guard against undue pressure on the cultivator on the one hand and undue loss to the revenue on the other.

31. As my criticism on the various points referred to by the Government of India has been somewhat discursive, I will endeavour to summarise briefly the suggestions which I have offered on each subject in the above report. They are :—

(1) Re-measurement and re-valuation of land at each revision of assessment are not contemplated in the Bombay system, and after the present work has been placed on a satisfactory footing, no such operations will be necessary at all.

(2) In order to place the work on a satisfactory footing in districts remaining to be dealt with, no general re-measurement or re-valuation is necessary. Partial re-measurement and re-valuation will ordinarily suffice.

(3) To ensure the absence of the necessity for field operation at future revisions it will be necessary to entertain at once a competent staff, in connection with the Agricultural Department, to take over the Settlement maps and records, to keep them fully up to date and to

collect year by year the statistics necessary to be considered at future revisions of rates.

(4) In all districts, or portions of a district, the soils of which were classified subsequent to A.D. 1854, the same area entered in a survey number as *pot kharab* at the first settlement shall be ordinarily allowed in any re-valuation which may be necessary for purposes of revision.

(5) As the revenue from the assessment of *pot kharab* is to be waived in future, and as all the heavy increases under that head have already been levied, it is not necessary to make any special provision regarding the gradual levy of such increases in future.

(6) Instead of awaiting the expiration of each settlement to undertake the field operations which are considered necessary to perfect the basis of our initial revenues, such operations should be executed at once in the remaining districts of the Presidency, and accurate field-to-field valuation registers made over to the custody of the Revenue or Agricultural Department.

(7) When the field operations are concluded throughout the Presidency there will be no necessity for a separate Survey and Settlement Department. The duties of fixing and tabulating the revised assessments may be performed by the Revenue and Agricultural Departments respectively.

(8) There is no material objection to introduce into the Bombay system of settlements some degree of certainty of future assessments as contemplated by the Government of India. But it is doubtful whether the character of the tenure in Bombay is in favour of such a change, and whether the sacrifice we would make would be productive of any real benefit.

(9) The principle of remissions and suspensions of revenue is so fully considered in the settlement system of Bombay, that its admittance into the system of collection as well would be superfluous, except to provide for the case of utterly abnormal failures of crops.

Read the following letter from the Government of India, Revenue and Agricultural Department, No. 953 R., dated 9th October 1883.

I am directed to acknowledge your letter No. 6340 of 27th August 1883, and to express the satisfaction with which Government of India has received the concurrence of His Excellency in Council in the views and principles enunciated in the letter to which you reply, and to convey its appreciation of the able review and careful suggestions supplied by Mr. Stewart, the Commissioner of Survey. I am now briefly to communicate, in accordance with request contained in your last paragraph, the views of the Government of India upon the most important points in your letter and in Mr. Stewart's proposals.

2. The future assessment of *pot kharab* or land escaping assessment as unarable at the time of settlement, will be abandoned in all talukas and groups classified since 1854. This concession will finally terminate the long-standing question opened by Sir P. Wodehouse in 1874, and with respect to which no definite conclusion had hitherto been recorded. The Government of India is willing to concur entirely in the present decision of the Bombay Government in this matter.

3. With reference to the assessment of *pot kharab* in districts and tracts assessed before 1854, i.e., in which a re-valuation of soil is required the Government of India agrees with the Bombay Government in accepting the assurance of Mr. Stewart that the amount of culturable *pot kharab* entered in the settlement record of the area still remaining to be assessed is of so small amount as to render any necessity for progressive revenues unlikely.

4. The division which has been suggested by Mr. Stewart of the districts of the Bombay Presidency into three classes will lead to the speedy and final termination of the settlement operations in nine districts, viz., seven in the first and two in the last class, leaving seven, those of the second class, subject to more or less re-classification. It is satisfactory to understand that the Bombay Government is able thus to guarantee the majority of the districts of the Presidency against re-valuation of soils.

5. The proposal of Mr. Stewart for the early disposal of the operations of the Survey Department in district of the second class appear to the

Government of India to be conducive both to the financial and administrative interests of the State as well as to the benefit of the agricultural population. His Excellency the Governor General in Council is glad to accord his approval to the scheme set forth in Mr. Stewart's letter. Its chief advantages seem to be these :—

(1) The concentration of settlement operations within a shorter period than would otherwise have been possible and the consequent diminution of the cost of superintendence.

(2) The earlier correction of the village records and maps—a measure of great administrative importance.

(3) The greater facility with which a revision of maps, soils and records can be made within the next few years than at any later date, in consequence of the fewer changes which will have taken place since the last survey.

(4) The greater knowledge which the agricultural population will be able at once to acquire of their future prospects at the termination of the present term of settlement.

6. I am to add that, with reference to the fourth advantage of Mr. Stewart's scheme indicated in the preceding paragraph, His Excellency the Governor General in Council observes that the Government of Bombay does not consider the time yet come for a decision as to the extent to which enhancement of revenue at future settlements can be based upon the limited grounds recorded in the 13th paragraph of the letter addressed to the North-Western Provinces. So far as classification of soils is concerned, it is understood that a fixed valuation of all soils as measured by the proportion they bear to a standard value will at the termination of the Survey Department's operations be openly declared, and that the percentage of enhancement in any one village or group of villages will be the same for all classes of soil at the next revision of settlement. But it is not at present decided that the rate should in all villages or groups of villages bear a uniform relation to a rise in prices, as contemplated by the Government of India in the paragraph above quoted. A decision on this point is deferred until the completion of the survey record. It is on this point only that there seems to be any material difference between the proposals of the Bombay Government and the scheme of assessment

suggested by the Government of India. I am, however to express the concurrence of His Excellency Governor General in Council with the view taken in the 15th paragraph of your letter, that uncertainty of assessment should not be retained merely in the hope that it may act as a deterrent on the moneylending class. This argument is based on the unquestionable fact that the value of an agricultural holding as a security is enhanced by attaching certainty to the principles of assessment, and in that view affords additional confirmation to the opinion of the Government of India expressed in the 2nd paragraph of the letter of North-Western Provinces, that the elimination of uncertainty is an important advantage to the holders of land.

A fair corollary from the proposition seems to be that the rate of interest at which agricultural loans could be obtained, would be reduced, and this deduction appears to be, to some extent, borne out by the reports lately submitted on the scheme for an Agricultural Bank in a Deccan taluka in which the high rate of interest is attributed to the uncertainty of future assessment. The Government of India cannot but thoroughly agree with the Government of Bombay that anything which may operate to hold back capital from agriculture is an evil, and trusts that His Excellency the Governor in Council may, when the time for decision arrives see his way to as close an approximation as possible to a fixed and certain method of enhancement.

7. In continuation of the remarks in the preceding paragraph, I am desired to make a brief reference to the tenth paragraph of your letter. As a rule a local increase in the profits of agriculture resulting from a better market secured by new roads or railways is accompanied by a rise in prices at that market. It was contemplated indeed by the Government of India that the local increase of profits would be sufficiently covered by a consideration of the local increase of prices. This view was not perhaps indicated with full clearness in the letter to the North-Western Provinces ; but the option given to the local Government in the 27th paragraph of choosing the market, at which prices should be registered was intended to meet the event of a local rise in prices which would justify the enhancement of revenue in a particular locality. Were this course not adopted, the Government of India apprehends that a consideration of rise in profits, apart from rise in prices, might sometimes lead to undue enhancement ; in

other words, that the same advantage might be charged for twice over, once as giving increased facilities, and once as an element in the increase of prices.

8. In the 16th paragraph of your letter the question of suspensions and remissions is dealt with. The views of the Government of India on this matter have already been explained in previous communications.

9. The assignment of the important duties indicated by Mr. Stewart to the Agricultural Department is so completely in accord with the scheme for an Agricultural Department advised by the Government of India in its Resolution of December 1881, that it is needless for His Excellency the Governor General in Council to assure the Bombay Government of his full acquiescence in this part of its proposals. The Government of India is glad to know that important administrative work will be found for the Department, which will at the same time ensure its more complete acquaintance with the agricultural condition of every portion of the Presidency, and also enable it to effect a considerable economy and accuracy in future revisions of settlement.

10. In conclusion, I am desired to accord the thanks of His Excellency the Governor General in Council to the Government of Bombay for the earnest and cordial manner in which it has given its consideration to the important questions placed before it in my communication of the 15th of May.

RESOLUTION.—Copies of the letter from the Government of India, No. 953R., dated 9th October last, and of the whole correspondence on the subject should be forwarded for information to the Commissioners of Divisions and in Sind, and the Survey and Settlement Commissioner.

J. MONTEATH,
Acting Under Secretary to Government.

NOTES

1. In the province of Gujarat's the utilization of the revenue survey maps has had a fair trial, for some years past, and has been found of the greatest value. The maps of that province, prepared by Colonel Haig, R.E., with the use of the revenue survey maps, were exhibited at the Venice Geographical Congress, and obtained a gold medal ; and the Government of India, while commenting upon this, remarked in their Resolution, Revenue and Agriculture Department, No. 168, dated 8th May 1882, as follows :-

   "The Government of India is extremely glad to notice that in this survey Colonel Haig has been able to take much of his topographical details from the field surveys of the Bombay Revenue Survey. The economy of this is obvious, and the more recent work done by the Survey Settlement Department of that Presidency approaches in its accuracy a scientific survey."

2. *Mushk* and *Peta bhagdars* are perfectly general terms. In Mehwasi villages the sub-shares are known a *bhayats.*

3. *Ghasdana* is a combined word meaning *ghas* (grass) and *dana* (corn). This was not *regularly* collected, but the Gaikwar's cavalry sallied out in one direction one year and in another direction next year. *Ghasdana* was always exacted by force (*vide* Book III, Chapter V of Ras Mala).

4. One rea = ½ pie.

5. One *moora* is equivalent to 25 maunds.

6. With regard to landowners or rayats who fall into difficulties in ordinary years, we do not consider that any radical change in the prevailing method of revenue collection is needed, though a reasonable indulgence may well be shown in a few exceptional cases of individual misfortune. The Collector should understand what Government looks to him to manage its estate to the best advantage, and that notwithstanding the general principle of the settlement he is entrusted with discretion to postpone the demand in the case of persons whom it is to the public interest to maintain on the land. The interest of the landowner and the interest of he Government as the chief landlord, are identical, and it should be understood that Collector is not to sacrifice a good tenant to the principle of the settlement by rigidly selling him up and ejecting him because his revenue is in arrear.

7. Letter from the Commissioner in Sind No. 2202, dated 18th June 1881. Joint letter from the Commissioners, Central, Southern and Northern Divisions, and the Survey and Settlement Commissioner, No. 2725, dated 28th September 1881.

   Note by the Commissioner, N.D.

Glossary

Abhavani	: A system of appraisement of the standing crops for the purpose of collecting rent.
Ardheli	: Cropsharer paying half the crop as rent.
Bagayat land	: Land cultivating garden crops with artificial irrigation facilities.
Bara baluta	: Twelve principal artisans and village servants entitled to receive a fixed share of produce from peasant households for services rendered.
Bhaichara	: Practice of allotting equal shares and holdings for individuals or families.
Dad Ilahi	: Land held since times immemorial, gift of providence.
Deshmukh	: Headman of the district.
Deshpande	: Chief accountant of the district.
Dharekari	: Free peasant proprietors in the Konkan region.
Gairan	: Common grazing land of the village.
Gam Shamlat	: Common land of the village.
Gatkuli land	: Land on which original landholding family had disappeared.
Huks	: Perquisites, remuneration, payment in kind to artisans and village servants.

Inams	: Alienated lands granted tax-free to the privileged landowners called inamdars by the state, also called muaphee or khairat (spelt as enam in the old text).
Jirayat land	: Dry crop land dependent on rainfall for cultivation.
Khot	: Headman and landlord of the village in the Konkan region.
Kulargi	: Villages of peasant proprietors.
Kulkarni	: Accountant of the village (also spelt as Coolkurnee in the old text).
Kunbi	: Generic term for a member of the agricultural class.
Maurusi Haris	: Occupancy tenants in Sind holding land on hereditary basis.
Miras	: Hereditary land owned by the privileged landowners called mirasdars (also spelt as meeras in the old text).
Nimbatai	: A system of cropsharing under which the produce and risk were shared equally by landowner and tenant.
Pagar	: Pay, wages, remuneration.
Patel	: Headman of the village in the Deccan.
Pattidars	: Sub-sharers having equal rights in the estate.
Pot kharab	: Culturable wasteland of the village.
Raiyat	: Cultivator, peasant (also spelt as rayat, or ryot), Persian term from riya meaning subjects of the ruler.
Talukdar	: Hereditary estate owners in Gujarat with full proprietary rights.
Upri (Oopri)	: Coming from outside the village, an inferior cultivator with tenant status.
Vatandar kuls	: Families of hereditary cultivators in the Konkan region.

Varkas	: Dry crop land.
Vethi	: Forced labour.
Waola Pasaita	: Service lands granted to the artisans in Gujarat in lieu of their services.
Watan land	: Alienated land gifted to watandars (village officials) by the state in lieu of their services.

cess, 19, 26, 30, 72, 89–90, 117, 148, 150, 158, 164, 173–5, 182, 184, 211
chakariat, 26, 159
chambhar, 64, 75, 79, 93
Chandra, Bipan, 15
China, 44, 48
Christianity, 47
colonialism, 43, 50
commodity, 14, 186; exchange of, 14
Cooke, Humphrey, 167–8
Cornwallis, Lord, 45
cultivation, 11, 20, 27, 29, 37, 65–6, 73, 81, 94–5, 103, 108–11, 131, 133, 137, 146, 161, 168, 169, 173–4, 178, 180, 182, 184–5, 188–9, 191, 194, 200, 204–6, 208, 219, 220–1, 227
cultivators, 13, 17, 19–20, 24–6, 28, 30, 32, 43, 50–1, 63–4, 70–1, 73–4, 79, 81, 84, 148, 150, 154, 158, 161, 164, 178–9, 182; petty, 30, 178

dad ilahi, see gift of providence
Dark Age, 46
daspatkari, 164
Deccan, 10, 16–18, 21, 24, 28–9, 31–2, 39–40, 53, 61, 67, 95, 109–10, 116, 131, 142, 147, 163, 165, 183, 188, 192, 195, 202–3, 222, 235; *inam*, 24–5, 32, 167; *irjik* in, 17; *muaphee*, 24; peasant uprising of 1875, 21; *Sama Patras*, 21, 22; Report of Captain D. Davidson, 61; village communities of, 95, 110
Desai, M.B., 36
deshmookh, 20, 30, 39, 51, 75, 84–5, 88
deshpande, 20, 30, 39, 51, 75, 84
Dewey, Clive, 16
dhal, 151
dharekari, 27–8, 37, 163–5
dharo, 151
dhungur, 89–90
Dickinson, Captain, 171
didhivala, 28
Dow, 45
Dumont, Louis, 16
dupatkari, 28, 164

East India Company, 31, 40, 50, 168
Elphinstone, [M.] 13, 81, 85; Report on Bombay in 1819, 13
employment, 28, 74, 187, 209
Engels, Frederick, 10
England, 44, 65, 167–8; Gairan, Sirkaree, 65; village commons in, 65
Europe, 10, 27, 42, 44, 48–9, 108, 117; Roman provincial land, 27; self-governing institutions in, 10; Teutonic Townships, 10

farmer, 12, 22, 31, 68, 75–7, 79, 96, 101, 160, 162, 174; capitalist, 31; distressed, 22; revenue, 12
feudalism, 27
fishing, 28
Fletcher, 138
Foras, 170, 172, 175
Francis, Colonel, 40, 45, 135, 138

Gamph Gangad, 25, 151
garden grants, 183–4
Germany, *junkers*, 31
ghasdana, 157
ghut, 77
gift of providence, 11
Godfrey, Colonel, 138
Goldsmid.132, 136, 140
gomastha, 40, 50
Gooddine, R.N., 10, 18–20, 40, 48, 120
goor, 87
grants; charitable, ·183–4; huri, 184; *inam*, 170–71; patadari, 183; ready-money, 96, 99, 100; seri, 184–5; village service, 184
Guha, Ranjit, 45
Gujarat, 17–18, 25, 31, 33–5, 39, 52–3, 149–50, 152–3, 156, 159, 165, 188, 192–3, 222–3; *sondhal* in, 17; *talati*, 39, 156–9; tenures in, 149
Gutkoolee, 61, 65–6, 69–70

Habib, Irfan, 15
handicrafts, 14–15
hari, 26, 30–31, 159, 181–2

Index

Hawkins, Lieutenant, 171
Hearn, 138
Hughes, Sir Edward, 170
huk, 18–20, 39, 61–2, 68–9, 71, 78, 84–9, 91–5, 100, 102, 104–11; kinds of, 62, 76, 87–90, 95–7, 104–9

imperialism, 41, 43, 49, 50
inam/enam, 19, 21, 24–5, 32, 33, 61-2, 65, 67, 78, 80, 83, 86, 92, 94, 96-100, 104-9, 135, 159–60, 165–6, 167, 170–72, 175 personal, 25, 167; political, 24; religious, 25; service, 25
inamdar, 21, 24, 31–3, 48, 51
indebtedness, 35, 41, 137
India, 9–10, 13–14, 16, 21, 23–4, 31, 33, 38, 40–1, 44–50, 52–3, 85, 119, 135–6, 145, 168, 170, 177, 204–9, 211–16, 218, 220–1, 227–9, 231–6; British rule in, 9, 11–13, 21–5, 36, 38, 40, 45, 131, 156–7, 161, policy, 23, right of the peasants, 13; colonial, famines in, 9; colonial rule, 18, 31–2, 39–40, 43, 50–3; communal ownership of land in, 16; merchants of, 40; Mohammedan invasions, 30; north, 10, 16, 53, landlord type villages in, 16; revolts, 21, 49, 51–3; southern, 13, 172; systems of landed property in, 23; uprising of 1857, 49; village communities in, 10, 13; western, 9, 13, 21, 23–4, 48, 52–3
Ireland, 10
irrigation, 14–15, 20, 141–2, 173, 178–80, 182, 193–4, 202, 211, 217; common tanks for, 15
izafat, 30, 160–2

jagir, 183
jagirdar, 34
Jamaican Revolt in 1865, 49
jukat, 90

Kambell, 36
kasht hasb maqdur, 11
Keatinge, G., 33
khairat, 183–4
khot, 24, 26–31, 36–8, 48, 51, 160, 162–5; pauperisation of, 38; power of, 37–8; right of, 27, 37; status of, 36
khot nisbat, 26–7, 29
Khoteputra, 90
khoti, 26–9, 36–8, 147, 160, 162–5
Khoti Association, 37
Khoti Commission, 37
Khoti Enquiry Committee, 38
khureed khut, 90
Kosambi, D.D., 15
Kumar, Ravinder, 32
kunbi, 19, 24, 29, 168–9, 174

labour, 14–18, 25–7, 29, 31, 37, 44–5, 47, 64, 90, 105, 107, 118, 151, 190–1, 193, 199; abundant, 16; agricultural, 44; co-operation, 17; demand for, 17; division of, 14–15, 17, social, 17; exchange of, 17, free, 17, system of, 17; family, 17; forced, 26–7, 29, 37; form of, 17, customary, 17, *irjik*, 17; manual, 25, 151; secured, 17; *sondhal*, 17; wage, 17, 31, contractual, 17
laissez-faire laissez aller, 42, 45, 47; free trade ideology of, 42
lambardar, 11
land; alienated, 24–6, 32, 33, 143, 159; arable, 10, 189; *bagayat*, 28; bhagdari , 26, 153, 155; book, 27; categories of, 21; charter, 27; classification of, 140; cultivable, 19, 26, 65, 146, 155, 179–81, 188, 221; demesne, 27; distribution of, 23; enam, 61, 65–7, 104, 106, *Gaw-Nisbut-Enam*, 67; fertility of, 16, 140; folk, 27; gairan, 61, 65; *garania*, 159; government, 24, right of occupancy of, 24; gutkoolee, 19, 61, 65–6, 69; *haria-garania-salamia*, 159; *Inam* Commissioners, 33; *khana khali, see* ownerless; khoti, 27–9, 37–8, 160, 162–3; *khot khasgi*, 26–7; khot nisbat, 26–7, 29; koorun, 65; management of, 27; measurement of, 12; Meeras, 61–2, 65–6,

69–70, 72, 111; mirasi, 24, 32; Mullaee, 65; mustjir, 12; *narva*, 26, 153–6; ownerless, 12; ownership of, 10–11, 16, 23–5, 149, ancestral shares, 11–12, *bara balutedari* system, 18, British system, 11, common, 10, 23, communal, 11, 16, gatkul, 24, 32, grant or gift, 19, hereditary, 19, household, 11, 27, 76, *inam/enam*, 19, 21, 33, 61, 65-7, 104, 106, 159, 160, 170–1, joint, 10, 24, *khairat*, 21, *miras*, 19, 20, 32, 148, 160, 163, mirasdari system, 24, mirasdar, 19–20, 24, 28, 31–2, 147–8, 164, *pattidari*, 12, rayatwari system, 11, 13, 24–5, 32, 39, 40, 48, 214; talukdari, 25, 33, 36, *zamindari*, 12, 30–31, 34–5, 45, 137, 178, 181–2, 228; *pasaita*, 17, 26, 159; *pasaitavechania-nakra*, 159; pasture, 10, 19, 65; preserved grass, 65; private property in, 14, 15; Purtun, 65; rent-free, 26, 66–8, 97–8, 156–9, 171, 177, 183–5, 194; repartition of, 16; revenue, 11, 13, 19, 20, 24–5, 27–8, 32–5, 37–41, 45, 51–2, 139, 143, 146, 149, 186, 189, 193–5, 197–200, 204–5, 208, 210–12, 214; revenue-free, 12, 24; *sadr-malguzar*, 12; *salamia*, 26, 159; salt batty, 170, 175; *sanadia*, 159; scarce, 16; service, 17; settlements, 134, 138–9, 142–5, 167, 178–80, 182, 187–9, 192–3, 197, 199, 201, 206, 209, 215, 218, 223–4, 226–7, 232, 234 ; term of, 142; shet, 65, 67, 78; *shilotri*, 30, 161; Sookhwustee, 69; thul, 65; tika, 65; *toka*, 174–5; unculturable, 65; varkas, 29, 37, 165; *vechania*, 159; village, 12; *wahiwatdar*, 34; *wazifa*, 159; woodland, 10

landed property, 45

landlord, 11–12, 16, 47–8, 146, 190, 193; grantee's right, 12; quasi, 12; single, 12; zamindars, 13, 31, 34–5, 48, 51, 162, 179–80, 182–3

Land Revenue Code, 144, 147, 152, 181, 183, 185, 194, 197, 203, 210, 212–4, 223, 228–9; amendment of, 144

land tenure, 9, 23; bhagdari, 25–6, 35, 153–7; customary, 26; *dharekari*, 27–8, 37, 163–4; Gamph Gangad, 151; *izafat*, 30, 160–62; khoti, 26–7, 29, 36–8, 147, 160, 162–5; *kularg*, 30, 162; *maurusi haripan*, 31, 181; mirasdari , 32; mirasi, 24, 32; *muksh bhag*, 25, 153; *narvadari*, 25–6, 35, 153–5, 157; occupancy, 27–8, 31, 37–8, 164–5; quasi-freehold, 27; *sanand*, 150–1; *shilotri*, 30, 160–2; survey, 24, 32, 147–8, 160–2, 164–5; talukdari, 34, 35, 147, 149–52, 156–8

lease, 137, 143, 162, 165, 168–71, 175–6, 183, 194

leasehold, 172, 175

lohar, 64, 75, 93

lugnamoohoort, 90

Mackay, Alexander, 17

Madras Presidency, 13

Maharashtra, 22, 32

Maine, Sir Henry Sumner, 10, 13, 16

makhal, 151

Mandlik, V.N., 37

maparkee, 88

Maratha, 29, 157

Maratha Aikyeehhu Sabha, 38

market, 15, 17, 21, 28, 31, 38, 51, 90, 96, 115, 171, 174, 190, 211–12, 227, 230, 235; economy, 17, 21, 31, 51; forces, 17

Marx, Karl, 14, 23; *Capital* (vol. I), 14

maurusi hari, 31, 181, 182

meeras, 66, 69–73, 81, 84, 104, 110–11

meerasdar/mirasdar, 19–20, 24, 28, 31–2, 66, 69–70, 73, 80–3, 107, 110–11, 114, 147–8, 164

Mehwasi, 26, 147, 156

Mercantilism, 43–4

Metcalfe, Charles, 13

Metcalf, T.R., 45

mirasi, 24, 32

moneylender, 22, 40

muhar, 67, 76–80, 86, 88–92, 94–5, 100, 113

Mukherjee, S.N., 16
muksh bhagdar, 26, 153, 156
mulkgiri, 157
mulkgirt, 150
Munro, Thomas, 13, 16

nagar vethi, 27, 37
mooshaheera, 88, 95–6, 105–9
nimboor, 76, 87
narva, 26, 153–6
narvadari, 25–6, 35, 153–5, 157
Northern Konkan, 159; tenures in, 159, *shilotri*, 161, survey, 159
North-Western Provinces, 11, 204–5, 208, 210, 234–5

obschina, see village community
occupation, 17, 22; caste-based hereditary, 17
Oudh, 11, 53
Ozanne, 136, 138, 213

pandree, 89, 104, 106
pansooparee, 70
pata, 183
patidar, 12, 26, 154
Pattullo, 45
pavnedonpatkari, 28
pavvini, 164
Pedder, 138
pension and tax, 16, 44–5, 47, 52, 115–16, 173; mohoturfa, 116–17; state, 16; tax-gatherer, 14
pewbood, 90
Phadke, Vasudev Balwant, 22
phalavni, 154–5
phaski, 37
police, 14, 42, 52, 86, 100, 103, 152, 156, 166
political crises, 10
pot-kharab, 188–90, 206
poverty, 12, 63–4, 83, 179
power, 10, 12, 18–20, 23, 30–3, 39, 42, 49, 51, 62–3, 71, 73–4, 81, 83, 85, 89–91, 105, 111, 116, 120, 150, 176, 186, 188, 194, 211; balance of, 20; *inamdar*, 33
Preston, Major, 138
Pringle, [R.K.] 131–2, 136
property, 9, 11, 14–15, 19, 21–3, 30, 34–5, 45, 47, 50, 62–3, 65–6, 70, 72–3, 78, 90, 103–4, 110, 162, 168, 170, 172–3, 178, 182, 184, 186, 192; auction, 12, 32, 171, 174; forms of, 45; landed, 9, 23, 45, 63, distribution of, 9 systems of, 23; nominal, 110; private, 14–15, 47, 168; tribal idea of, 11
Punjab, 11, 53, 194
puragunda, 63
purbhara , 91, 105, 107–10

Ratnagiri, 26–7, 36, 37, 162, 164, 222, 223, 224
Record of Rights, 136, 139, 145, 150
rent; ground, 169, 171, 173, 174, 175; quit, 26, 31, 173, 174
revenue, 11, 12, 13, 19, 20, 24, 25, 27, 28, 32, 33, 34, 35, 37, 38, 39, 40, 41, 45, 51, 52, 139, 143, 146, 149, 186, 189, 193, 194, 195, 197, 198, 199, 200, 204, 205, 208, 210, 211, 212, 214; *ardheli*, 29; *bighoti*, 26, 155; *chakariat*, 26, 159; *chautheli*, 29; *deh khurch*, 31; dewusthan, 112; *dharekari*, 27, 28, 163, 165; dhurmadee, 112; *gaon khurch*, 29; *ghurputtee*, 29; government, 21, 26, 27, 34, 77, 78, 88, 96, 97, 101, 108, 148, 153, 154, 215, 228; jama, 25, 26, 33, 34, 37, 149, 153, 156, 157, 158 ; *judi*, 24; *karsai*, 30; *khand*, 30; *khar*, 30, 161, 162; khoti *watan*, 27; *khotki*, 37; land, collection of, 27, 146, fixation of, 51, settlement of, 24, zamindari, 45; *lapo*, 31, 181, 182; *makta*, 30; *malkano*, 31, 181, 182; management, 24, 73, village system of, 24; *maurusi hari*, 31, 181, 182; *nakra*, 26, 159; *pasaita*, 17, 26, 159; payment of, 11, 24, 32, 33, 35, 156, 216; principal payers, 12; quit rent, 24, 67, 80, 149, 152, 153, 159, 166, 168, 169, 181, 221; rights, 24; *salami*, 24,

153, *numbervar*, 153; *tirdhelis*, 29; *tobro*, 31, 181; *udhad*, 25, 26, 147, 149, 153, 156, 157, 158; *udhad jama*, 26, 149, 153, 156; *ukta tharav*, 30; *wazifa*, 26; zamindari, 12, 30, 31, 34, 35, 45, 137, 178, 181, 182, 228
Revenue Survey, 61, 120, 131, 172, 185, 188, 201; origin of the measure, 131; survey and settlement, 135, 143, 185, 201, 213, 229, 232, 236
Ricardo, David, 47
rights, 10, 13, 18–19, 22–6, 28–31, 33–4, 36–7, 61–3, 65, 71–2, 74, 101–2, 139, 142–3, 145–6, 149, 151, 153, 155, 157, 160, 162–4, 168, 173, 175, 178, 180, 200; civil, 10, 101; hereditary, 22, 36, 102; inheritance, 19; mirasi, 24; occupancy, 29; proprietary, 25, 37, 149, 162; residence, 18; tenant, 31, 180; *watan*, 36; zamindari, 30, 34, 178
ryots, 13, 20, 30, 36, 39–40, 61, 88, 92, 94–5, 98, 100, 103, 107–8, 111

sadilwar, 62, 96–7
sahukar, 38, 40, 50
sallee koshtee, 90
Sanadi, 172, 176
Seth, Jagat, 50
settlement; irrigation, 179–80; original, 137, 179, 187, 189, 195, 209, 211, 220, 222, 225, 230; revision, 179–80, 189, 193, 209
shewsubjee, 90
Sind, 30–1, 34, 135, 142, 177–8, 180–1, 183–4, 199, 236; tenure in, 177; zamindars in, 31, 34
society, 9, 14–15, 17–8, 22–3, 41–2, 46, 51–2, 63, 101; civil, 41; economic elements of, 15; Indian, 14; rural, 9, 17, 18, 22, 23, 51, 52 ; constitution of, 9, groups and classes of, 23
Sootar, 64, 75, 93
Southern Konkan, 162; tenures in, 162
Stewart, Theodore, 135, 136, 138, 205, 208, 209, 212, 213, 233, 234, 236
Survey, 32, 36, 61, 120, 131, 133, 135, 136, 137, 138, 139, 140, 142, 143, 145, 146, 147, 159, 164, 165, 172, 174, 175, 185, 187, 188, 195, 201, 202, 203, 208, 213, 226, 229, 232, 233, 234, 236; Great Trigonometrical Survey, 172; tenure, 147, definition of, 147, *miras*, 147

talukdar, 11, 12, 24, 25, 31, 34, 35, 36, 48, 51, 149, 150, 151, 152, 153; alienations, 151, 165, 174, 183, 184; origin of, 150
Tate, Lieutenant, 171
Temple, Sir Richard, 40
tenant, 17, 19, 24, 26, 27, 28, 29, 30, 31, 34, 35, 36, 37, 38, 40, 41, 51, 64, 66, 69, 79, 87, 88, 145, 146, 147, 151, 155, 157, 160, 161, 162, 163, 164, 165, 168, 170, 174, 176, 177, 178, 180, 181, 182, 193, 198; demands on, 30; *dulandi*, 29; *gayal*, 29; hereditary, 31, 181; *khand kari*, 30; kunbi, 19, 29, 174; Marathas, 29, 157; tenants-at-will, 26, 29, 37, 151, 170
tenures; maleki, 157; mehwasi, 156; narva, 154, 155; narvadari, 153, 155; personal, 167; political, 166; religious endowment, 167; *sarakati*, 158; *senja*, 153; service, 166; *talpad*, 152, 153; talukdari, 149, 152; *udhad jamabandi*, 158; *vanta*, 152, 153, 158
Thapar, Romila, 15
thulwaheek, 69, 71, 72, 73, 82
trade, 31, 40, 42, 43, 44, 45, 47, 50, 61, 212; foreign, 43; free, 42, 45, 47; international, 31, 44

udhad jama, 26, 149, 153, 156
udhad jamabandi, 25, 26, 147, 157, 158
upri, 18, 19, 20, 24, 29, 32, 147, 148
utilitarianism, 48
vatandar kul, 164
veth, 37
village community; artisans, 13, 17–18, 20, 50–2, 71, 74–6, 87, 91–2, 101, 115; backwardness, irrational and features of,

16; *barabaluta* system, 17; caste system, 12, 16–17, 21–2, 78, 90, communal responsibility, 17; dominance, 16; class polarisation, 17; class struggles, 15; cohesive, 14; constitution, 9, 13–14, 50, 166, 168, 174, self-governing, 13; coolkurnee, 64, 74–5, 79, 83–5, 88–93, 95–7, 105–8, 112–13; cultivators, 13, 17, 19–20, 24–6, 28, 30, 32, 43, 50–1, 63–4, 70–1, 73–4, 79, 81, 84, 148, 150, 154, 158, 161, 164, 178–9, 182; proprietary, 26, 154, yeoman, 25; decline and decay of, 13; deshmookh/deshmukh, 20, 30, 39, 51, 75, 84–5, 88; deshpande 20, 30, 39, 51; 75, 84; expenditure, 96; feature of, 11; headman, 13; hereditary, 117, 119, 177; hudola, 80; hukdar, 78, 94; *jajmani* system, 16; joint, 12; khoti, 28, 37, 160, 162; kulkarni, 13, 18, 20, 22, 39, 51–2; moneylenders in, 40; *moolana*, 74–5, 77, 93, *hulal*, 77, *moordar*, 77; muhar, 64, 67, 75–6, 78–80, 86, 88–9, 93–5, 100, 113, gaow, 80; mirasdar, privileges of, 20; notions of, 15; officials, 10, 17–18, 39, 63, 67, 98, 118; patel, 13, 18–20, 22, 39–40, 51–2, 61, 64, 66, 68–76, 79–85, 87–93, 95–7, 102–16, 156–7, huks and perks of, 20; power and authority of, 19; pottery of, 15; revenue, 11–12; rights of, 61; self-sufficing, 15; servant, 13, 17–18, 20, 22, 74, 78, 87, 92, 151, astrologer, 15, 18, 20, 64, 76; barber, 13, 15, 17, 18, 20, 76, bhaichara, 11–12, bheel, 74, 78, 93, bhut, 64, 75–7, 86, 93, blacksmith, 13, 17–18, 20, chambar, 79, carpenter, 13, 15, 17–18, 20, customary rights, 18; *dharekari*, 27, *gaokari*, 18, goldsmith, 18, 77, goorow, 64, 75, 77, 93, karoonaroo, 74–5, kazee, 77, 86, 97, 113; kolee, 74, 78, 93, *koombhar*, 75–6, 93, *kulargi*, 27–8, kunbi, 19, 24, 29, 168–9, 174, mahar, 18, 20, 22, 29, mamlatdar, 52, mang, 78, 89, 93, marwari, 21, 40–1, meer, 78, mehwasi, 26, 147, 156, mundwahik, 19, 65, naeekwadee, 86, narva, 153–4, nhawee, 64, 75–6, 93, oopree, 64–5, 69, 72–3, 81, 101, 111, owandkari, 19, 65, 69, pandree, 87, 91–2, 94, 100, 107, potter, 15, 17–18, 20, priest, 13, 18, 20, 22, 64, 76–7, pureet, 64, 75–6, 93, remunerations, 17–20, 39, 61–2, 68–9, 71–2, 75–83, 86–9, 91–4, 95–7, 100–2, 104–11, 119, 151, 161, 163, 177, shoemaker, 18, 89, 90, sonar, 64, 77, 93, tanner, 17, 18, 20, washerman, 15, 18, 20, 22, 76; settlement of, 18; sizes of, 15; social cohesion, 16, 49; talukdari, 25–6, 33–4, 36, *gamph*, 25, *sanand*, 25; tax-gathering agency, 11; village commons in, 65

Vohra, Virji, 50

Wadia, Bomanji Lowji, 170
Wadia, Khan Bahadur Jamshedji Dhunjibhai, 171
Wadia, Manekji Lowji, 170
Wadia, Nowroji Jamshedji, 170
wanwula, 87, 95
waola pasaita, 17
wartala, 37
waste, 10, 26–7, 29, 34, 39, 99, 111, 133, 137, 157, 168, 174, 178–9, 182, 190, 193–4, 219, 226–7; arable, 10; *gam shamlat*, 10; *gaveek*, 26, 29; land, 26, 133, 137, 168, 174, 178–9, 190, 193–4, 227; tillers, 29; village common, 10, 19
watandar kul, 28
water, 14–15, 28, 76, 78, 115–16, 141, 146, 165, 180, 184, 186, 191–4, 199, 202, 210–11; rain, 191; subsoil, 191, 193–4
weaving, 14
Wingate, Lieutenant, 36, 132, 135–6, 140

zamindar, 11–12, 31, 178, 180–2, 217, 228